Taste of Home

GRANDMA'S FAVORITES

TASTE OF HOME BOOKS • RDA ENTHUSIAST BRANDS, LLC • MILWAUKEE, WI

© 2022 RDA Enthusiast Brands, LLC.
1610 N. 2nd St., Suite 102,
Milwaukee WI 53212-3906
All rights reserved. Taste of Home
is a registered trademark of
RDA Enthusiast Brands, LLC.

Visit us at **tasteofhome.com** for other
Taste of Home books and products.

International Standard Book Number:
D 978-1-62145-824-1
U 978-1-62145-825-8

Component Number:
D 117600106H
U 117600108H

Executive Editor: Mark Hagen
Senior Art Director: Raeann Thompson
Senior Editor: Christine Rukavena
Art Director: Courtney Lovetere
Senior Designer: Jazmin Delgado
Deputy Editor, Copy Desk:
Dulcie Shoener
Copy Editor: Kara Dennison

Cover Photography:
Photographer: Dan Roberts
Set Stylist: Stacey Genaw
Food Stylist: Josh Rink

Pictured on front cover:
All-American Turkey Potpie, p. 126

Pattern: MarinaMays/Getty Images

Pictured on back cover:
Mom's Buttermilk Biscuits, p. 89;
The Best Beef Stew, p. 197; Layered
Strawberry Pound Cake Dessert, p. 286

Printed in China
1 3 5 7 9 10 8 6 4 2

CONTENTS

Legendary is how many describe Grandma's cooking—it's tasty, old-fashioned, and packed with homemade flavor and good nutrition. Nobody cooks quite like Grandma—but home cooks of the next generation always aspire to learn.

That's why you'll love cooking from *Grandma's Favorites*. All the cherished classics are here, from antipasto bites and zucchini au gratin to icebox cake and strawberry pie.

You're sure to relish:

- **Grandma's Favorite Main Courses.** Dig into cheesy lasagna, chicken-fried steak, meat pies and Grandma's signature cabbage rolls, just to name a few. Whether it's one-pot spaghetti for a weeknight or holiday glazed ham, every dinner at Grandma's is made with love.

- **Grandma's Favorite Breakfasts.** Power through until lunchtime with wholesome oatmeal, golden waffles, home-style biscuits and gravy, and so many others.

- **Grandma's Favorite Soups & Stews.** From meaty chili to elegant bisque, Grandma's specialty is a cozy bowlful of steaming soup—everyone's favorite comfort food. Just add buttery bread and you'll be in heaven!

- **Grandma's Cakes & Pies.** More than two dozen showstopping delights are sure to be the talk of the table! These recipes are so treasured that they'll become a part of your own tradition.

Create new memories to cherish and savor the flavors of times gone by with the 298 recipes inside *Grandma's Favorites*. Preparing recipes from this collection is the next best thing to cooking at Grandma's side!

CHERRY NUT CAKE,
PAGE 262

SUNDAY DINNER MENUS

Whether you're new to meal planning or a longtime pro, consider this handy guide
that relies on recipes from this book to create complete meals.

Mom's Roast Beef, p. 110
• Seasoned Mashed
Potatoes, p. 151
• Cauliflower-Broccoli
Cheese Bake, p. 159
• Cinnamon-Pear Rustic
Tart, p. 238

Shrimp Mozambique,
p. 108 • Orange & Olives
Salad, p. 138 • Mom's
Tangerine Iced Tea, p. 57
• Lemon Oatmeal Cookies,
p. 215

Apple & Herb Roasted
Turkey, p. 111 • Grilled
Apple Tossed Salad, p. 143
• Icebox Rolls, p. 70
• Healthy Spinach Dip,
p. 52 • Praline Pumpkin
Pecan Pie, p. 267

Hungarian Goulash, p. 132
• Mom's Pickled Carrots,
p. 38 • Greens with Hot
Bacon Dressing, p. 149
• Apple Kolaches, p. 275

Breaded Pork Chops,
p. 113 • Sliced Tomato
Salad, p. 159 • Zucchini
Onion Pie, p. 161 • Lemon
Ricotta Cake, p. 236

Mom's Meat Loaf, p. 108
• Mom's Macaroni &
Cheese, p. 152 • Blooming
Onions, p. 49 • Mexican Ice
Cream, p. 275

Parmesan Baked Cod,
p. 121 • Red Potatoes with
Beans, p. 167 • Sweet
Onion Skillet Bread, p. 79
• Lime Pudding Cakes,
p. 285

Grilled Onion & Skirt Steak
Tacos, p. 105 • Corn on the
Cob with Lemon-Pepper
Butter, p. 168 • Grandma's
Fruit Salad, p. 154
• Mexican Chocolate Sugar
Crisps, p. 204

French Meat & Vegetable
Pie, p. 123 •Loaded
Potato-Leek Soup, p. 181
• Olive-Stuffed Celery, p. 65
• Rice Pudding, p. 270

Spiced Lime & Cilantro
Chicken, p. 102 • Festive
Rice, p. 141 • Grandma's
Gelatin Fruit Salad, p. 160
• Quick & Easy Baklava
Squares, p. 291

Bacon-Colby Lasagna,
p. 124 • Zucchini
Panzanella Salad, p. 138
• Savory Stuffed Cherry
Peppers, p. 36 • Tender
Garlic Cheese Breadsticks,
p. 76 • Salted Dark
Chocolate Tart, p. 241

Speedy Salmon Patties,
p. 105 • Beet & Sweet
Potato Fries, p. 164
• Mom's Chopped
Coleslaw, p. 165
• Grandma's Strawberry
Pie, p. 255

PB&J FRENCH TOAST,
PAGE 11

BREAKFASTS

Dig in to fluffy, creamy scrambled eggs, sweet and
nutty candied bacon, and bubbly baked cheese grits.
When these homey comfort foods are piled high on
your plate, you must be at Grandma's house!

CREAM CHEESE SCRAMBLED EGGS

My mother-in-law introduced me to this recipe, and now it's my kids' favorite breakfast.
The rich taste makes it special enough for Christmas morning, but it won't take up a lot of time.
—*Jacque Hunt, Heyburn, ID*

TAKES: 15 MIN. • MAKES: 4 SERVINGS

3 oz. cream cheese, softened
2 Tbsp. half-and-half cream
8 large eggs
⅓ cup grated Parmesan cheese
½ tsp. lemon-pepper seasoning
⅛ tsp. salt
½ cup crumbled cooked bacon
2 Tbsp. butter
Minced chives, optional

1. In a small bowl, beat cream cheese and cream until smooth. Beat in eggs, Parmesan cheese, lemon pepper and salt. Stir in the bacon.

2. In a large skillet, melt butter over medium heat. Pour in egg mixture; cook and stir until eggs are thickened and no liquid egg remains. Garnish with chives, if desired.

¾ CUP: 362 cal., 28g fat (14g sat. fat), 483mg chol., 954mg sod., 3g carb. (3g sugars, 0 fiber), 23g pro.

PECAN BACON

Crispy, sweet bacon dresses up any breakfast. When my girls see this,
they call it a special breakfast. The big flavor punch may just surprise you.
—*Catherine Ann Goza, Charlotte, NC*

PREP: 10 MIN. • BAKE: 30 MIN. • MAKES: 1 DOZEN

12 bacon strips
¼ cup packed brown sugar
¼ cup finely chopped pecans
⅛ tsp. ground cinnamon
⅛ tsp. pepper

1. Preheat oven to 375°. Place bacon in a single layer in a foil-lined 15x10x1-in. baking pan. Bake until lightly browned, 16-18 minutes.

2. Remove bacon from pan. Discard drippings from pan, wiping clean if necessary.

3. In a shallow bowl, mix remaining ingredients. Dip both sides of bacon in brown sugar mixture, patting to help coating adhere; return to pan.

4. Bake until caramelized, 8-10 minutes longer. Remove immediately from pan.

1 BACON STRIP: 142 cal., 12g fat (4g sat. fat), 18mg chol., 186mg sod., 4g carb. (4g sugars, 0 fiber), 4g pro.

GRANDMA'S SECRET

Try mixing some fresh veggies, crumbled cooked sausage or breakfast potatoes into the scrambled eggs.

CREAM CHEESE
SCRAMBLED EGGS

HEARTY SAUSAGE & SWEET POTATOES

Sweet potatoes with sausage and sage make a happy dish.
I get a lot of recipe requests when I serve this down-home hash.
—*Courtney Stultz, Weir, KS*

PREP: 20 MIN. • **COOK:** 25 MIN. • **MAKES:** 6 SERVINGS

- **2 large sweet potatoes, peeled and cut into ½-in. pieces.**
- **2 Tbsp. olive oil, divided**
- **½ tsp. salt**
- **1 lb. bulk pork sausage**
- **1 large tart apple, peeled and chopped**
- **1 large carrot, cut into ½-in. pieces**
- **½ tsp. dried sage leaves**
- **½ tsp. ground cinnamon**
- **½ tsp. pepper**
- **⅛ tsp. pumpkin pie spice**

1. In a large microwave-safe bowl, combine potatoes, 1 Tbsp. oil and salt. Microwave, covered, on high for 6-8 minutes or until tender, stirring every 2 minutes.

2. Meanwhile, in a large skillet, cook sausage over medium heat 6-8 minutes or until no longer pink, breaking into crumbles; remove with a slotted spoon.

3. In same skillet, heat remaining oil over medium-low heat. Add apple and carrot; cook, covered, 5-7 minutes or until carrot is just tender, stirring occasionally. Return sausage to pan. Stir in sweet potatoes and seasonings; cook, covered, 10-12 minutes or until carrot is tender.

NOTE: This recipe was tested in a 1,100-watt microwave.

1 CUP: 409 cal., 25g fat (7g sat. fat), 51mg chol., 793mg sod., 34g carb. (15g sugars, 4g fiber), 12g pro.

FROM GRANDMA'S KITCHEN: If you don't have pumpkin pie spice, you can make your own with a blend of 2 tsp. cinnamon, 1 tsp. ginger, and ½ tsp. each ground nutmeg and cloves or allspice. Use in recipes that call for the spice blend.

PB&J FRENCH TOAST
PICTURED ON PAGE 6

My grandpa made an awesome breakfast for us grandkids: French toast
that started on the griddle as peanut butter and jelly sandwiches.
—*Lindsey Folsom, Dorsey, IL*

TAKES: 15 MIN. • MAKES: 4 SERVINGS

¼ cup creamy peanut butter
¼ cup grape jelly or
    jelly of your choice
8 slices sandwich bread
2 large eggs
¼ cup 2% milk
2 Tbsp. butter
    Optional: Sliced
    fresh strawberries and
    chopped salted peanuts
    Confectioners' sugar or
    maple syrup

1. Spread peanut butter and jelly over 4 slices of bread. Top
with remaining bread. In a shallow bowl, whisk eggs and milk
until blended.

2. On a griddle, melt butter over medium heat. Dip both sides of
sandwiches in egg mixture. Place on griddle; toast 2-3 minutes on
each side or until golden brown. If desired, top with strawberries
and peanuts. Dust with confectioners' sugar or serve with syrup.

1 SANDWICH: 370 cal., 19g fat (7g sat. fat), 109mg chol., 416mg sod.,
40g carb. (18g sugars, 2g fiber), 11g pro.

RHUBARB COMPOTE WITH YOGURT & ALMONDS

My Grandma Dot used to make rhubarb compote and always had some in the freezer when I came to visit.
This breakfast is a tribute to her. No two stalks of rhubarb are exactly alike, so make sure to taste the
compote before you chill it. It should be tart, but sometimes it needs a little extra sugar.
—*Michael Hoffman, Brooklyn, NY*

PREP: 10 MIN. • COOK: 15 MIN. + CHILLING • MAKES: 6 SERVINGS

2 cups finely chopped
    fresh rhubarb
¼ cup sugar
2 Tbsp. water
3 cups reduced-fat plain
    Greek yogurt
2 Tbsp. honey
¾ cup sliced almonds,
    toasted

1. In a small saucepan, combine rhubarb, sugar and water. Bring
to a boil. Reduce heat; simmer, uncovered, 10-15 minutes or until
rhubarb is tender, stirring occasionally. Transfer to a bowl; cool
slightly. Refrigerate until cold.

2. In a small bowl, whisk yogurt and honey until blended. Spoon
into serving dishes. Top with compote; sprinkle with almonds.

NOTE: To toast nuts, bake in a shallow pan in a 350° oven for
5-10 minutes or cook in a skillet over low heat until lightly
browned, stirring occasionally.

½ CUP YOGURT WITH ABOUT 2 TBSP. COMPOTE AND 2 TBSP.
ALMONDS: 218 cal., 8g fat (2g sat. fat), 7mg chol., 49mg sod.,
23g carb. (20g sugars, 2g fiber), 14g pro. DIABETIC EXCHANGES:
1 starch, 1 reduced-fat milk, 1 fat.

HOT SPICED FRUIT

HOT SPICED FRUIT

My baked pears, apples and cranberries have a touch of spice and sweetness—
just like a pie without the crust. Serve them over waffles or yogurt.
—*Lin Koppen, Orchard Park, NY*

PREP: 25 MIN. • BAKE: 30 MIN. + COOLING • MAKES: 12 SERVINGS

¼ cup packed brown sugar
2 Tbsp. cornstarch
¼ tsp. ground cinnamon
¼ tsp. ground ginger
⅛ tsp. ground cloves
1 cup cranberry or
  white grape juice
3 medium pears, peeled
  and sliced
3 medium apples, peeled
  and sliced
1 cup fresh or frozen
  cranberries, thawed
  and chopped
1 can (11 oz.) mandarin
  oranges, drained

1. Preheat oven to 375°. In a small bowl, mix the first
5 ingredients; gradually whisk in cranberry juice.

2. In a greased 13x9-in. baking dish, combine remaining
ingredients. Pour cranberry juice mixture over top.

3. Bake, uncovered, 30-35 minutes or until pears and apples
are tender, stirring once. Let stand 10 minutes before serving.
Serve warm or cold.

½ CUP: 88 cal., 0 fat (0 sat. fat), 0 chol., 5mg sod., 23g carb.
(17g sugars, 3g fiber), 1g pro.

CHICKEN SAUSAGE & POTATO HASH

This hash is total comfort food, whether it's for breakfast, lunch or dinner.
We like it with fried or poached eggs on top.
—*Lisa Speer, Palm Beach, FL*

TAKES: 30 MIN. • MAKES: 4 SERVINGS

3 Tbsp. canola oil, divided
1 pkg. (12 oz.) fully cooked
  sun-dried tomato
  chicken sausage links
  or flavor of your choice,
  coarsely chopped
1 pkg. (20 oz.) refrigerated
  diced potatoes with onion
½ cup chopped sweet onion
¼ tsp. plus ⅛ tsp. pepper,
  divided
½ cup chopped roasted
  sweet red pepper
1 Tbsp. butter
4 large eggs

1. In a large nonstick skillet, heat 1 Tbsp. oil over medium-high
heat. Add sausage; cook and stir 4-6 minutes or until lightly
browned. Remove from pan.

2. In same pan, heat remaining oil over medium heat. Add
potatoes, sweet onion and ¼ tsp. pepper; cook, covered,
10-12 minutes or until golden brown, turning potatoes every
2 minutes. Stir in red pepper and sausage; heat through.

3. Meanwhile, in another large nonstick skillet, heat butter
over medium-high heat. Break eggs, 1 at a time, into pan;
immediately reduce heat to low. Cook, covered, 5-6 minutes or
until whites are completely set and yolks just begin to thicken.
If desired, carefully turn eggs and cook second side to desired
doneness. Remove from heat; sprinkle with remaining pepper.
Serve over hash.

1 SERVING: 446 cal., 25g fat (6g sat. fat), 264mg chol., 1045mg sod.,
27g carb. (4g sugars, 2g fiber), 23g pro.

PEACH PANCAKES WITH BUTTER SAUCE

I am 10 and I enjoy helping my grandma in the kitchen.
I love pancakes and peaches, so we came up with this recipe.
—*Mikayla Blackstar, Ponca City, OK*

PREP: 20 MIN. • COOK: 5 MIN./BATCH • MAKES: 16 PANCAKES (2 CUPS SAUCE)

2 cups all-purpose flour
2 Tbsp. sugar
4 tsp. baking powder
1 tsp. ground cinnamon
½ tsp. salt
2 cups 2% milk
2 large eggs, lightly beaten
¼ cup canola oil
1 can (15¼ oz.) peach
   halves, drained and
   finely chopped

SAUCE
1 cup corn syrup
½ cup sugar
⅓ cup butter, cubed
1 large egg
2 to 3 tsp. vanilla extract

1. In a large bowl, combine the flour, sugar, baking powder, cinnamon and salt. Combine the milk, eggs and oil; add to dry ingredients just until moistened. Fold in peaches.

2. Pour batter by ¼ cupfuls onto a greased hot griddle; turn when bubbles form on top. Cook until the second side is golden brown.

3. Meanwhile, in a small saucepan, combine the corn syrup, sugar, butter and egg. Cook and stir over medium heat until mixture is thickened and coats the back of a spoon. Stir in vanilla. Serve with pancakes.

2 PANCAKES WITH ¼ CUP SAUCE: 507 cal., 18g fat (7g sat. fat), 104mg chol., 485mg sod., 82g carb. (37g sugars, 1g fiber), 8g pro.

FRENCH VANILLA-PEAR FRENCH TOAST

My handyman, who is originally from Nicaragua, shared this classic breakfast dish his mother
used to prepare. He says he makes it frequently for his children and they clean their plates!
—*Gail Borczyk, Boca Raton, FL*

PREP: 20 MIN. + CHILLING • BAKE: 40 MIN. • MAKES: 6 SERVINGS

1 cup packed brown sugar
½ cup butter, melted
1 large pear, peeled and
   sliced (about 1½ cups)
¾ cup raisins
4 cups cubed day-old
   French bread
   (1½ in. pieces)
¾ cup finely chopped
   pecans
4 large eggs
2 cups French vanilla
   ice cream, melted
2 tsp. ground cinnamon
2 tsp. vanilla extract

1. In a small bowl, mix brown sugar and butter. Spread onto bottom of a greased 8-in. square baking dish. Layer with pear, raisins, bread cubes and pecans.

2. In a large bowl, whisk eggs, ice cream, cinnamon and vanilla until blended; pour over top. Refrigerate, covered, several hours or overnight.

3. Preheat oven to 350°. Remove casserole from refrigerator while oven heats. Bake, uncovered, 40-45 minutes or until golden brown and a knife inserted in the center comes out clean. Let stand 5-10 minutes before serving.

1 SERVING: 701 cal., 38g fat (16g sat. fat), 339mg chol., 390mg sod., 80g carb. (61g sugars, 4g fiber), 15g pro.

CREAMY, CHEESY GRITS WITH CURRIED POACHED EGGS

I first tried curried poached eggs when I lived in Germany. They were delicious with that rich, runny yolk, and serving them over cheesy grits seemed like the next best move to try. I'm happy to say that my instincts were right!
—*Shannon Copley, Upper Arlington, OH*

PREP: 20 MIN. • **COOK:** 15 MIN. • **MAKES:** 4 SERVINGS

2 **bacon strips, coarsely chopped**	¼ **tsp. salt**
2 **cups vegetable broth**	¼ **tsp. pepper**
½ **cup quick-cooking corn grits**	2 **tsp. white vinegar**
1 **cup shredded sharp cheddar cheese**	2 **tsp. curry powder**
2 **oz. reduced-fat cream cheese**	4 **large eggs**
	Additional shredded cheddar cheese, optional
	1 **to 2 Tbsp. minced chives or parsley**

1. In a large saucepan, cook bacon over medium heat until crisp, stirring occasionally. Remove with a slotted spoon; drain on paper towels. Discard drippings.

2. In same saucepan over medium heat, bring vegetable broth to a boil. Slowly stir in grits. Reduce heat to low; simmer, covered, stirring occasionally, until thickened, about 7 minutes. Add cheeses, salt and pepper; stir well. Cover and remove from heat.

3. Place 2-3 in. water in a large saucepan or skillet with high sides. Stir in vinegar and curry powder. Bring to a boil; adjust heat to maintain a gentle simmer. Break each cold egg into a separate small bowl; 1 at a time, hold bowls close to surface of water, and slip eggs into water.

4. Cook eggs, uncovered, until whites are completely set and yolks begin to thicken but are not hard, 3-5 minutes. Using a slotted spoon, lift eggs out of water.

5. Meanwhile, divide grits evenly among 4 bowls. Place 1 egg on top of each serving of grits; top with chopped bacon and, if desired, additional shredded cheese. Sprinkle with chives or parsley. Serve immediately.

1 EGG AND ¾ CUP GRITS: 316 cal., 19g fat (9g sat. fat), 228mg chol., 870mg sod., 18g carb. (2g sugars, 1g fiber), 18g pro.

FROM GRANDMA'S KITCHEN: For perfect poached eggs, use the freshest eggs possible. Vinegar in the water keeps the eggs nice and compact, preventing them from spreading.

MOM'S FLUFFY SCRAMBLED EGGS

I make these fluffy scrambled eggs when family comes for breakfast or when
I just want to do something extra special for myself in the morning. My favorite cheese for
this recipe is freshly grated white cheddar, but whatever you have in the fridge works!
—*Kailey Thompson, Palm Bay, FL*

TAKES: 30 MIN. • MAKES: 8 SERVINGS

8 bacon strips
12 large eggs, beaten
6 Tbsp. butter, divided
2 cups shredded
white cheddar cheese
¼ cup minced fresh parsley
¼ cup snipped fresh dill
½ tsp. salt
¼ tsp. pepper
8 bread slices, toasted
Hot pepper sauce

1. In a large nonstick skillet, cook bacon over medium heat until crisp, stirring occasionally. Remove; drain on paper towels and break into 1-in. pieces. Discard drippings. In the same pan, cook and stir eggs over medium heat until almost set. Stir in 2 Tbsp. butter; cook and stir until no liquid egg remains. Add cheese, parsley, dill, salt, pepper and remaining 4 Tbsp. butter; stir gently until cheese is melted.

2. Top toast with eggs and bacon; drizzle with hot pepper sauce.

1 SERVING: 403 cal., 29g fat (14g sat. fat), 338mg chol., 772mg sod., 14g carb. (2g sugars, 1g fiber), 21g pro.

PEAR QUINOA BREAKFAST BAKE

In an effort to eat healthier, I've been trying to incorporate more whole grains into our diet.
My husband and I enjoy quinoa, so I created this breakfast bake for our
Sunday brunch. The quinoa is a nice change of pace from oatmeal.
—*Sue Gronholz, Beaver Dam, WI*

PREP: 15 MIN. • BAKE: 55 MIN. + STANDING • MAKES: 2 SERVINGS

1 cup water
¼ cup quinoa, rinsed
¼ cup mashed peeled
ripe pear
1 Tbsp. honey
¼ tsp. ground cinnamon
¼ tsp. vanilla extract
Dash ground ginger
Dash ground nutmeg

TOPPING
¼ cup sliced almonds
1 Tbsp. brown sugar
1 Tbsp. butter, softened
Plain Greek yogurt,
optional

1. Preheat oven to 350°. In a small bowl, combine the first 8 ingredients; transfer to a greased 3-cup baking dish. Cover and bake for 50 minutes. In another small bowl, combine the almonds, brown sugar and butter; sprinkle over quinoa mixture.

2. Bake, uncovered, until lightly browned, 5-10 minutes longer. Let stand 10 minutes before serving. If desired, serve with yogurt.

1 SERVING: 267 cal., 13g fat (4g sat. fat), 15mg chol., 49mg sod., 35g carb. (18g sugars, 4g fiber), 6g pro. DIABETIC EXCHANGES: 2½ fat, 2 starch.

"Delicious recipe, and one I will definitely remember when our pear tree bears fruit. It was easy to make, and both my husband and I enjoyed it even though it was our first time eating quinoa."
—GRAMMYDEBBIE, TASTEOFHOME

MOM'S FLUFFY
SCRAMBLED EGGS

SLOW-COOKED BREAKFAST APPLE COBBLER

This is a fabulous recipe to serve on Christmas or any other cold morning. The apples can be peeled if preferred.
—*Marietta Slater, Justin, TX*

PREP: 15 MIN. • COOK: 6 HOURS • MAKES: 6 SERVINGS

6 medium apples, cut into ½-in. wedges
1 Tbsp. butter
3 Tbsp. honey
½ tsp. ground cinnamon
¼ cup dried cranberries
2 cups granola without raisins
Optional: Milk and maple syrup

1. Place apples in a greased 3-qt. slow cooker. In a microwave, melt butter; stir in honey and cinnamon. Drizzle over apples. Sprinkle cranberries and granola over top.

2. Cook, covered, on low until apples are tender, 6-8 hours. If desired, serve with milk and syrup.

¾ CUP: 289 cal., 8g fat (1g sat. fat), 5mg chol., 31mg sod., 58g carb. (31g sugars, 11g fiber), 7g pro.

EGG BISCUIT BAKE

This all-in-one brunch bake is a variation of a simple cheesy egg dish my mother used to make. It's become our favorite comfort food.
—*Alice Le Duc, Cedarburg, WI*

TAKES: 30 MIN. • MAKES: 6 SERVINGS

1 can (5 oz.) evaporated milk
8 oz. Velveeta, cubed
1 tsp. prepared mustard
¾ cup cubed fully cooked ham
½ cup frozen peas
2 Tbsp. butter
10 large eggs, lightly beaten
1 tube (12 oz.) refrigerated buttermilk biscuits

1. Preheat oven to 375°. In a large saucepan, combine milk, cheese and mustard; cook over low heat until smooth, stirring constantly. Stir in ham and peas.

2. Melt butter in a large skillet; heat butter until hot. Add eggs; cook and stir over medium heat until eggs are completely set. Add cheese sauce and stir gently.

3. Spoon into an ungreased shallow 2-qt. baking dish. Separate biscuits and cut each in half. Place with cut sides down around outer edge of dish.

4. Bake, uncovered, 15-20 minutes or until a knife inserted in the center comes out clean and biscuits are golden brown.

1 SERVING: 486 cal., 26g fat (13g sat. fat), 405mg chol., 1347mg sod., 35g carb. (7g sugars, 1g fiber), 28g pro.

SIMPLY INCREDIBLE GRITS

Since moving to the South, I have come to love grits! I also love my slow cooker,
and I worked to find a way to make perfect grits without stirring on the stovetop.
I knew this recipe was a winner when my mother-in-law overheard someone say at a
church potluck that it just wasn't right that a Midwesterner could make such good grits!
—Tacy Fleury, Clinton, SC

PREP: 10 MIN. • COOK: 2½ HOURS • MAKES: 6 SERVINGS

2⅔ cups water
1½ cups uncooked
    old-fashioned grits
1½ cups 2% milk
3 Tbsp. butter, cubed
2 tsp. chicken bouillon
    granules
½ tsp. salt
1 cup shredded
    cheddar cheese
⅓ cup grated
    Parmesan cheese

Combine the first 6 ingredients in a greased 3-qt. slow cooker.
Cook, covered, on low until liquid is absorbed and grits are tender,
2½-3 hours, stirring every 45 minutes. Stir in the cheeses until
melted. Serve immediately.

¾ CUP: 334 cal., 15g fat (9g sat. fat), 43mg chol., 755mg sod.,
38g carb. (3g sugars, 2g fiber), 11g pro.

SMOKED SAUSAGE BREAKFAST HASH

This hash full of red potatoes, sweet potatoes and sausage brightens up any day.
We spread the love throughout the week and pile leftovers into burritos and casseroles.
—Jamie Burton, Highlands Ranch, CO

PREP: 15 MIN. • BAKE: 25 MIN. • MAKES: 4 SERVINGS

1 lb. red potatoes
    (about 3 medium),
    cut into ½-in. cubes
1 medium sweet potato,
    peeled and cut into
    ½-in. cubes
1 medium onion, chopped
1½ cups sliced smoked
    turkey sausage
    (about 8 oz.)
4 garlic cloves, minced
1 tsp. Creole seasoning
2 cups chopped fresh
    spinach
1 Tbsp. butter
4 large eggs

1. Preheat oven to 425°. In a large bowl, toss together the first
6 ingredients. Spread evenly in a greased 15x10x1-in. baking pan.
Roast 20-25 minutes or until vegetables are tender, stirring once.
Stir in spinach; roast 5 minutes longer.

2. Meanwhile, in a large nonstick skillet, heat butter over medium-
high heat. Break eggs, 1 at a time, into pan; immediately reduce
heat to low. Cook until whites are completely set and yolks begin
to thicken but are not hard, about 5 minutes. Serve over hash.

1¼ CUPS HASH WITH 1 EGG: 317 cal., 11g fat (4g sat. fat), 229mg
chol., 842mg sod., 35g carb. (8g sugars, 4g fiber), 19g pro.

SALMON
QUICHE

SALMON QUICHE

This recipe came to me from my mother—it's the kind you request after just one bite! Unlike some quiches, this one is hearty enough to appeal to everyone. Cooking is something that I've always liked to do. I pore over cookbooks the way other people read novels!
—Deanna Baldwin, Bermuda Dunes, CA

PREP: 15 MIN. • BAKE: 55 MIN. • MAKES: 8 SERVINGS

1 sheet refrigerated
   pie crust
1 medium onion, chopped
1 Tbsp. butter
2 cups shredded
   Swiss cheese
1 can (14¾ oz.) salmon,
   drained, flaked and
   cartilage removed
5 large eggs
2 cups half-and-half cream
¼ tsp. salt
   Minced fresh parsley,
   optional

1. Line unpricked pie crust with a double thickness of heavy-duty foil. Bake at 450° for 8 minutes. Remove foil; bake 5 minutes longer. Cool on a wire rack.

2. In a small skillet, saute onion in butter until tender. Sprinkle cheese in the crust; top with salmon and onion.

3. In a small bowl, whisk the eggs, cream and salt; pour over salmon mixture. Bake at 350° for 45-50 minutes or until a knife inserted in the center comes out clean. Sprinkle with parsley if desired. Let stand 5 minutes before cutting.

1 PIECE: 448 cal., 29g fat (15g sat. fat), 219mg chol., 610mg sod., 18g carb. (5g sugars, 0 fiber), 26g pro.

JAM & CREAM FRENCH TOAST

My grandmother used to make this for me when I was a child. You can experiment with other flavors of jam and bread.
—B. MacKinnon, Kodak, TN

TAKES: 15 MIN. • MAKES: 1 SERVING

2 Tbsp. cream cheese,
   softened
2 thick slices
   cinnamon-raisin bread
2 Tbsp. strawberry jam
1 large egg
1 Tbsp. butter
   Maple syrup, optional

1. Spread cream cheese on 1 slice of bread. Spread jam on the other slice; place jam side down over the cream cheese. In a shallow bowl, beat egg. Dip both sides of bread into egg.

2. In a small skillet, melt butter; toast bread for 3-4 minutes on each side or until golden brown. Serve with syrup if desired.

2 SLICES: 376 cal., 26g fat (15g sat. fat), 275mg chol., 264mg sod., 27g carb. (25g sugars, 0 fiber), 9g pro.

"My grandson loves this and always requests it when he comes for a sleepover. Easy to make and very tasty."
—JKCOACH98, TASTEOFHOME.COM

HAM STEAKS WITH GRUYERE, BACON & MUSHROOMS

This meat lover's breakfast has a big wow factor. The Gruyere,
bacon and fresh mushrooms in the topping are an amazing combination.
—*Lisa Speer, Palm Beach, FL*

TAKES: 25 MIN. • MAKES: 4 SERVINGS

2 Tbsp. butter
½ lb. sliced fresh
  mushrooms
1 shallot, finely chopped
2 garlic cloves, minced
⅛ tsp. coarsely ground
  pepper
1 fully cooked boneless
  ham steak (about 1 lb.),
  cut into 4 pieces
1 cup shredded
  Gruyere cheese
4 bacon strips, cooked
  and crumbled
1 Tbsp. minced fresh
  parsley, optional

1. In a large nonstick skillet, heat butter over medium-high heat. Add mushrooms and shallot; cook and stir 4-6 minutes or until tender. Add garlic and pepper; cook 1 minute longer. Remove from pan; keep warm. Wipe skillet clean.

2. In same skillet, cook ham over medium heat 3 minutes. Turn; sprinkle with cheese and bacon. Cook, covered, 2-4 minutes longer or until cheese is melted and ham is heated through. Serve with mushroom mixture. If desired, sprinkle with parsley.

1 SERVING: 352 cal., 22g fat (11g sat. fat), 113mg chol., 1576mg sod., 5g carb. (2g sugars, 1g fiber), 34g pro.

DUTCH CREAM WAFFLES

Originally made by my grandmother on a wood-burning stove, these crispy
waffles are also special to me for another reason. I served them to my
husband more than 50 years ago when I first cooked for him in our new home.
—*Barbara Syme, Peoria, AZ*

TAKES: 20 MIN. • MAKES: 3 SERVINGS

1 cup all-purpose flour
¼ tsp. salt
3 large eggs, separated
1 cup heavy whipping
  cream
  Maple syrup

1. In a large bowl, combine the flour and salt. In a small bowl, beat egg yolks on low speed; gradually add cream and beat for 1 minute. Add to flour mixture; combine on low speed, then beat on medium-high until smooth.

2. In another bowl with clean beaters, beat egg whites on high until stiff peaks form. Gently fold into batter.

3. Bake in a preheated waffle iron according to manufacturer's directions. Serve with syrup.

1 WAFFLE: 500 cal., 35g fat (20g sat. fat), 321mg chol., 291mg sod., 35g carb. (4g sugars, 1g fiber), 12g pro.

CHEESY BACON & GRITS CASSEROLE

I was craving grits for breakfast, so I created this masterpiece with fresh corn and leftover bacon.
—*Rebecca Yankovich, Springfield, VA*

PREP: 30 MIN. • **BAKE:** 35 MIN. + STANDING • **MAKES:** 8 SERVINGS

6 bacon strips, chopped
3 cups water
1 cup whole milk
¾ tsp. salt
1 cup uncooked old-fashioned grits
2 cups shredded Colby-Monterey Jack cheese, divided
2 large eggs, room temperature, lightly beaten
1 cup fresh or frozen corn, thawed
¼ tsp. pepper
Sliced avocado, optional

1. Preheat oven to 350°. In a large skillet, cook bacon over medium heat until crisp, stirring occasionally. Remove with a slotted spoon; drain on paper towels.

2. Meanwhile, in a Dutch oven, bring water, milk and salt to a boil. Slowly stir in grits. Reduce heat to low; cook, covered, until thickened, 15-20 minutes, stirring occasionally. Remove from heat. Stir in 1½ cups cheese until melted. Slowly stir in eggs until blended. Stir in bacon, corn and pepper. Transfer to a greased 2-qt. baking dish. Sprinkle with remaining ½ cup cheese.

3. Bake, uncovered, until edges are golden brown and cheese is melted, 35-40 minutes. Let stand 10 minutes before serving. If desired, serve with avocado.

FREEZE OPTION: Cool unbaked casserole; cover and freeze. To use, partially thaw in refrigerator overnight. Remove casserole from refrigerator 30 minutes before baking. Preheat oven to 350°. Bake grits as directed until heated through and a thermometer inserted in center reads 165°, increasing time to 45-55 minutes.

¾ CUP: 261 cal., 13g fat (8g sat. fat), 81mg chol., 534mg sod., 23g carb. (3g sugars, 1g fiber), 13g pro.

TRIPLE-SAUSAGE BREAKFAST BAKE

This over-the-top breakfast has marvelous flavors—smoky,
sweet and spicy—that'll really warm you up. It's a truly meaty meal.
—*Thomas Faglon, Somerset, NJ*

PREP: 20 MIN. • BAKE: 35 MIN. • MAKES: 6 SERVINGS

½ **lb. fully cooked
Italian sausage links,
sliced**
½ **lb. fully cooked
andouille sausage links,
sliced**
½ **lb. fully cooked
bratwurst links, sliced**
1 **medium onion, chopped**
1 **medium sweet
red pepper, chopped**
1 **serrano pepper, seeded
and finely chopped**
6 **large eggs**
1 **cup heavy
whipping cream**
1 **tsp. hot pepper sauce
Rye bread, toasted**

1. Preheat oven to 350°. In a large skillet, cook and stir sausages over medium heat until browned, 6-8 minutes. Remove with a slotted spoon to a greased 11x7-in. baking dish.

2. In same skillet, cook and stir onion and peppers over medium heat until tender, 5-6 minutes. Sprinkle over sausages. Whisk together the eggs, cream and hot sauce; pour over top. Bake, uncovered, until golden brown and set, 35-40 minutes. Serve with toasted rye bread.

TO MAKE AHEAD: Refrigerate, covered, several hours or overnight. To use, preheat oven to 350°. Remove casserole from refrigerator while oven heats. Bake as directed.

NOTE: Wear disposable gloves when cutting hot peppers; the oils can burn skin. Avoid touching your face.

1 CUP: 695 cal., 59g fat (24g sat. fat), 387mg chol., 1441mg sod., 10g carb. (3g sugars, 1g fiber), 36g pro.

WAFFLE MONTE CRISTOS

Adults love the sweet, smoky flavor. I use frozen waffles to save time,
but have at it if you want to put your waffle iron to good use.
—*Kelly Reynolds, Urbana, IL*

TAKES: 20 MIN. • MAKES: 4 SERVINGS

½ **cup apricot preserves**
8 **frozen waffles**
4 **slices deli turkey**
4 **slices deli ham**
4 **slices Havarti cheese
(about 3 oz.)**
4 **bacon strips, cooked**
2 **Tbsp. butter, softened
Maple syrup**

1. Preheat griddle over medium heat. Spread preserves over 4 waffles. Layer with turkey, ham, cheese and bacon; top with remaining waffles. Lightly spread outsides of waffles with butter.

2. Place on griddle; cook 4-5 minutes on each side or until golden brown and heated through. Serve with syrup for dipping.

1 SANDWICH: 511 cal., 23g fat (10g sat. fat), 70mg chol., 1163mg sod., 57g carb. (22g sugars, 2g fiber), 21g pro.

TRIPLE-SAUSAGE
BREAKFAST BAKE

SPICED APRICOT BAKED OATMEAL

Eat these spiced oatmeal squares while they're still warm for a cozy morning treat. I freeze mine in single servings so I can grab, go and microwave when I get to work. I'm not too humble to say I have the best breakfast in the office.

—*Ellie Martin Cliffe, Milwaukee, WI*

PREP: 15 MIN. • **BAKE:** 25 MIN. • **MAKES:** 12 SERVINGS

¾ cup packed brown sugar
3 tsp. pumpkin pie spice
2 tsp. baking powder
½ tsp. salt
¼ tsp. ground cardamom
3 cups old-fashioned oats
½ cup chopped
    dried apricots
½ cup chopped pecans,
    toasted
3 large eggs,
    room temperature

1½ cups fat-free milk
½ cup unsweetened
    applesauce
1½ tsp. vanilla extract
¼ cup butter, melted

TOPPINGS

3 cups vanilla yogurt
½ cup apricot preserves,
    warmed

1. Preheat oven to 350°. In a large bowl, mix first 5 ingredients; stir in oats, apricots and pecans. In another bowl, whisk together eggs, milk, applesauce and vanilla; gradually whisk in melted butter. Stir into oat mixture.

2. Transfer to a greased 11x7-in. baking dish. Bake, uncovered, 25-30 minutes or until set and edges are lightly browned. Cut into 12 portions; serve with toppings.

FREEZE OPTION: Freeze cooled portions of oatmeal in airtight freezer containers. To use, microwave each portion on high for 20-30 seconds or until heated through. Serve with toppings.

NOTE: To toast nuts, bake in a shallow pan in a 350° oven for 5-10 minutes or cook in a skillet over low heat until lightly browned, stirring occasionally.

1 PIECE WITH ¼ CUP YOGURT AND 2 TSP. PRESERVES: 327 cal., 11g fat (4g sat. fat), 60mg chol., 280mg sod., 52g carb. (33g sugars, 3g fiber), 9g pro.

"Fall is oatmeal time, and this recipe is delicious! I will make it again. I cut the recipe down and baked the smaller amount in 4 ramekins. Thank you for sharing this recipe."
—ORBS, TASTEOFHOME.COM

ZUCCHINI & GOUDA SKILLET FRITTATA

This is a version of a skillet dish that my mother-in-law created to use up all that extra summertime zucchini. The Gouda melts beautifully, but you can make it with Swiss or sharp cheddar, too.
—*Susan Marshall, Colorado Springs, CO*

TAKES: 30 MIN. • **MAKES:** 6 SERVINGS

6 **large eggs**
2 **Tbsp. 2% milk**
1 **tsp. chopped**
   fresh oregano
½ **tsp. salt**
⅛ **tsp. pepper**
2 **Tbsp. butter**
2 **medium zucchini (7 to**
   8 oz. each), thinly sliced
1 **medium onion, chopped**
2 **Tbsp. olive oil**
1 **medium tomato, diced**
1 **cup shredded**
   Gouda cheese
2 **Tbsp. minced fresh basil**

1. Combine the first 5 ingredients; set aside. In a large nonstick skillet, melt butter over medium heat. Add zucchini and onion. Cook until tender, 6-8 minutes; remove.

2. In same skillet, heat oil over medium heat. Add egg mixture. Cook until set, gently lifting edges of cooked egg to allow liquid to run underneath. Top with zucchini mixture, diced tomato and cheese. Cover and cook until cheese is melted, 2-3 minutes. Sprinkle basil on top.

1 WEDGE: 238 cal., 19g fat (8g sat. fat), 218mg chol., 462mg sod., 6g carb. (4g sugars, 1g fiber), 12g pro.

SAUSAGE-SWEET POTATO HASH & EGGS

When I first began making this dish for breakfast, I served it with fried eggs on top.
Now I sometimes make it for supper and serve it without eggs.
It's fantastic when I want a dish I can make quickly with minimal cleanup.
—*Nancy Murphy, Mount Dora, FL*

TAKES: 25 MIN. • **MAKES:** 4 SERVINGS

½ **lb. Italian turkey sausage**
   links, casings removed
2 **medium sweet potatoes,**
   peeled and cut into
   ¼-in. cubes
2 **medium Granny Smith**
   apples, chopped
¼ **cup dried cranberries**
¼ **cup chopped pecans**
¼ **tsp. salt**
4 **green onions, sliced**
4 **large eggs**

1. In a large nonstick skillet coated with cooking spray, cook sausage and sweet potatoes over medium-high heat 8-10 minutes or until sausage is no longer pink, breaking sausage into crumbles.

2. Add apples, cranberries, pecans and salt; cook and stir 4-6 minutes longer or until potatoes are tender. Remove from pan; sprinkle with green onions. Keep warm.

3. Wipe skillet clean and coat with cooking spray; place skillet over medium-high heat. Break eggs, 1 at a time, into pan. Reduce heat to low. Cook to desired doneness, turning after whites are set if desired. Serve with hash.

1 SERVING: 338 cal., 14g fat (3g sat. fat), 207mg chol., 465mg sod., 42g carb. (23g sugars, 6g fiber), 15g pro. **DIABETIC EXCHANGES:** 2 starch, 2 medium-fat meat, ½ fruit.

SUNRISE SAUSAGE
ENCHILADAS

SUNRISE SAUSAGE ENCHILADAS

These delicious enchiladas are equally good made with cubed ham or sausage.
Prepare ahead, refrigerate and bake when ready for a convenient breakfast twist.
—*Deb LeBlanc, Phillipsburg, KS*

PREP: 30 MIN. + CHILLING • BAKE: 40 MIN. • MAKES: 10 SERVINGS

- **1 lb. bulk pork sausage**
- **2 Tbsp. canola oil**
- **7 cups frozen shredded hash brown potatoes, thawed (20 oz.)**
- **½ tsp. salt**
- **½ tsp. chili powder**
- **¼ tsp. cayenne pepper**
- **¼ tsp. pepper**
- **1 can (4 oz.) chopped green chiles**
- **2 cups shredded cheddar cheese, divided**
- **10 flour tortillas (6 in.)**
- **2 cans (10 oz. each) green enchilada sauce**
- **Optional toppings: Chopped red onion, chopped sweet red pepper and chopped fresh cilantro**

1. In a large skillet, cook and crumble the sausage over medium heat until no longer pink, 5-7 minutes. Remove from pan with a slotted spoon; discard drippings.

2. In same pan, heat oil over medium-high heat; saute the potatoes until lightly browned, 8-10 minutes. Remove from the heat; stir in seasonings, chiles, sausage and ½ cup cheese.

3. Place ½ cup filling on each tortilla; roll up and place in a greased 13x9-in. baking dish, seam side down. Top with sauce. Refrigerate, covered, several hours or overnight.

4. Preheat oven to 375°. Remove enchiladas from the refrigerator while oven heats. Bake, covered, 30 minutes. Sprinkle with remaining cheese. Bake, uncovered, 10-15 minutes or until lightly browned and heated through. If desired, serve with toppings.

1 ENCHILADA: 398 cal., 25g fat (9g sat. fat), 48mg chol., 1116mg sod., 30g carb. (2g sugars, 2g fiber), 14g pro.

GRANDMA'S SECRET

Green enchilada sauce is a blend of tomatillos, oil and spices thickened with flour or cornstarch. Red enchilada sauce, made from tomatoes instead of tomatillos, is also available.

SAVORY FRENCH TOAST

I was tired of sweet French toast, so I made a savory version with sausage,
cheddar and chives for Christmas one year. Now my family asks for it regularly.
—*Carol Grant, Freehold, NJ*

PREP: 20 MIN. • BAKE: 25 MIN. • MAKES: 10 SERVINGS

10 slices French bread
   (1 in. thick)
 1 lb. bulk pork sausage
 8 large eggs
 2 cups 2% milk
 ½ cup grated
   Parmesan cheese
 1 Tbsp. minced chives
 ½ tsp. pepper
 1 cup shredded
   cheddar cheese
   Additional minced chives

1. Preheat oven to 350°. Arrange bread in a single layer in a greased 13x9-in. baking dish. In a large skillet, cook sausage over medium heat 6-8 minutes or until no longer pink, breaking into crumbles; drain.

2. In a large bowl, whisk eggs, milk, Parmesan, chives and pepper; pour over bread. Add sausage; sprinkle with cheese.

3. Bake, uncovered, 25-30 minutes or until edges are golden and a knife inserted in the center comes out clean. Let stand 5 minutes before cutting. Sprinkle with additional chives.

TO MAKE AHEAD: Prepare casserole as directed. Refrigerate, covered, several hours or overnight. To use, preheat oven to 350°. Remove casserole from refrigerator while oven heats. Bake as directed. Sprinkle with additional chives.

1 SERVING: 316 cal., 20g fat (8g sat. fat), 192mg chol., 638mg sod., 16g carb. (4g sugars, 1g fiber), 18g pro.

APPLE BUTTER BISCUIT BREAKFAST BAKE

My grandmother created this recipe to use up the leftovers from Christmas Eve dinner.
By combining the leftover ham and biscuits with her homemade apple butter, milk and eggs, she could
serve us all a warm, delicious breakfast and still have time to spend with the grandchildren.
—*Mary Leverette, Columbia, SC*

PREP: 30 MIN. + CHILLING • BAKE: 50 MIN. + STANDING • MAKES: 12 SERVINGS

10 leftover biscuits
   (3-in. diameter)
 ¾ cup apple butter
 2 cups shredded sharp
   cheddar cheese
1½ cups cubed
   fully cooked ham
 ¼ cup minced fresh parsley
 6 large eggs
2½ cups 2% milk
 1 tsp. salt
 ½ tsp. pepper
 ¼ tsp. ground mustard

1. Cut biscuits crosswise in half. Spread apple butter over cut sides of biscuits. Replace tops. Cut each biscuit into quarters; arrange in a single layer in a greased 13x9-in. baking dish. Top with cheese, ham and parsley.

2. In a large bowl, whisk eggs, milk, salt, pepper and mustard. Pour over biscuits. Cover and refrigerate overnight.

3. Preheat oven to 325°. Remove strata from refrigerator while oven heats. Bake, uncovered, until puffed and edges are golden brown, 50-60 minutes. Let stand 10 minutes before cutting.

1 PIECE: 331 cal., 15g fat (7g sat. fat), 126mg chol., 976mg sod., 31g carb. (12g sugars, 1g fiber), 16g pro.

SAUSAGE TORTILLA BREAKFAST BAKE

This casserole is perfect for a special brunch. It combines the spices of the Southwest with the comfort of a hearty breakfast. You can spice it up by adding cayenne and hot peppers, or mellow it by replacing the tomatoes and green chiles with mild salsa. It's versatile and easy—no wonder it's a longtime family favorite.
—*Darlene Buerger, Peoria, AZ*

PREP: 25 MIN. • BAKE: 25 MIN. + STANDING • MAKES: 6 SERVINGS

8 oz. bulk lean turkey breakfast sausage
½ cup canned diced tomatoes and green chiles
6 corn tortillas (6 in.)
½ cup shredded Monterey Jack cheese
¼ cup shredded pepper jack cheese
2 green onions, chopped
6 large eggs
¾ cup fat-free milk
¾ tsp. paprika
¼ tsp. ground cumin
Optional: Reduced-fat sour cream, salsa and additional chopped green onions

1. Preheat oven to 350°. In a large skillet, cook and crumble sausage over medium heat until no longer pink, 4-6 minutes. Stir in tomatoes.

2. Coat a 9-in. deep-dish pie plate with cooking spray. Line the pie plate with half the tortillas. Sprinkle with half each of the following: sausage mixture, cheeses and green onions. Repeat the layers.

3. In a bowl, whisk together eggs, milk, paprika and cumin; pour slowly over layers. Bake, uncovered, until set, 25-30 minutes. Let stand 10 minutes. Cut into wedges. If desired, serve with sour cream, salsa and additional green onions.

1 PIECE: 268 cal., 14g fat (5g sat. fat), 240mg chol., 646mg sod., 14g carb. (2g sugars, 2g fiber), 22g pro. DIABETIC EXCHANGES: 3 medium-fat meat, 1 starch.

MIXED FRUIT WITH LEMON-BASIL DRESSING

A slightly savory dressing really compliments the sweet
fruit in this recipe. I also use the dressing on salad greens.
—*Dixie Terry, Goreville, IL*

TAKES: 15 MIN. • **MAKES:** 8 SERVINGS

2 Tbsp. lemon juice
½ tsp. sugar
¼ tsp. salt
¼ tsp. ground mustard
⅛ tsp. onion powder
Dash pepper
6 Tbsp. olive oil
4½ tsp. minced fresh basil
1 cup cubed fresh
pineapple
1 cup sliced fresh
strawberries
1 cup sliced peeled
kiwifruit
1 cup seedless
watermelon balls
1 cup fresh blueberries
1 cup fresh raspberries

1. Place the lemon juice, sugar, salt, mustard, onion powder and pepper in a blender; cover and pulse until blended. While processing, gradually add oil in a steady stream. Stir in basil.

2. In a large bowl, combine the fruit. Drizzle with dressing and toss to coat. Refrigerate until serving.

¾ CUP: 145 cal., 11g fat (1g sat. fat), 0 chol., 76mg sod., 14g carb. (9g sugars, 3g fiber), 1g pro. **DIABETIC EXCHANGES:** 2 fat, 1 fruit.

HOME-STYLE SAUSAGE GRAVY & BISCUITS

My mother-in-law introduced me to her hamburger gravy,
and I modified it slightly. We have this every weekend.
—*Michele Bapst, Jacksonville, NC*

TAKES: 30 MIN. • **MAKES:** 8 SERVINGS

1 tube (16.3 oz.)
large refrigerated
flaky biscuits
1 lb. bulk pork sausage
1 cup chopped sweet onion
2 Tbsp. butter
1 envelope
country gravy mix
1 Tbsp. all-purpose flour
Dash each garlic powder,
Italian seasoning, onion
powder and pepper
1½ cups 2% milk
1 cup reduced-sodium
chicken broth

1. Bake biscuits according to package directions.

2. Meanwhile, in a large skillet, cook sausage and onion over medium heat until sausage is no longer pink; drain. Add butter; cook until melted. Stir in the gravy mix, flour and seasonings until blended. Gradually add milk and broth. Bring to a boil; cook and stir for 1 minute or until thickened. Serve with biscuits.

1 SERVING: 412 cal., 26g fat (8g sat. fat), 31mg chol., 1208mg sod., 33g carb. (9g sugars, 1g fiber), 10g pro.

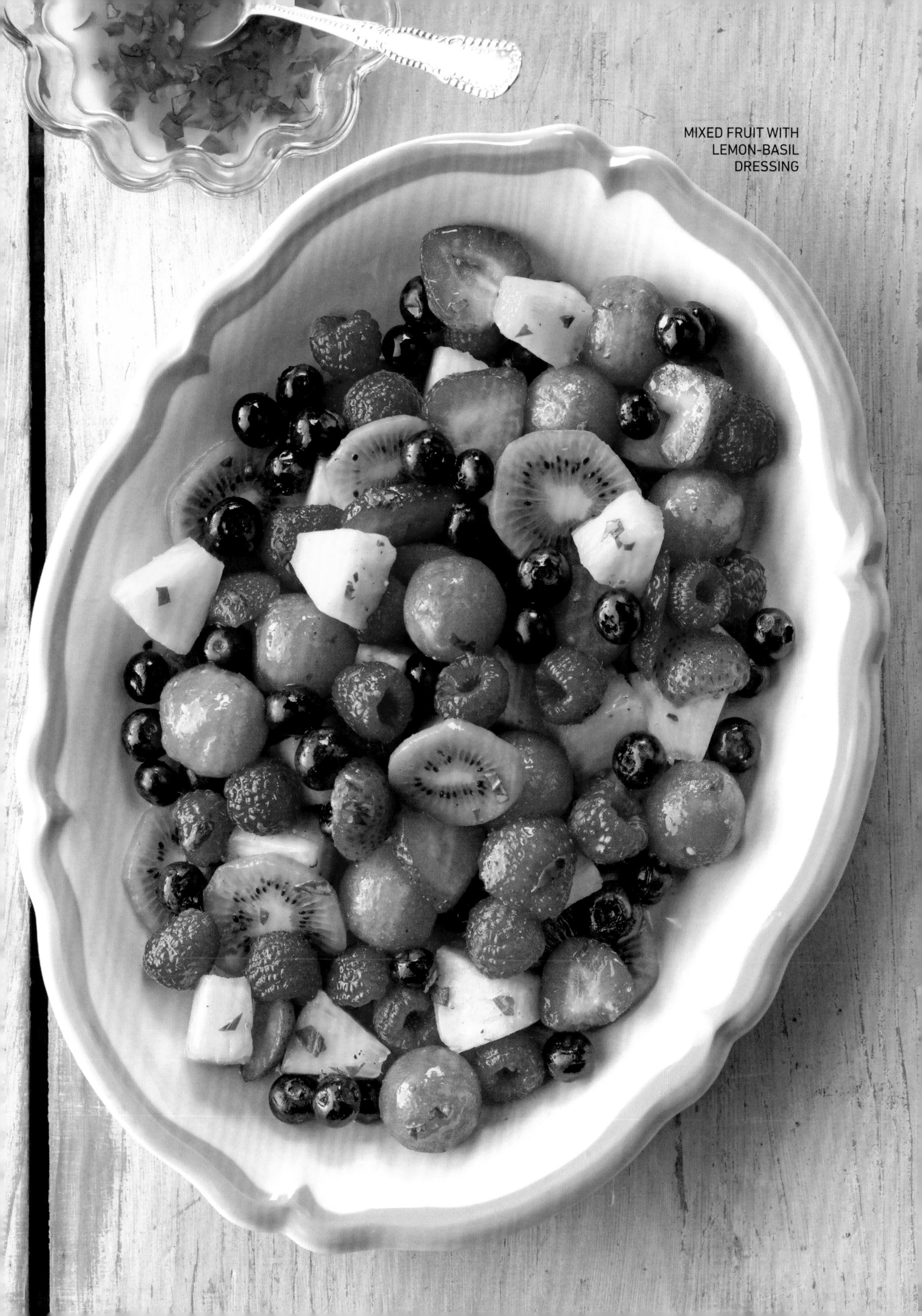
MIXED FRUIT WITH LEMON-BASIL DRESSING

CAJUN CRAB
POPPERS, PAGE 44

GRANDMA'S FAVORITE
SNACKS

—⟫✦⟪—

No one puts on a wonderful appetizer spread like
Grandma! From traditional samosas and palmiers
to surprising pork buns and pickled carrots,
turn here for noshes that inspire.

SAVORY STUFFED CHERRY PEPPERS

Our family's holiday dinners always include a giant antipasto tray, and the showpiece when we were growing up was Mom's stuffed hot peppers on top of the display. Regardless of how spicy the peppers were, every year we would sneak into the refrigerator and steal one of those thrilling little flavor bombs! There isn't a holiday that we don't make them in her honor. These stuffed peppers are remarkable hot or cold. Serve with a nice loaf of Italian bread and a glass of wine.

—Donna Scarano, East Hanover, NJ

PREP: 20 MIN. • BAKE: 40 MIN. • MAKES: ABOUT 3 DOZEN

3 jars (16 oz. each) pickled hot cherry peppers, drained

1 can (2 oz.) anchovy fillets

1 large tomato, seeded and finely chopped

1 cup pimiento-stuffed olives, finely chopped

1 cup ripe olives, finely chopped

3 Tbsp. olive oil, divided

¼ cup grated Parmesan cheese

2 Tbsp. seasoned bread crumbs

1 tsp. capers, drained

1 Tbsp. minced fresh parsley or 1 tsp. dried parsley flakes

1 tsp. garlic powder

½ tsp. pepper

½ tsp. dried basil

1. Preheat oven to 350°. Cut tops off peppers and remove seeds; set aside. Drain and chop anchovies, reserving oil.

2. In a large bowl, combine tomato, olives, 1 Tbsp. olive oil, Parmesan cheese, anchovies, anchovy oil, bread crumbs, capers, parsley and seasonings. Spoon into peppers.

3. Place in a greased 13x9-in. baking dish. Drizzle with the remaining 2 Tbsp. olive oil. Bake until tops are light golden brown, about 40 minutes.

FREEZE OPTION: Cover and freeze cooled peppers in a greased 13x9-in. baking dish. To use, partially thaw in refrigerator overnight. Remove from refrigerator 30 minutes before baking. Preheat oven to 350°. Reheat peppers, covered, until heated through, 20-30 minutes.

1 APPETIZER: 49 cal., 3g fat (0 sat. fat), 2mg chol., 612mg sod., 4g carb. (1g sugars, 1g fiber), 2g pro.

FROM GRANDMA'S KITCHEN: To quickly seed a tomato, cut it into wedges. Swipe your finger over each wedge to remove the gel pocket and seeds. This is nice for when you don't need perfectly seeded tomatoes.

MOM'S PICKLED CARROTS

My mother is the only other person I've known to make this recipe.
In fact, when I take it to a potluck or picnic, no one has ever heard
of pickled carrots. But once they try them, they are hooked.
—*Robin Koble, Fairview, PA*

PREP: 15 MIN. + CHILLING • **COOK:** 20 MIN. • **MAKES:** 6 CUPS

2 lbs. carrots, cut
lengthwise into
¼-in.-thick strips
1½ cups sugar
1½ cups water
1½ cups cider vinegar
¼ cup mustard seed
3 cinnamon sticks (3 in.)
3 whole cloves

1. Place carrots in a large saucepan; add enough water to cover.
Bring to a boil. Cook, covered, until crisp-tender, 3-5 minutes.
Drain. Transfer to a large bowl. In another large saucepan,
combine remaining ingredients. Bring to a boil. Reduce heat;
simmer, uncovered, for 20 minutes. Pour mixture over carrots.
Refrigerate, covered, overnight to allow flavors to blend.

2. Transfer mixture to jars. Cover and refrigerate up to 1 month.

¼ **CUP:** 30 cal., 0 fat (0 sat. fat), 0 chol., 170mg sod., 7g carb.
(6g sugars, 1g fiber), 1g pro.

FRIED LEMON-PEPPER WINGS

These lemon-pepper wings are perfect for game day. Try these out if you've been stuck in a chicken
wing rut. Add grated lemon zest to the butter mixture if you want a more pronounced lemon flavor.
—Taste of Home *Test Kitchen*

PREP: 20 MIN. • **COOK:** 10 MIN./BATCH • **MAKES:** 2 DOZEN

2½ lbs. chicken wings
½ cup all-purpose flour
2 tsp. salt
¼ tsp. pepper
Oil for deep-fat frying
2 Tbsp. butter, melted
1½ tsp. lemon-pepper
seasoning
2 Tbsp. minced
fresh parsley

1. Cut wings into 3 sections; discard wing tip sections. In a large
bowl, combine flour, salt and pepper. Add wings, a few at a time,
and toss to coat.

2. In an electric skillet or deep fryer, heat oil to 375°. Fry wings, a
few at a time, until no longer pink, 3-4 minutes on each side. Drain
on paper towels. In a large bowl, combine butter and seasoning.
Add wings; toss to coat. Sprinkle with parsley. Serve immediately.

1 **PIECE:** 107 cal., 9g fat (2g sat. fat), 18mg chol., 92mg sod., 1g carb.
(0 sugars, 0 fiber), 5g pro.

MANDARIN TURKEY PINWHEELS

Curry, smoked turkey and mandarin oranges give these pinwheels their flavor twist.
My cousin and I made them for an open house and people came back for seconds—and thirds!
—*Lorie Miner, Kamas, UT*

PREP: 15 MIN. + CHILLING • **MAKES:** 2½ DOZEN

1 pkg. (8 oz.) reduced-fat cream cheese
½ tsp. curry powder
½ cup mandarin oranges, drained and chopped
3 flour tortillas (12 in.), room temperature
½ lb. sliced deli smoked turkey
3 cups fresh baby spinach
2 green onions, chopped

1. In a small bowl, beat cream cheese and curry powder until blended. Stir in oranges. Spread over tortillas. Layer with turkey, spinach and green onions; roll up tightly. Wrap in waxed paper and refrigerate for 2 hours or until firm enough to cut.

2. Unwrap and cut each roll into 10 slices.

1 PIECE: 50 cal., 2g fat (1g sat. fat), 8mg chol., 149mg sod., 4g carb. (1g sugars, 1g fiber), 3g pro.

GRANDPA'S PIZZA BREAD

My grandmother made this pan bread often but never wrote down the recipe. Eventually,
my dad experimented until he came up with precise measurements. Now my kids love it.
—*Barbara Schimke, Etna, NH*

PREP: 20 MIN. + RISING • **BAKE:** 20 MIN. • **MAKES:** 16-20 SERVINGS

1 pkg. (¼ oz.) active dry yeast
1½ cups warm water (110° to 115°), divided
4 tsp. sugar
4 tsp. plus 2 Tbsp. olive oil, divided
1½ tsp. salt
3½ to 4 cups all-purpose flour
Salt and coarsely ground pepper to taste

1. In a large bowl, dissolve the yeast in ½ cup warm water. Add sugar; let stand for 5 minutes. Add 4 tsp. of oil, salt, remaining water and 2 cups flour. Beat until smooth. Stir in enough remaining flour to form a soft dough.

2. Turn onto a floured surface; knead until smooth and elastic, about 6-8 minutes. Place in a greased bowl, turning once to grease top. Cover and let rise in a warm place until doubled, about 1 hour.

3. Punch dough down. Brush a 13x9-in. baking pan with 1 Tbsp. oil. Press dough into pan. Brush with remaining oil and sprinkle with salt and pepper. Cover and let rise in a warm place until doubled, about 45 minutes.

4. Bake at 375° for 20-25 minutes or until lightly browned. Cut in squares. Serve warm or at room temperature.

1 SERVING: 104 cal., 2g fat (0 sat. fat), 0 chol., 178mg sod., 18g carb. (1g sugars, 1g fiber), 2g pro.

SAMOSAS

This samosa recipe is one of my family's absolute favorites. The crispy dough pockets are stuffed with potatoes and peas and then air-fried to give them a healthier twist. They'd make a perfect starter, side dish or buffet food for your next party.
—*Soniya Saluja, Chantilly, VA*

PREP: 20 MIN. + RISING • COOK: 15 MIN./BATCH • MAKES: 1 DOZEN

2 cups all-purpose flour
3 Tbsp. ghee or canola oil
½ tsp. salt
½ tsp. caraway seeds
¾ cup cold water

FILLING
5 medium potatoes, peeled and chopped
6 Tbsp. canola oil, divided
1 cup fresh or frozen peas, thawed
1 tsp. minced fresh gingerroot
1 tsp. garam masala
½ tsp. cumin seeds
½ tsp. salt
Optional: Fennel seeds, crushed coriander seeds, caraway seeds or amchur (dried mango powder)

1. In a large bowl, combine flour, ghee, salt and caraway seeds until mixture resembles bread crumbs. Gradually stir in enough water to form a firm dough. Turn onto a lightly floured surface; knead until smooth and elastic, 6-8 minutes. Cover and let rest for 1 hour.

2. Place potatoes in a large saucepan and cover with water. Bring to a boil. Reduce heat and cook until just tender, 8-10 minutes; drain. Set aside to cool slightly. In a large skillet, heat 3 Tbsp. oil over medium heat. Add potatoes and cook until potatoes start to cling to the skillet, about 5 minutes. Stir in peas, ginger, garam masala, cumin seeds and salt; cook until heated through, about 2 minutes. Stir in optional ingredients as desired. Set aside.

3. Divide dough into 6 pieces. Roll 1 piece of dough into a 10x6-in. oval. Cut dough in half. Moisten straight edge with water. Bring 1 corner of half moon up to meet the other corner of half moon, forming a cone. Pinch seam to seal. Fill with 3-4 Tbsp. potato mixture. Moisten curved edge of dough with water; fold over top of filling and press seam to seal. Gently press the bottom of each samosa to flatten slightly. Repeat with remaining dough and filling.

4. Preheat air fryer to 350°. Brush samosas with the remaining 3 Tbsp. oil. In batches, arrange samosas in a single layer, without touching, on tray in air-fryer basket. Cook until golden brown, about 15 minutes.

1 SAMOSA: 280 cal., 14g fat (3g sat. fat), 10mg chol., 203mg sod., 33g carb. (1g sugars, 3g fiber), 5g pro.

FROM GRANDMA'S KITCHEN: After stuffing the samosas (before frying them), you can freeze them in a freezer-safe container or bag. When you're ready to cook, take them out of the freezer and let them stand at room temperature for a few minutes. Then cook them directly in an air fryer, adding a few extra minutes to the cooking time.

MINI TERIYAKI TURKEY SANDWICHES

Preparing pulled turkey in a delicious teriyaki sauce for these snack-size sandwiches is a breeze using a slow cooker. Serve them on lightly toasted sweet dinner rolls for the finishing touch.
—*Amanda Hoop, Seaman, OH*

PREP: 20 MIN. • COOK: 5½ HOURS • MAKES: 20 SANDWICHES

2 boneless skinless turkey breast halves (2 lbs. each)
⅔ cup packed brown sugar
⅔ cup reduced-sodium soy sauce
¼ cup cider vinegar
3 garlic cloves, minced
1 Tbsp. minced fresh gingerroot
½ tsp. pepper
2 Tbsp. cornstarch
2 Tbsp. cold water
20 Hawaiian sweet rolls
2 Tbsp. butter, melted

1. Place turkey in a 5- or 6-qt. slow cooker. In a small bowl, combine brown sugar, soy sauce, vinegar, garlic, ginger and pepper; pour over turkey. Cook, covered, on low 5-6 hours or until meat is tender.

2. Remove turkey from slow cooker. In a small bowl, mix cornstarch and cold water until smooth; gradually stir into cooking liquid. When cool enough to handle, shred meat with 2 forks and return meat to slow cooker. Cook, covered, on high until sauce is thickened, 30-35 minutes.

3. Preheat oven to 325°. Split rolls and brush cut sides with butter; place on an ungreased baking sheet, cut side up. Bake 8-10 minutes or until toasted and golden brown. Spoon ⅓ cup turkey mixture on roll bottoms. Replace tops.

1 SANDWICH: 252 cal., 5g fat (2g sat. fat), 70mg chol., 501mg sod., 25g carb. (13g sugars, 1g fiber), 26g pro.

FROM GRANDMA'S KITCHEN: This recipe also works perfectly with boneless skinless chicken breasts. (Cut the cooking time to 2 hours.) To spice things up, add crushed red pepper flakes or slices of fresh jalapeno.

CREAMY IRISH COFFEE

My maternal grandmother usually never drank more than a glass of champagne at Christmas, but she couldn't resist creamy Irish coffee.
—*Rebecca Little, Park Ridge, IL*

TAKES: 10 MIN. • MAKES: 4 SERVINGS

3 cups hot strong brewed coffee
4 oz. Irish cream liqueur
Sweetened whipped cream, optional
Chocolate shavings, optional

Divide coffee and liqueur among 4 mugs; stir. If desired, top with whipped cream and chocolate shavings.

1 SERVING : 118 cal., 4g fat (0 sat. fat), 0 chol., 1mg sod., 8g carb. (6g sugars, 0 fiber), 0 pro.

GRUYERE & CRAB PALMIERS

I keep these little bursts of flavor in my freezer so they can be pulled out and popped into the oven whenever needed. Crab, pancetta and Gruyere make a sophisticated, elegant appetizer, and you can make your own variations on the filling. Try chicken and pesto, or a Mediterranean version with spinach and feta.

—Grace Voltolina, Westport, CT

PREP: 30 MIN. + CHILLING • BAKE: 15 MIN. + COOLING • MAKES: 3 DOZEN

1 large egg, lightly beaten
1 Tbsp. mayonnaise
1 tsp. minced fresh thyme or ¼ tsp. dried thyme
1 tsp. Dijon mustard
½ tsp. pepper
½ tsp. smoked paprika
½ tsp. prepared horseradish
¼ tsp. Worcestershire sauce
1 can (6 oz.) lump crabmeat, drained
4 oz. sliced pancetta, chopped
1 pkg. (17.3 oz.) frozen puff pastry, thawed
½ cup shredded Gruyere or Swiss cheese

1. Preheat oven to 400°. In a small bowl, combine the first 8 ingredients; fold in crab. In a small skillet, cook pancetta over medium heat until partially cooked but not crisp; drain on paper towels.

2. Unfold 1 sheet puff pastry. Spread half of the crab mixture to within ½ in. of edges. Sprinkle with half the cheese and half the pancetta.

3. Roll up the left and right sides toward the center, jelly-roll style, until rolls meet in the middle. Repeat with remaining pastry and ingredients. Refrigerate until firm enough to slice, about 30 minutes.

4. Cut each roll crosswise into ½-in. slices. Place 2 in. apart on parchment-lined baking sheets. Bake until golden and crisp, 15-20 minutes. Cool on pans 2 minutes. Remove to wire racks to cool.

FREEZE OPTION: Cover and freeze unbaked sliced palmiers on waxed paper-lined baking sheets until firm. Transfer to freezer containers; close tightly and return to freezer. To use, bake palmiers as directed.

1 PALMIER: 93 cal., 6g fat (2g sat. fat), 14mg chol., 149mg sod., 8g carb. (0 sugars, 1g fiber), 3g pro.

FLORENTINE ALMOND ARTICHOKE MOUNDS

I always enjoyed traditional spinach artichoke dip. For a party, I wanted to make a new appetizer that was a spin on that. This original creation is a bit reminiscent of the dip recipe and works well on a buffet.
—*Sherry Johnston, Green Cove Springs, FL*

PREP: 20 MIN. • **BAKE:** 20 MINUTES • **MAKES:** 8 SERVINGS

2 cans (14 oz. each) artichoke bottoms, drained
1 pkg. (16 oz.) frozen leaf spinach, thawed and squeezed dry
¾ cup heavy whipping cream
¾ cup shredded Swiss cheese
¾ cup chopped or sliced almonds, divided
2 large garlic cloves, minced
2 tsp. prepared horseradish
½ tsp. salt
¼ tsp. coarsely ground pepper

1. Preheat oven to 400°. Rinse artichoke bottoms; pat dry with paper towels. Combine spinach with cream, Swiss cheese and ½ cup almonds; mix in garlic, horseradish, salt and pepper. Place artichoke bottoms on a parchment-lined baking sheet. Mound spinach mixture on artichokes; sprinkle with remaining almonds.

2. Bake until almonds turn golden brown, 20-25 minutes. Serve hot or at room temperature.

1 APPETIZER: 243 cal., 18g fat (8g sat. fat), 35mg chol., 461mg sod., 12g carb. (3g sugars, 4g fiber), 10g pro.

CAJUN CRAB POPPERS
PICTURED ON PAGE 34

I visit my brother and his family in New Orleans whenever I can. These easy jalapeno poppers are stuffed with crab, Cajun seasonings and bacon. They're a little hot and spicy, just like a visit to New Orleans!
—*Elizabeth Lubin, Huntington Beach, CA*

PREP: 20 MIN. • **BAKE:** 15 MIN. • **MAKES:** 16 APPETIZERS

4 oz. cream cheese, softened
1 large egg, lightly beaten
2 Tbsp. minced fresh parsley
1 garlic clove, minced
½ tsp. Cajun seasoning
1½ cups shredded sharp cheddar cheese
1 can (8 oz.) lump crabmeat, drained
2 bacon strips, cooked and crumbled
8 jalapeno peppers
Additional fresh parsley

1. Preheat oven to 375°. In a small bowl, beat the first 5 ingredients until blended. Stir in shredded cheese, crab and bacon.

2. Cut jalapenos in half lengthwise and remove seeds. Spoon filling into pepper halves. Place on an ungreased baking sheet. Bake until lightly browned, 15-20 minutes. Sprinkle with additional parsley.

NOTE: Wear disposable gloves when cutting hot peppers; the oils can burn skin. Avoid touching your face.

1 POPPER: 88 cal., 7g fat (4g sat. fat), 41mg chol., 187mg sod., 1g carb. (1g sugars, 0 fiber), 6g pro.

FLORENTINE ALMOND
ARTICHOKE MOUNDS

GRANDMA'S SECRET
For less mess and drier spinach, try using a cone-shaped coffee filter. Simply place a small portion of thawed spinach in the coffee filter, wring dry and repeat. Easy squeezy!

MAPLE PULLED PORK BUNS

Maple syrup is the sweet secret to these irresistible buns.
Slow-cooking the flavorful pork couldn't be easier,
and the buns are quick to roll up. We love these
for parties because they serve a packed house.
—*Rashanda Cobbins, Milwaukee, WI*

PREP: 25 MIN. + RISING • COOK: 5½ HOURS • MAKES: 16 SERVINGS

1 boneless pork shoulder
  butt roast (2½ lbs.)
1½ tsp. ground mustard
1 tsp. salt
½ tsp. cayenne pepper
½ tsp. ground ginger
1 cup thinly sliced onion
2 garlic cloves, peeled
1 cup maple syrup, divided
½ cup water

3 Tbsp. cider vinegar
2 loaves (1 lb. each) frozen
  bread dough, thawed
1 cup barbecue sauce
1 cup shredded pepper
  jack cheese
  Chopped green onions
  and crushed red pepper
  flakes

1. Season pork with mustard, salt, cayenne pepper and ginger;
place in a 4-qt. slow cooker. Top with onion and garlic; pour in
½ cup maple syrup, water and cider vinegar. Cook, covered, on
low 5-7 hours or until meat is tender. Shred meat with 2 forks;
discard cooking liquid and vegetables.

2. On a lightly floured surface, roll 1 loaf dough into a 16x10-in.
rectangle. Combine barbecue sauce with remaining syrup; brush
¼ cup sauce mixture to within ½ in. of dough edges. Top with half
the pork. Roll up jelly-roll style, starting with a long side; pinch
seam to seal. Cut crosswise into 8 slices. Place in a 9-in. pie plate,
cut sides down. Repeat with remaining dough and additional pie
plate. Cover with kitchen towels; let rise in a warm place until
doubled, about 1 hour. Reserve remaining sauce mixture. Preheat
oven to 400°.

3. Bake until golden brown, about 20 minutes. Sprinkle with
cheese and bake until melted, 5-10 minutes longer. Serve with
reserved sauce mixture; sprinkle with green onions and red
pepper flakes.

1 ROLL: 358 cal., 12g fat (4g sat. fat), 50mg chol., 727mg sod.,
41g carb. (14g sugars, 2g fiber), 20g pro.

FROM GRANDMA'S KITCHEN: You can make the pork quickly in
an electric pressure cooker instead of a slow cooker. Select
Manual, high pressure and set time for 75 minutes. Allow
to naturally release for 10 minutes, then quick-release any
remaining pressure.

HONEY-KISSED SAVORY SHORTBREAD CRACKERS

It may seem like a lot of work to make homemade crackers. However, after you've tasted these sweet and savory honey-kissed shortbread crackers, I think you'll admit that it's worth every minute you spent making them. They're crispy, cheesy and salty and have a lovely sweet honey finish. They are basically cracker perfection.

—Colleen Delawder, Herndon, VA

PREP: 45 MIN. • **BAKE:** 15 MIN./BATCH + COOLING • **MAKES:** 7 DOZEN

1 cup unsalted butter, softened
⅓ cup minced fresh parsley
2 cups all-purpose flour
1 Tbsp. sugar
1 tsp. paprika
½ tsp. kosher salt
½ tsp. garlic powder
½ tsp. pepper
1 cup grated shredded cheddar cheese
¼ cup heavy whipping cream

HONEY-KISSED TOPPING
1 Tbsp. unsalted butter
1 Tbsp. honey
⅔ cup confectioners' sugar
⅓ cup minced fresh parsley
Flaky sea salt, such as Maldon, optional

1. Preheat oven to 350°. In a large bowl, beat butter for 2 minutes. Mix in parsley. In another bowl, whisk flour, sugar, paprika, kosher salt, garlic powder and pepper. Add cheese; toss to coat. Add to butter mixture alternately with cream, beating until mixture comes together. Divide dough into 3 portions.

2. On a lightly floured surface, roll each portion of dough to ¼-in. thickness. Cut with a floured 1½-in. round cookie cutter. Place 1 in. apart on parchment-lined baking sheets. Reroll and chill the scraps as needed. Bake until crisp, 15-20 minutes. Cool completely on wire racks.

3. In a microwave, melt butter and honey; stir until smooth. Stir in confectioners' sugar until smooth; fold in parsley. Top crackers with honey mixture; if desired, sprinkle with flaky sea salt. Let stand until set. Store crackers between layers of waxed paper in an airtight container at room temperature.

1 SERVING: 45 cal., 3g fat (2g sat. fat), 8mg chol., 21mg sod., 4g carb. (1g sugars, 0 fiber), 1g pro.

GRANDMA'S SECRET

These baked blooming onions are lighter than traditional ones that are floured, battered and then fried. For crispy, decadent results, make these in your air fryer.

BLOOMING ONIONS

Instead of being battered and deep-fried, these onions are brushed with
melted butter and mustard, sprinkled with bread crumbs and seasonings and baked.
This makes an impressive-looking appetizer, and the dip can be used for veggies and crackers, too.
—Kendra Doss, Colorado Springs, CO

PREP: 20 MIN. • **BAKE:** 40 MIN. • **MAKES:** 8 SERVINGS

2 **large sweet onions**
1 **Tbsp. butter, melted**
2 **tsp. Dijon mustard**
3 **Tbsp. dry bread crumbs**
¼ **tsp. salt**
¼ **tsp. pepper**

SAUCE
¼ **cup fat-free sour cream**
¼ **cup fat-free mayonnaise**
1½ **tsp. dried minced onion**
¼ **tsp. garlic powder**
¼ **tsp. dill weed**

1. Preheat oven to 425°. With a sharp knife, slice ½ in. off the top of the onions; peel onions. Cut each into 16 wedges to within ½ in. of root end.

2. Place each onion on a double thickness of heavy-duty foil (about 12 in. square). Fold foil around onions and seal tightly. Place in an ungreased 11x7-in. baking dish. Bake, uncovered, for 20 minutes.

3. In a small bowl, combine butter and mustard. Open foil; fold foil around onions. Brush butter mixture over onions; sprinkle with bread crumbs, salt and pepper.

4. Bake until crisp-tender, 18-22 minutes. Meanwhile, in a small bowl, combine sauce ingredients. Serve with onions.

1 SERVING: 65 cal., 2g fat (1g sat. fat), 6mg chol., 205mg sod., 11g carb. (5g sugars, 1g fiber), 2g pro. **DIABETIC EXCHANGES:** 1 vegetable, ½ starch.

"Very good! The family liked them. Now I'm looking forward to serving these at a party."
— NIFERSCHMIDT, TASTEOFHOME.COM

GARLIC MUSHROOM APPETIZER

My grandfather, who was a hotel chef for many years, created this recipe. He prepared
these mushrooms for big family gatherings, and they always disappeared quickly.
—*Rosanna Houlton, Fort Collins, CO*

PREP: 15 MIN. • COOK: 30 MIN. + CHILLING • MAKES: 3½ CUPS

1 cup chopped onion
½ cup canola oil
3 Tbsp. butter
2 lbs. fresh mushrooms, sliced
1 can (28 oz.) crushed tomatoes in puree, undrained
1 tsp. salt
¼ tsp. pepper
½ cup red wine vinegar
1 bunch fresh parsley, finely chopped (about 1½ cups)
3 garlic cloves, minced
  Sliced French bread

1. In a large saucepan, saute onion in oil and butter until crisp-tender. Add mushrooms; cook for 2 minutes or until vegetables are tender. Add the tomatoes, salt and pepper; cover and simmer for 20-30 minutes.

2. Stir in the vinegar, parsley and garlic. Cover and simmer for 10 minutes. Cover and refrigerate for several hours or overnight. To serve, spoon onto slices of French bread.

ABOUT 3 TBSP.: 118 cal., 9g fat (2g sat. fat), 6mg chol., 240mg sod., 8g carb. (1g sugars, 2g fiber), 3g pro.

HOMEMADE TORTILLA CHIPS

I make these homemade tortilla chips to serve with roasted tomatillo salsa.
They have a little heat from the chipotle. If you prefer plain, just sprinkle with salt after frying.
—*David Ross, Spokane Valley, WA*

TAKES: 25 MIN. • MAKES: 4 SERVINGS

¾ tsp. salt
½ tsp. ground chipotle pepper
10 corn tortillas (6 in.)
  Canola or corn oil for deep-fat frying

1. In a small bowl, mix salt and chili powder. Cut each tortilla into 4 wedges. In an electric skillet, heat 1 in. of oil to 350°. Fry chips, several at a time, 2-3 minutes on each side or until golden brown. Drain on paper towels.

2. Transfer chips to a large bowl; sprinkle with salt mixture and gently toss to coat.

10 CHIPS: 183 cal., 8g fat (1g sat. fat), 0 chol., 479mg sod., 27g carb. (1g sugars, 4g fiber), 3g pro.

STICKY HONEY CHICKEN WINGS

This honey chicken wings recipe was given to me by
a special lady who was like a grandmother to me.

—*Marisa Raponi, Vaughan, ON*

PREP: 25 MIN. + MARINATING • BAKE: 30 MIN. • MAKES: 3 DOZEN

½ cup orange blossom
   honey
⅓ cup white vinegar
2 Tbsp. paprika

2 tsp. salt
1 tsp. pepper
4 lbs. chicken wings

1. Combine the honey, vinegar, paprika, salt and pepper in a small bowl.

2. Cut through the 2 wing joints with a sharp knife, discarding wing tips. Add remaining wing pieces and honey mixture to a large bowl; stir to coat. Cover and refrigerate 4 hours or overnight.

3. Preheat oven to 375°. Remove wings; reserve honey mixture. Place wings on greased 15x10x1-in. baking pans. Bake until juices run clear, about 30 minutes, turning halfway through.

4. Meanwhile, place reserved honey mixture in a small saucepan. Bring to a boil; cook 1 minute.

5. Remove wings from oven; preheat broiler. Place wings on a greased rack in a broiler pan; brush with honey mixture. Broil 4-5 in. from heat until crispy, 3-5 minutes. Serve with remaining honey mixture.

1 PIECE: 71 cal., 4g fat (1g sat. fat), 16mg chol., 147mg sod., 4g carb. (4g sugars, 0 fiber), 5g pro.

HEALTHY SPINACH DIP

I needed to take something healthy and low in fat to a get-together, so I experimented and came up with this dip. Packed full of flavorful veggies, it's always a hit, whether it's served with bread, crackers or additional veggies. Somebody asks for the recipe every time.
—*Noelle Myers, Grand Forks, ND*

PREP: 15 MIN. + CHILLING • **MAKES:** 1 CUP

½ cup fat-free plain yogurt
1 oz. fat-free cream cheese
2 tsp. thinly sliced green onion
2 tsp. finely chopped sweet yellow pepper
2 tsp. finely chopped sweet red pepper
2 tsp. Italian salad dressing mix
⅛ tsp. ground nutmeg
1 cup frozen leaf spinach, thawed and squeezed dry
Radishes and carrot sticks

In a small bowl, combine the first 7 ingredients; stir in spinach. Cover and refrigerate at least 1 hour before serving. Serve with fresh vegetables.

½ CUP: 62 cal., 0 fat (0 sat. fat), 2mg chol., 499mg sod., 9g carb. (5g sugars, 1g fiber), 6g pro.

"Delicious and tastes just like its high-fat version you can buy in the grocery store. My husband is on a strict diet and this is the ticket. If you want any quantity, we recommend doubling or quadrupling the recipe. However, we used only one packet of Italian dressing mix, which kept it spicy and delicious without overdoing the flavor. This will be on our regular rotation of holiday appetizers. Yum!"
— LLHEATH, TASTEOFHOME.COM

CHOCOLATY CHIPS

My two little guys can't get enough of this sweet and salty snack that uses just three ingredients and is ready to eat in 15 minutes. The boys like to drizzle on the melted chocolate. Sometimes we replace the potato chips with apple slices.
—*Jami Geittmann, Greendale, WI*

TAKES: 15 MIN. • **MAKES:** 6 SERVINGS

3 cups regular or kettle-cooked potato chips
½ cup semisweet chocolate chips
1 tsp. shortening

1. Arrange potato chips in a single layer on a waxed paper-lined baking sheet.

2. In a microwave, melt chocolate chips and shortening; stir until smooth. Drizzle over chips. Refrigerate 5 minutes or until set.

½ CUP: 140 cal., 9g fat (4g sat. fat), 0 chol., 75mg sod., 16g carb. (8g sugars, 1g fiber), 1g pro.

HEALTHY
SPINACH DIP

FRIED CHICKEN & PULLED PORK CORNBREAD POPPERS

These fun little apps are an instant conversation starter wherever they're served. We love them on game day, but they'd be a hit at brunch, too.
—*Crystal Schlueter, Northglenn, CO*

TAKES: 25 MIN. • **MAKES:** 2 DOZEN

2 oz. frozen popcorn chicken
1 pkg. (8½ oz.) cornbread/muffin mix
4 seeded jalapeno peppers or pickled jalapeno peppers, cut into 6 slices each
¼ cup refrigerated fully cooked barbecued pulled pork
½ cup maple syrup or honey
1 tsp. Sriracha chili sauce, optional

1. Preheat oven to 400°. Bake popcorn chicken according to package directions. When cool enough to handle, cut chicken into 12 pieces.

2. Meanwhile, prepare cornbread mix according to package directions. Place a jalapeno slice in each of 24 foil-lined mini muffin cups. Fill each cup with 1 Tbsp. batter. Gently press a piece of popcorn chicken into the centers of half the cups. Spoon 1 tsp. pulled pork into the centers of remaining cups.

3. Bake until golden brown, about 12 minutes. Serve with maple syrup; if desired, whisk chili sauce into syrup.

NOTE: Wear disposable gloves when cutting hot peppers; the oils can burn skin. Avoid touching your face.

1 MINI MUFFIN: 74 cal., 2g fat (1g sat. fat), 10mg chol., 120mg sod., 13g carb. (7g sugars, 1g fiber), 2g pro.

SECRET INGREDIENT DEVILED EGGS

My Grandma Phyllis's secret in many of her savory dishes is the maraschino cherry. Her deviled eggs are unrivaled by any of the ones I've tried. The sweetness of the cherries balances the heat of the jalapeno; celery and pickles give a nice crunch. It's always a party-pleaser, and the cherries will make your guests wonder what the secret is!

—*Adrienne Vradenburg, Bakersfield, CA*

TAKES: 30 MIN. • MAKES: 2 DOZEN

12 **hard-boiled large eggs**
⅓ **cup mayonnaise**
3 **Tbsp. finely chopped celery**
3 **Tbsp. finely chopped sweet pickles**
3 **Tbsp. finely chopped maraschino cherries**
2 **Tbsp. Dijon mustard**
1 **Tbsp. finely chopped seeded jalapeno pepper**
¼ **tsp. salt**
¼ **tsp. pepper**
½ **tsp. smoked paprika**
¼ **tsp. ground chipotle pepper**
¼ **tsp. black sesame seeds**
24 **maraschino cherries**

Cut eggs in half lengthwise. Remove yolks, reserving whites. In a small bowl, mash yolks. Stir in mayonnaise, celery, pickles, chopped cherries, mustard, jalapeno, salt and pepper. Spoon or pipe into egg whites. Sprinkle with paprika, chipotle pepper and sesame seeds. Top each with a cherry. Refrigerate until serving.

NOTE: Wear disposable gloves when cutting hot peppers; the oils can burn skin. Avoid touching your face.

1 STUFFED EGG HALF: 74 cal., 5g fat (1g sat. fat), 93mg chol., 109mg sod., 4g carb. (4g sugars, 0 fiber), 3g pro.

SAVORY CRACKER SNACK MIX

A *Taste of Home* recipe inspired this one! Because I love everything bagel seasoning, I decided to give this a try. A friend later suggested I make the mix more versatile, and now it's a deliciously addictive snack!

—*Cyndy Gerken, Naples, FL*

PREP: 15 MIN. • BAKE: 15 MIN. + COOLING • MAKES: 4½ CUPS

1½ **cups potato sticks**
1½ **cups cheddar-flavored snack crackers**
1½ **cups sourdough pretzel nuggets**
3 **Tbsp. butter**
¼ **cup grated Parmesan cheese**
3 **Tbsp. olive oil**
1½ **tsp. sesame seeds**
1½ **tsp. dried minced garlic**
1½ **tsp. dried minced onion**
1½ **tsp. poppy seeds**
¼ **tsp. kosher salt**

1. Preheat oven to 350°. In a large bowl, combine potato sticks, crackers and pretzels. In a small saucepan, melt butter; stir in remaining ingredients. Drizzle over pretzel mixture; toss to coat.

2. Spread in a greased 15x10x1-in. baking pan. Bake until crisp and lightly browned, 12-15 minutes, stirring every 4 minutes. Cool completely in pan on a wire rack. Store in an airtight container.

¾ CUP: 306 cal., 20g fat (7g sat. fat), 20mg chol., 468mg sod., 26g carb. (1g sugars, 1g fiber), 5g pro.

PARTY CHEESE BALLS

PARTY CHEESE BALLS

These tangy cheese balls are guaranteed to spread cheer at your next gathering.
The ingredients create a colorful presentation and a savory combination of flavors.
As a grandmother who loves to cook, I send many pantry presents off to college.
—*Shirley Hoerman, Nekoosa, WI*

PREP: 20 MIN. + CHILLING • MAKES: 2 CHEESE BALLS (1¾ CUPS EACH)

1 pkg. (8 oz.) cream cheese, softened
2 cups shredded cheddar cheese
1 jar (5 oz.) sharp American cheese spread
1 jar (5 oz.) pimiento spread
3 Tbsp. finely chopped onion
1 Tbsp. lemon juice
1 tsp. Worcestershire sauce
  Dash garlic salt
½ cup chopped pecans, toasted
½ cup minced fresh parsley
  Assorted crackers

1. In a large bowl, beat the first 8 ingredients until blended. Cover and refrigerate until easily handled, about 45 minutes.

2. Shape into 2 balls; roll in parsley and pecans. Cover and refrigerate. Remove from the refrigerator 15 minutes before serving with crackers.

2 TBSP.: 99 cal., 9g fat (5g sat. fat), 25mg chol., 188mg sod., 2g carb. (1g sugars, 0 fiber), 4g pro.

MOM'S TANGERINE ICED TEA

Take a sip of this sweet tea with a citrus twist. You'll love it.
—*Mary Miller, Poplarville, MS*

PREP: 10 MIN. • COOK: 5 MIN. + CHILLING • MAKES: 4 SERVINGS

2¾ cups water, divided
4 individual black tea bags
⅔ cup sugar
2 cups fresh tangerine juice (about 12 tangerines)
  Ice cubes
  Tangerine slices and mint sprigs, optional

1. In a small saucepan, bring 2 cups water to a boil. Remove from the heat; add tea bags. Steep for 3-5 minutes. Discard tea bags; cool tea slightly.

2. In another saucepan, combine remaining water and sugar; bring to a boil. Cook and stir until sugar is dissolved. Remove from the heat; cool slightly.

3. Transfer tea and sugar syrup to a large pitcher; stir in tangerine juice. Refrigerate until chilled.

4. Serve over ice; add tangerine slices and mint if desired.

1 CUP: 182 cal., 0 fat (0 sat. fat), 0 chol., 1mg sod., 46g carb. (46g sugars, 0 fiber), 1g pro.

BABY SWISS APPETIZER CHEESECAKE

This beautiful cheesecake appetizer can be refrigerated up to 24 hours before serving, so it's the perfect make-ahead recipe for holidays, game days or special occasions.
—*Marilyn Edelman, Sabetha, KS*

PREP: 35 MIN. + COOLING • **BAKE:** 35 MIN. + CHILLING • **MAKES:** 24 SERVINGS

1½ **cups crushed Ritz crackers (about 36 crackers)**
3 **Tbsp. butter, melted**
3 **pkg. (8 oz. each) cream cheese, softened**
¼ **cup heavy whipping cream**
1 **Tbsp. oil from sun-dried tomatoes**
3 **large eggs, room temperature, lightly beaten**
6 **oz. baby Swiss cheese, shredded**
½ **cup oil-packed sun-dried tomatoes, patted dry and thinly sliced**
4 **green onions, chopped Crackers**

1. Preheat oven to 375°. In a small bowl, mix cracker crumbs and butter. Press onto the bottom of a greased 9-in. springform pan. Place pan on a baking sheet. Bake until golden brown, about 10 minutes. Cool on a wire rack. Reduce oven setting to 325°.

2. In a large bowl, beat cream cheese until smooth. Beat in cream and oil. Add eggs; beat on low speed just until blended. Fold in cheese, tomatoes and green onions. Pour over crust. Return pan to baking sheet.

3. Bake until center is almost set, 35-40 minutes. Cool on a wire rack 10 minutes. Loosen sides from pan with a knife. Cool 1 hour longer. Refrigerate overnight, covering when completely cooled.

4. Remove rim from pan. Serve cheesecake with crackers.

1 PIECE: 197 cal., 17g fat (9g sat. fat), 65mg chol., 176mg sod., 6g carb. (2g sugars, 0 fiber), 5g pro.

FROM GRANDMA'S KITCHEN: This appetizer has a mild Swiss cheese flavor. For a more intense flavor, substitute aged Swiss or Gruyere cheese.

BACON, ONION & APPLE STRUDEL

This is such a fun recipe—an appetizer twist on what's traditionally a dessert. It can be served hot out of the oven, warm or cold, and either alone or with a side salad. Yummy! Different types of cheese, such as goat, feta or jack, can also be used.
—*Donna-Marie Ryan, Topsfield, MA*

PREP: 30 MIN. • BAKE: 25 MIN. • MAKES: 10 SERVINGS

2 **Tbsp. butter**
2 **large sweet onions, halved and sliced**
2 **medium Granny Smith apples, peeled and thinly sliced**
½ **cup chopped walnuts, toasted**
2 **Tbsp. honey Dijon mustard**
2 **Tbsp. honey**
1 **tsp. salt**
½ **tsp. pepper**
1 **pkg. (17.3 oz.) frozen puff pastry, thawed**
2 **cups shredded sharp cheddar cheese**
4 **bacon strips, cooked and crumbled**
1 **large egg**
1 **Tbsp. water**

1. Preheat oven to 400°. In a large skillet, heat butter over medium-high heat. Add onions and apples; cook and stir until tender, 12-15 minutes. Stir in walnuts, mustard, honey, salt and pepper. Remove from heat; cool slightly.

2. On 2 parchment-lined baking sheets, roll out each pastry into a 14x12-in. rectangle. Place half the onion mixture down the center of each rectangle; top with cheese and bacon.

3. On each long side, cut eight 1¾-in.-wide strips. Starting at 1 end, fold alternating strips at an angle across filling; pinch ends to seal. Whisk egg with water; brush over braids. Bake until golden brown, 25-28 minutes. Let stand 5 minutes before cutting.

1 PIECE: 463 cal., 29g fat (10g sat. fat), 41mg chol., 656mg sod., 42g carb. (11g sugars, 5g fiber), 12g pro.

TOASTED RAVIOLI

While visiting a friend who just moved to St. Louis, Missouri, I tried these toasted ravioli at almost every restaurant! When I got home, I had to try to replicate them, and this recipe comes pretty close.
—*Cristina Carrera, Kenosha, WI*

PREP: 15 MIN. • COOK: 20 MIN. • MAKES: ABOUT 1½ DOZEN

1 **cup seasoned bread crumbs**
¼ **cup shredded Parmesan cheese**
2 **tsp. dried basil**
1 **cup all-purpose flour**
2 **large eggs, lightly beaten**
1 **pkg. (9 oz.) frozen beef ravioli, thawed**
Oil for deep-fat frying
Fresh minced basil and additional shredded Parmesan cheese, optional
1 **cup marinara sauce**

1. In a shallow bowl, mix bread crumbs, Parmesan cheese and basil. Place flour and eggs in separate shallow bowls. Dip ravioli in flour to coat both sides; shake off excess. Dip in egg, then in crumb mixture, patting to help coating adhere.

2. In a deep cast-iron or electric skillet, heat ½ in. oil to 375°. Fry ravioli, a few at a time, until golden brown, 1-2 minutes on each side. Drain on paper towels. If desired, immediately sprinkle with basil and cheese. Serve warm with marinara sauce.

1 PIECE: 73 cal., 5g fat (1g sat. fat), 6mg chol., 117mg sod., 6g carb. (1g sugars, 1g fiber), 2g pro.

"Very good and accurate expression of the dish. As a lifelong St. Louisan, I can say that toasted ravioli is a local staple ... if you are a visitor to St. Louis, it is a rite of passage. It is typically offered in restaurants as an appetizer with marinara sauce and Parmesan on the side (though I've had it as my entree from time to time)."
—BILL742, TASTEOFHOME.COM

BRIE TOASTS WITH CRANBERRY COMPOTE

Just six ingredients are all I need to create an elegant appetizer perfect for entertaining. The tart cranberry compote pairs well with creamy Brie cheese.
—*Katherine Watson, Omaha, NE*

PREP: 30 MIN. • BAKE: 5 MIN. • MAKES: ABOUT 2 DOZEN

1 **cup dried cranberries**
1 **cup balsamic vinegar**
½ **cup jellied cranberry sauce**
1 **Tbsp. sugar**
1 **loaf (1 lb.) French bread, cut into ½-in. slices**
3 **Tbsp. butter, melted**
½ **lb. Brie cheese, thinly sliced**

1. In a small saucepan, combine the cranberries, vinegar, cranberry sauce and sugar. Cook and stir over medium heat until thickened, about 12 minutes.

2. Brush bottoms of bread with butter; place on ungreased baking sheets. Bake at 350° for 1-2 minutes or until lightly toasted. Top bread with Brie. Bake for 4-6 minutes or until cheese is melted. Spoon cranberry mixture over cheese, about 1 Tbsp. on each.

1 APPETIZER: 145 cal., 5g fat (3g sat. fat), 14mg chol., 218mg sod., 21g carb. (7g sugars, 1g fiber), 4g pro.

TOASTED
RAVIOLI

FIG & GOAT CHEESE MEATBALLS

Around the holidays, saucy cocktail meatballs are always the first appetizer to go. In this dish, the sweet flavor of the fig glaze goes perfectly with the pork and tangy goat cheese. Serve the meatballs hot from the skillet or freeze and gently reheat.
—*Kim Banick, Turner, OR*

PREP: 45 MIN. • **BAKE:** 25 MIN. • **MAKES:** 3 DOZEN

1 cup panko bread crumbs	1 cinnamon stick (3 in.)
2 large eggs, lightly beaten	4 whole cloves
2 lbs. bulk Italian sausage	1 whole star anise
1 log (4 oz.) fresh goat cheese	1 cup dried figs, chopped
	1 cup water
1 cup red wine vinegar	Chopped fresh chives, optional
½ cup sugar	

1. Preheat oven to 350°. In a large bowl, combine bread crumbs and eggs. Add sausage; mix lightly but thoroughly. Divide into 36 portions. Shape each portion around ½ tsp. cheese to cover completely. Place meatballs on a greased rack in a 15x10x1-in. baking pan. Bake until cooked through, 25-30 minutes.

2. Meanwhile, in a large saucepan, bring vinegar, sugar, cinnamon, cloves and star anise to a boil. Reduce heat; simmer 5 minutes. Discard cinnamon, cloves and star anise. Add figs; cook until softened, 8-10 minutes. Remove from heat; cool slightly. Transfer to a blender. Add 1 cup water; process until almost smooth. Serve with meatballs. If desired, top meatballs with chopped chives.

FREEZE OPTION: Freeze cooled meatballs and sauce in freezer containers. To use, partially thaw in refrigerator overnight. Heat through in a covered saucepan, stirring gently; add a little water if necessary.

1 MEATBALL: 97 cal., 6g fat (2g sat. fat), 26mg chol., 175mg sod., 7g carb. (5g sugars, 0 fiber), 4g pro.

NANA REBA'S POTATO KNISHES

I grew up eating these appetizers every holiday. My grandmother had to show up with at least four dozen because they were devoured within minutes. You cannot eat just one!
—*Ellie Brandon, Tucson, AZ*

PREP: 35 MIN. • **BAKE:** 25 MIN./BATCH • **MAKES:** 5 DOZEN

1 pkg. (24 oz.) refrigerated mashed potatoes
2 Tbsp. butter
1 small onion, chopped
¼ tsp. salt
¼ tsp. pepper
4 sheets refrigerated pie crust
  Spicy brown mustard

1. Preheat oven to 350°. Prepare potatoes according to package directions. Meanwhile, in a small skillet, heat butter over medium heat. Add onion; cook and stir just until tender, 4-6 minutes. Remove from heat. Stir in salt and pepper. Stir onion mixture into potatoes. Cool slightly.

2. Meanwhile, on a work surface, unroll crusts. Roll each to a 12x10-in. rectangle. Spread half the potato mixture evenly over 1 crust; top with another crust. Repeat with remaining crusts and potato mixture. Cut each rectangle lengthwise into 2-in. strips. Carefully transfer strips to parchment-lined baking sheets, separating slightly. Press opposite edges of strips with a fork to seal. Cut strips crosswise into 2-in. squares.

3. Bake until golden brown, 25-30 minutes. Serve knishes warm with mustard.

1 SERVING: 82 cal., 5g fat (2g sat. fat), 5mg chol., 97mg sod., 8g carb. (1g sugars, 0 fiber), 1g pro.

BBQ POPCORN

With this quick-fix BBQ popcorn, you can experience a summer barbecue any time of the year!
—*Rashanda Cobbins, Milwaukee, WI*

TAKES: 10 MIN. • **MAKES:** 8 SERVINGS

8½ cups popped popcorn
2 Tbsp. butter, melted
2 Tbsp. honey
2 tsp. paprika
2 tsp. chili powder
1½ tsp. salt
½ tsp. onion powder
½ tsp. garlic powder
⅛ tsp. cayenne pepper

Place popcorn in a large bowl. In a small bowl, combine butter and honey; drizzle over popcorn and toss to coat. Sprinkle with remaining spices; toss to coat.

1 CUP: 115 cal., 8g fat (3g sat. fat), 18mg chol., 565mg sod., 211g carb. (5g sugars, 2g fiber), 1g pro.

OLIVE-STUFFED
CELERY

OLIVE-STUFFED CELERY

My grandmother taught both me and my mom this appetizer recipe.
We always serve it at Christmas and Thanksgiving. The stuffing is so yummy that even
if you don't normally care for the ingredients on their own, you'll love the end result.
—*Stacy Powell, Santa Fe, TX*

TAKES: 25 MIN. • MAKES: 2 DOZEN

1 dill pickle spear plus
  1 tsp. juice
3 sweet pickles plus
  1 tsp. juice
6 pitted ripe olives plus
  1 tsp. juice
6 pimiento-stuffed olives
  plus 1 tsp. juice
1 pkg. (8 oz.) cream cheese,
  softened
⅓ cup Miracle Whip
¼ tsp. salt
¼ cup finely chopped
  pecans, toasted
6 celery ribs, cut into
  2-in. pieces

1. Finely chop pickles and olives; set aside. In a small bowl, beat the cream cheese, Miracle Whip, juices and salt until blended. Stir in the pickles, olives and pecans.

2. Pipe or stuff filling into celery sticks. Store in the refrigerator.

1 PIECE: 61 cal., 5g fat (2g sat. fat), 12mg chol., 228mg sod., 2g carb. (1g sugars, 0 fiber), 1g pro.

FROM GRANDMA'S KITCHEN: Give limp celery a second chance to season entrees, soups and stews. Cut the ends from the limp celery stalks and place the stalks in a glass of cold water in the refrigerator for several hours or overnight. You'll be surprised how refreshed the celery will be.

ITALIAN OYSTER CRACKERS

My friends and family love these crackers that are easily made in the slow cooker.
Often I leave them in the slow cooker and everyone eats them warm.
—*Angela Lively, Conroe, TX*

PREP: 10 MIN. • COOK: 1 HOUR • MAKES: 8 SERVINGS

2 pkg. (9 oz. each)
  oyster crackers
¼ cup canola oil
3 garlic cloves, minced
1 envelope Italian salad
  dressing mix
1 tsp. dill weed
¼ cup butter, melted
½ cup grated Parmesan
  cheese

1. Combine crackers, oil, garlic, Italian seasoning and dill weed in a 6-qt. slow cooker. Cook, covered, on low 1 hour.

2. Drizzle melted butter over crackers; sprinkle with cheese. Stir to coat.

3. Transfer mixture to a baking sheet; let stand until cool. Store in an airtight container.

¾ CUP: 407 cal., 20g fat (6g sat. fat), 20mg chol., 1057mg sod., 49g carb. (2g sugars, 2g fiber), 8g pro.

GARLIC KNOTTED
ROLLS, PAGE 68

GRANDMA'S FAVORITE

BREADS, BISCUITS & MORE

Does anything declare "Welcome home" like the heavenly aroma of fresh-baked bread? Grandma has a way with classic yeast breads, in-a-snap biscuits and garlicky dinner rolls.

SAVORY SKILLET POPOVER

This showstopping recipe delivers comfort and flavor, and it brings a smile.
It's the perfect vehicle for using up little bits of leftovers, as long as they are fully
cooked and heated in the bottom of the skillet prior to adding the batter and cheese.
—*Susan Anderson, Helena, MT*

PREP: 25 MIN. • **BAKE:** 20 MIN. • **MAKES:** 6 SERVINGS

6 **Tbsp. butter**
2 **Tbsp. chopped shallot**
8 **large eggs, room temperature**
¾ **cup 2% milk**
1 **cup plus 2 Tbsp. all-purpose flour**
½ **tsp. kosher salt**
½ **tsp. pepper**
1 **Tbsp. minced fresh thyme or 1 tsp. dried thyme**
¾ **cup grated Parmesan cheese**

1. Preheat oven to 425°. In a 12-in. cast-iron or other ovenproof skillet, melt butter over medium-high heat. Add shallot; cook and stir until tender, 1-2 minutes.

2. In a large bowl, whisk eggs and milk until blended. Whisk in flour, salt and pepper until smooth; stir in thyme. Pour batter into hot pan; sprinkle with Parmesan.

3. Bake until top is puffed and sides are golden brown and crisp, 20-25 minutes. Serve immediately.

1 PIECE: 343 cal., 21g fat (11g sat. fat), 290mg chol., 542mg sod., 22g carb. (2g sugars, 1g fiber), 15g pro.

GARLIC KNOTTED ROLLS

PICTURED ON PAGE 66

Using frozen yeast dough is an easy way to make homemade rolls.
These cute knots add a special touch to any menu.
—*Kathy Harding, Richmond, MO*

PREP: 15 MIN. + RISING • **BAKE:** 15 MIN. • **MAKES:** 10 ROLLS

1 **loaf (1 lb.) frozen bread dough, thawed**
1½ **tsp. dried minced onion**
3 **Tbsp. butter**
4 **garlic cloves, minced**
⅛ **tsp. salt**
1 **large egg, beaten**
Poppy seeds, optional

1. Pat out dough on a work surface; sprinkle with minced onion and knead until combined. Divide dough in half. Shape each half into 5 balls. To form knots, roll each ball into a 10-in. rope; tie into a knot. Tuck ends under. Place rolls 2 in. apart on a greased baking sheet.

2. In a small skillet over medium heat, melt butter. Add garlic and salt; cook and stir 1-2 minutes. Brush over rolls. Cover and let rise until doubled, about 30 minutes.

3. Preheat oven to 375°. Brush tops with egg; if desired, sprinkle with poppy seeds. Bake until golden brown, 15-20 minutes.

1 ROLL: 168 cal., 6g fat (2g sat. fat), 30mg chol., 315mg sod., 22g carb. (2g sugars, 2g fiber), 5g pro.

SAVORY SKILLET
POPOVER

ICEBOX ROLLS

I remember my mom making these rolls almost every Saturday so they'd be ready to bake on Sunday for company. Of course, when the company was there, we'd get to enjoy them, too! Although they take a little time to prepare, they're not difficult to make. And there's nothing in the stores that can compare with them!
—*Jean Fox, Welch, MN*

PREP: 30 MIN. + CHILLING • **BAKE:** 15 MIN. • **MAKES:** 36 ROLLS

- 1 pkg. (¼ oz.) active dry yeast
- 2½ cups water, divided
- ½ cup shortening
- 2 large eggs, room temperature, beaten
- 1½ tsp. salt
- ½ cup sugar
- 8½ to 9 cups all-purpose flour
- ⅓ cup butter, melted

1. Dissolve yeast in ½ cup warm water (110°-115°). In a separate bowl, combine 1 cup boiling water and shortening. Add remaining (room-temperature) water, eggs, salt, sugar and yeast mixture.

2. Stir in 1 cup of flour at a time, mixing well after each addition, until a soft dough forms. Turn dough onto a floured surface; knead until smooth and elastic, 6-8 minutes. Place in a greased bowl, turning once to grease top. Cover and refrigerate overnight.

3. Turn onto a lightly floured surface; divide dough into 9 portions. Divide and shape each portion into 12 balls. Place 3 balls in each cup of 3 greased muffin tins. Cover with kitchen towels; let rise in a warm place until doubled, about 1 hour.

4. Preheat oven to 375°. Brush rolls with half of melted butter; bake until golden brown, 15-20 minutes. Remove from oven; brush with remaining butter.

1 ROLL: 162 cal., 5g fat (2g sat. fat), 15mg chol., 117mg sod., 25g carb. (3g sugars, 1g fiber), 4g pro.

GRANDMA'S CINNAMON ROLLS

The secret to these rolls is the brown sugar sauce they're baked in.
I serve them as dinner rolls as well as for a special breakfast treat.
—*Della Talbert, Howard, CO*

PREP: 30 MIN.+ RISING • BAKE: 25 MIN. • MAKES: 15 ROLLS

DOUGH
- **1 pkg. (¼ oz.) active dry yeast**
- **¼ cup sugar, divided**
- **1 cup warm water (110° to 115°), divided**
- **2 Tbsp. butter, softened**
- **1 large egg**
- **1 tsp. salt**
- **3¼ to 3¾ cups all-purpose flour**

TOPPING
- **1 cup heavy whipping cream**
- **1 cup packed brown sugar**

FILLING
- **½ cup sugar**
- **2 tsp. ground cinnamon**
- **½ cup butter, softened**

1. In a large bowl, dissolve yeast and ½ tsp. sugar in ¼ cup warm water. Let stand for 5 minutes. Add the remaining sugar and water, butter, egg, salt and 1½ cups of flour; beat until smooth. Stir in enough remaining flour to form a soft dough.

2. Turn onto a lightly floured surface; knead until smooth and elastic, 6-8 minutes. Place in a greased bowl, turning once to grease top. Cover and let rise in a warm place until doubled, about 1 hour.

3. Meanwhile, combine topping ingredients; pour into a greased 13x9-in. baking pan; set aside. Combine the filling ingredients; set aside.

4. Punch dough down and turn onto a lightly floured surface. Roll into a 15x8-in. rectangle; spread filling over dough. Roll up from the long side. Seal seam. Slice into 15 rolls; place, with cut side down, over topping. Cover and let rise until nearly doubled, 30-45 minutes.

5. Bake at 375° for 25 minutes or until golden brown. Cool 3 minutes; invert pan onto a serving plate.

1 SERVING: 321 cal., 14g fat (9g sat. fat), 56mg chol., 251mg sod., 46g carb. (25g sugars, 1g fiber), 4g pro.

"Really fluffy and delicious cinnamon rolls. I didn't have whipping cream, so I substituted vanilla ice cream and reduced the brown sugar to ⅔ cup. The brown sugar-ice cream sauce was a really nice touch! Next time, I will hopefully have whipping cream handy and try it according to the original recipe. I will definitely make these again."
—DONORDOUG, TASTEOFHOME.COM

GRANDMA'S SECRET

Hickory, the wood traditionally used for smoking Gouda cheese and many other foods, lends a sweet flavor similar to maple wood with the pungency of mesquite.

GOUDA & ROASTED POTATO BREAD

Our family tried roasted potato bread at a bakery on a road trip, and I came up with
my own recipe when we realized we lived much too far away to have it regularly.
It makes for a really amazing roast beef sandwich and is also delicious with soups.

—*Elisabeth Larsen, Pleasant Grove, UT*

PREP: 45 MIN. + RISING • **BAKE:** 40 MIN. • **MAKES:** 1 LOAF (16 PIECES)

½ **lb. Yukon Gold potatoes,
chopped (about ¾ cup)**
1½ **tsp. olive oil**
1½ **tsp. salt, divided**
1 **pkg. (¼ oz.) active dry
yeast**
2½ **to 3 cups all-purpose
flour**
1 **cup warm water (120° to
130°)**
½ **cup shredded smoked
Gouda cheese**

1. Arrange 1 oven rack at lowest rack setting; place second rack in middle of oven. Preheat oven to 425°. Place potatoes in a greased 15x10x1-in. baking pan. Drizzle with oil; sprinkle with ½ tsp. salt. Toss to coat. Roast until tender, 20-25 minutes, stirring occasionally.

2. In a large bowl, mix yeast, remaining 1 tsp. salt and 2 cups flour. Add warm water; beat on medium speed until smooth. Stir in enough remaining flour to form a soft dough (dough will be sticky). Turn dough onto a floured surface; knead until smooth and elastic, 6-8 minutes. Gently knead in roasted potatoes and cheese. Place in a greased bowl, turning once to grease the top. Cover and let rise in a warm place until doubled, about 1 hour.

3. Punch down dough. Shape into a 7-in. round loaf. Place on a parchment-lined baking sheet. Cover with a kitchen towel; let rise in a warm place until dough expands to a 9-in. loaf, about 45 minutes.

4. Heat an oven-safe skillet on bottom oven rack. Meanwhile, in a teakettle, bring 2 cups water to a boil. Using a sharp knife, make a slash (¼ in. deep) across top of loaf. Place bread on top rack. Pull bottom rack out by 6-8 in.; add boiling water to skillet. (Work quickly and carefully, pouring water away from you. Don't worry if some water is left in the kettle.) Carefully slide bottom rack back into place; quickly close door to trap steam in oven. Bake 10 minutes.

5. Reduce oven setting to 375°; remove skillet from oven. Bake bread until deep golden brown, 30-35 minutes longer. Remove loaf to a wire rack to cool.

1 PIECE: 101 cal., 2g fat (1g sat. fat), 4mg chol., 253mg sod., 18g carb. (0 sugars, 1g fiber), 3g pro.

RAISIN SCONES

Several years ago, my parents went to Scotland, where Mom was born. Mom asked Dad to re-create the scones they had on the trip. Mom agrees eating these is like being back in Scotland!
—*Art Winter, Trumbull, CT*

TAKES: 30 MIN. • MAKES: 1 DOZEN

2 cups all-purpose flour
2 Tbsp. sugar
2 tsp. baking powder
½ tsp. salt
½ tsp. baking soda
½ tsp. ground nutmeg
½ cup cold butter, cubed
1 cup raisins
¾ cup buttermilk
1 egg white
    Additional sugar

1. In a large bowl, combine dry ingredients. Cut in butter until mixture resembles coarse crumbs. Stir in raisins and buttermilk just until moistened.

2. Turn onto a floured surface; knead gently 6-8 times. Pat into an 8-in. circle and cut into 12 wedges. Place 1 in. apart on a greased baking sheet. Beat egg white until foamy; brush over scones. Sprinkle with sugar. Bake at 425° for 12-15 minutes or until golden brown.

1 SCONE: 196cal., 8g fat (5g sat. fat), 21mg chol., 327mg sod., 28g carb. (10g sugars, 1g fiber), 3g pro.

NOTE: To substitute for each cup of buttermilk, use 1 Tbsp. white vinegar or lemon juice plus enough milk to measure 1 cup. Stir, then let stand 5 minutes. Or, use 1 cup plain yogurt or 1¾ tsp. cream of tartar plus 1 cup milk.

EASY BRAN MUFFINS

My granddaughter Kelsey has always loved cooking. At age 4, she entered Easy Bran Muffins in a baking contest. The recipe Kelsey used is ideal for kids. The ingredients are measured in whole amounts. Though it makes a lot of batter, you can store it in the refrigerator and make the muffins in batches. By the way, I also entered muffins in the contest, competing against Kelsey. Kelsey won the blue ribbon and I took second place!
—*Peggy Reed, Vergennes, VT*

PREP: 15 MIN. + STANDING • BAKE: 15 MIN. • MAKES: 5 DOZEN

6 cups All-Bran
2 cups boiling water
1 cup butter, softened
3 cups sugar
4 large eggs, room temperature
5 cups all-purpose flour
5 tsp. baking soda
1 tsp. salt
1 qt. buttermilk

Combine cereal and water; let stand 10 minutes. In a bowl, cream butter and sugar. Add the eggs, 1 at a time, beating well after each addition. Combine flour, baking soda and salt; add to creamed mixture alternately with buttermilk. Fold in the cereal mixture. Fill greased or paper-lined muffin cups two-thirds full. Bake at 400° for 15-20 minutes.

NOTE: Batter may be stored, covered, in refrigerator for 2 weeks; do not stir. Bake as directed.

1 MUFFIN: 131 cal., 4g fat (2g sat. fat), 21mg chol., 221mg sod., 23g carb. (12g sugars, 2g fiber), 3g pro. DIABETIC EXCHANGES: 1½ starch, 1 fat.

SPICED PISTACHIO PUMPKIN BREAD

This savory loaf is a nice surprise compared with sweet pumpkin loaves. Serve it with soup and salad, or toast a slice and slather it with butter.

—*Mary Leverette, Columbia, SC*

PREP: 30 MIN. • BAKE: 65 MIN. + COOLING
MAKES: 2 LOAVES (16 PIECES EACH)

3 Tbsp. butter	**BATTER**
1 cup chopped shelled pistachios	⅔ cup butter, softened
½ tsp. ground turmeric	2⅔ cups sugar
½ tsp. ground cumin	4 large eggs, room temperature
¼ tsp. cayenne pepper	1 can (15 oz.) pumpkin
	⅔ cup water
	3½ cups self-rising flour
	1 tsp. pumpkin pie spice

1. Preheat oven to 350°. In a small saucepan, melt butter over medium heat. Cook until butter is golden brown, 5-7 minutes, stirring constantly. Remove from heat; stir in pistachios, turmeric, cumin and cayenne. Let cool.

2. For batter, in a large bowl, beat ⅔ cup butter and sugar until crumbly. Add eggs, 1 at a time, beating well after each addition. Beat in pumpkin and water. In another bowl, whisk flour and pie spice; add to butter mixture just until moistened. Fold in pistachio mixture.

3. Transfer to 2 greased 9x5-in. loaf pans. Bake until a toothpick inserted in center comes out clean, 65-70 minutes. Cool in pans 10 minutes before removing to wire rack to cool completely.

FREEZE OPTION: Securely wrap cooled loaves in foil, then freeze. To use, thaw at room temperature.

1 PIECE: 193 cal., 7g fat (4g sat. fat), 36mg chol., 228mg sod., 29g carb. (18g sugars, 1g fiber), 3g pro.

TENDER GARLIC CHEESE BREADSTICKS

Garlic breadsticks complement so many dishes and they're so easy to make!
You can use bread flour in place of the all-purpose flour .

—Ann Volner, Maryville, MO

PREP: 45 MIN. + RISING • **BAKE:** 10 MIN. • **MAKES:** 32 BREADSTICKS

1 pkg. (¼ oz.) active
dry yeast
1½ cups warm water (110° to
115°)
½ cup warm 2% milk
(110° to 115°)
3 Tbsp. sugar
3 Tbsp. butter, melted
1½ tsp. salt
½ tsp. baking soda
4½ to 5½ cups all-purpose
flour

TOPPING

½ cup butter, melted
1 cup grated Parmesan
cheese
4½ tsp. Italian seasoning
1 tsp. garlic powder

1. In a large bowl, dissolve yeast in warm water and milk. Add the sugar, butter, salt, baking soda and 3 cups flour. Beat until smooth. Stir in enough remaining flour to form a firm dough.

2. Turn onto a floured surface; knead until smooth and elastic, 6-8 minutes. Place in a greased bowl, turning once to grease the top. Cover and let rise in a warm place until doubled, about 1 hour.

3. Turn onto a lightly floured surface; cover and let rest for 10 minutes. Divide into 32 pieces. Shape each into a 4½-in. rope.

4. Place melted butter in a shallow bowl. Place cheese in a second shallow bowl. Dip ropes in butter, then coat with cheese. Place 3 in. apart on lightly greased baking sheets. Combine Italian seasoning and garlic powder; sprinkle over breadsticks. Cover and let rise until doubled, about 30 minutes.

5. Bake at 375° for 10-15 minutes or until golden brown. Remove to wire racks. Serve warm.

1 BREADSTICK: 117 cal., 5g fat (3g sat. fat), 13mg chol., 199mg sod., 15g carb. (2g sugars, 1g fiber), 3g pro.

"We cut this recipe in half, but other than subbing in ½ cup of whole wheat flour, followed exactly. It's amazing! We'll definitely make these again!"
—ABBY, TASTEOFHOME.COM

TRADITIONAL HOT CROSS BUNS

On Easter morning, our family always looked forward to a breakfast of dyed hard-boiled eggs and Mom's hot cross buns. I still serve these for special brunches or buffets.
—*Barbara Jean Lull, Fullerton, CA*

PREP: 25 MIN. + RISING • **BAKE:** 15 MIN. • **MAKES:** 2½ DOZEN

2 pkg. (¼ oz. each) active dry yeast
2 cups warm whole milk (110° to 115°)
2 large eggs, room temperature
⅓ cup butter, softened
¼ cup sugar
1½ tsp. salt
1 tsp. ground cinnamon
¼ tsp. ground allspice

6 to 7 cups all-purpose flour
½ cup dried currants
½ cup raisins
1 large egg yolk
2 Tbsp. water

ICING
1½ cups confectioners' sugar
4 to 6 tsp. whole milk

1. In a small bowl, dissolve yeast in warm milk. In a large bowl, combine eggs, butter, sugar, salt, spices, yeast mixture and 3 cups flour; beat on medium speed until smooth. Stir in currants, raisins and enough remaining flour to form a soft dough (dough will be sticky).

2. Turn onto a floured surface; knead until dough is smooth and elastic, 6-8 minutes. Place in a greased bowl, turning once to grease the top. Cover and let rise in a warm place until doubled, about 1 hour.

3. Punch down dough. Turn onto a lightly floured surface; divide and shape into 30 balls. Place 2 in. apart on greased baking sheets. Cover with kitchen towels; let rise in a warm place until doubled, 30-45 minutes. Preheat oven to 375°.

4. Using a sharp knife, cut a cross on top of each bun. In a small bowl, whisk egg yolk and water; brush over tops of rolls. Bake for 15-20 minutes or until golden brown. Remove from pans to wire racks to cool slightly.

5. For icing, in a small bowl, mix confectioners' sugar and enough milk to reach desired consistency. Pipe a cross on top of each bun. Serve warm.

1 BUN: 171 cal., 3g fat (2g sat. fat), 28mg chol., 145mg sod., 31g carb. (12g sugars, 1g fiber), 4g pro.

GRANDMA'S SECRET

While some hot cross buns are still made in the traditional way by cutting an "X" into the dough, many modern versions get a pretty cross of sweet icing on top.

SWEET ONION SKILLET BREAD

Because there are just a few ingredients in this recipe, you'll get the best results if you use the finest-quality foods, such as a fresh Vidalia onion and aged Parmesan cheese.
—*Lisa Speer, Palm Beach, FL*

PREP: 25 MIN. • **BAKE:** 10 MIN. • **MAKES:** 4 SERVINGS

1 large sweet onion,
   thinly sliced
2 Tbsp. butter
2 Tbsp. olive oil, divided
1 can (13.8 oz.) refrigerated
   pizza crust
¼ cup grated Parmesan
   cheese

1. In a large cast-iron or other ovenproof skillet, saute onion in butter and 1 Tbsp. oil until softened. Reduce heat to medium-low; cook, stirring occasionally, until golden brown, 15-20 minutes. Set aside.

2. Brush bottom and sides of skillet with remaining oil. Unroll crust into skillet; flatten crust and build up edge slightly. Top with onion mixture and cheese. Bake at 450° until golden brown, 10-12 minutes. Cut into 4 wedges.

1 WEDGE: 415 cal., 17g fat (5g sat. fat), 19mg chol., 776mg sod., 53g carb. (9g sugars, 2g fiber), 11g pro.

SOUR CREAM YEAST ROLLS

These tender, golden brown rolls are the perfect finishing touch for any meal. There's nothing like returning to Mom's table, and these represent genuine home comfort.
—*Christine Frazier, Auburndale, FL*

PREP: 35 MIN. + RISING • **BAKE:** 25 MIN. • **MAKES:** 1 DOZEN

2½ to 3 cups all-purpose
   flour
2 Tbsp. sugar
1 pkg. (¼ oz.) active
   dry yeast
1 tsp. salt
1 cup sour cream
¼ cup water
3 Tbsp. butter, divided
1 large egg, room
   temperature

1. In a large bowl, combine 1½ cups flour, sugar, yeast and salt. In a small saucepan, heat the sour cream, water and 2 Tbsp. butter to 120°-130°; add to dry ingredients. Beat on medium speed for 2 minutes. Add egg and ½ cup flour; beat 2 minutes longer. Stir in enough remaining flour to form a soft dough.

2. Turn onto a floured surface; knead until smooth and elastic, 6-8 minutes. Place in a greased bowl, turning once to grease top. Cover and let rise in a warm place until doubled, about 1 hour.

3. Punch dough down. Turn onto a lightly floured surface; divide into 12 pieces. Shape each into a ball. Place in a greased 13x9-in. baking pan. Cover and let rise until doubled, about 30 minutes.

4. Bake at 375° for 25-30 minutes or until golden brown. Melt the remaining butter; brush over rolls. Remove from pan to a wire rack.

1 ROLL: 176 cal., 7g fat (4g sat. fat), 38mg chol., 230mg sod., 23g carb. (3g sugars, 1g fiber), 4g pro.

CORN PONE

CORN PONE

My husband's grandmother gave me this corn pone recipe years ago. She always made it with bacon drippings, which is heavenly, but if you're trying to be a little more health-conscious, you can use canola oil or a combination of the two. I cook it until it's crisp almost all the way through. It's delicious hot, warm or cold.
—*Tina Quiggle, LaGrange, GA*

PREP: 10 MIN. • BAKE: 35 MIN. • MAKES: 10 SERVINGS

½ to ¾ cup canola oil or
  bacon drippings
2 cups yellow or white
  cornmeal
1 tsp. salt
1¼ cups water
  Optional: Butter
  and honey

Preheat oven to 375°. Add oil to a 12-in. cast-iron or other ovenproof skillet; place in oven. In a large bowl, whisk together all cornmeal, salt and water. Mixture will be thick. Remove skillet from oven. Carefully spread mixture evenly in preheated skillet, spooning some of the oil on top of batter. Bake until edges start to brown, about 35 minutes. To serve, break into pieces and serve with butter and honey if desired.

1 SERVING: 215 cal., 12g fat (1g sat. fat), 0 chol., 238mg sod., 25g carb. (1g sugars, 1g fiber), 2g pro.

FROM GRANDMA'S KITCHEN: Think of corn pone as a simple version of cornbread. Corn pone consists of cornmeal, water, salt, and oil or bacon drippings, while cornbread adds eggs, sugar, butter, milk, flour and baking powder into the mix. Corn pone's consistency is usually a bit heavier and thicker compared to fluffy and light cornbread.

GRANDMA'S MOLASSES BREAD

This dark, slightly sweet bread is delicious toasted.
—*Jeannie Thomas, Kokomo, IN*

PREP: 5 MIN. • BAKE: 3-4 HOURS • MAKES: 1 LOAF (16 PIECES, ABOUT 1½ LBS.)

1 cup warm milk
  (70° to 80°)
2 Tbsp. butter, softened
2 Tbsp. molasses
1 large egg, room
  temperature
1½ tsp. salt
2½ cups bread flour
4½ tsp. sugar
½ cup rye flour
¼ cup whole wheat flour
2¼ tsp. active dry yeast

In bread machine pan, place all ingredients in order suggested by manufacturer. Select basic bread setting. Choose crust color and loaf size if available. Bake according to bread machine directions (check dough after 5 minutes of mixing; add 1 to 2 Tbsp. of water or flour if needed).

1 PIECE: 120 cal., 2g fat (1g sat. fat), 19mg chol., 249mg sod., 21g carb. (4g sugars, 1g fiber), 4g pro.

GRANDMA'S ORANGE ROLLS

Our children and grandchildren love these fine-textured sweet rolls. We have our own orange,
lime and grapefruit trees, and it's such a pleasure to go out and pick fruit to use in our recipes!
—*Norma Poole, Auburndale, FL*

PREP: 20 MIN. + RISING • **BAKE:** 20 MIN. • **MAKES:** 2½ DOZEN

1 pkg. (¼ oz.) active
  dry yeast
¼ cup warm water (110° to
  115°)
1 cup warm 2% milk (110°
  to 115°)
¼ cup shortening
¼ cup sugar
1 tsp. salt
1 large egg, room
  temperature, lightly
  beaten
3½ to 3¾ cups all-purpose
  flour

FILLING
1 cup sugar
½ cup butter, softened
2 Tbsp. grated orange zest

GLAZE
1 cup confectioners' sugar
4 tsp. butter, softened
½ tsp. lemon extract
4 to 5 tsp. 2% milk

1. In a large bowl, dissolve yeast in water. Add milk, shortening,
sugar, salt, egg and 3 cups flour. Beat until smooth. Stir in enough
remaining flour to form a soft dough.

2. Knead on a lightly floured surface until smooth and elastic,
6-8 minutes. Place in a greased bowl, turning once to grease top.
Cover and let rise in a warm place until doubled, about 1 hour.
Meanwhile, in a small bowl, combine filling ingredients; set aside.

3. Punch dough down; divide in half. Roll each half into a 15x10-in.
rectangle. Spread half the filling on each rectangle. Roll up,
jelly-roll style, starting with a long end. Cut each into 15 rolls.

4. Place, cut side down, in 2 greased 11x7-in. baking pans. Cover
and let rise until doubled, about 45 minutes.

5. Bake at 375° for 20-25 minutes or until lightly browned. In
a small bowl, combine the confectioners' sugar, butter, extract
and enough milk to achieve desired consistency; spread over
warm rolls.

FREEZE OPTION: Cover and freeze unrisen rolls. To use, thaw in
refrigerator overnight. Let rise, covered, in a warm place until
doubled, about 1½ hours. Bake and frost rolls as directed.

1 ROLL: 156 cal., 6g fat (3g sat. fat), 18mg chol., 122mg sod.,
24g carb. (12g sugars, 0 fiber), 2g pro.

MAKE-AHEAD CINNAMON ROLLS: For filling, substitute 1 cup
packed brown sugar for the sugar and 2 tsp. ground cinnamon
for the orange peel. In glaze, substitute vanilla extract for the
lemon extract.

*"You can also add some orange or lemon zest to the icing.
Very tasty rolls!"*
—SHARENE, TASTEOFHOME.COM

BANANA-ZUCCHINI BREAD

My grandmother made this bread for as long as I can remember, and I've been making it ever since I learned how to bake. Children love it for a snack, and it's good to serve at any meal. It's another delicious way to use zucchini, which is so abundant in late summer.

—*Eva Mae Hebert, Lafayette, LA*

> PREP: 20 MIN. • BAKE: 45 MIN. + COOLING
> MAKES: 2 LOAVES (16 PIECES EACH)

3 cups all-purpose flour	2 medium ripe bananas,
1½ tsp. baking powder	mashed (about 1 cup)
1½ tsp. baking soda	2 cups sugar
1½ tsp. ground cinnamon	1 cup vegetable oil
1 tsp. salt	1½ cups shredded unpeeled
4 large eggs, room	zucchini
temperature	1 cup chopped pecans

1. Preheat oven to 350°. In a large bowl, whisk flour, baking powder, baking soda, cinnamon and salt. In another bowl, whisk eggs, bananas, sugar and oil. Add to flour mixture; stir just until moistened. Fold in zucchini and pecans.

2. Pour into 2 greased 9x5-in. loaf pans. Bake until a toothpick inserted in center comes out clean, 45-50 minutes. Cool in pans for 10 minutes before removing to wire racks to cool completely.

1 PIECE: 193 cal., 10g fat (1g sat. fat), 23mg chol., 165mg sod., 24g carb. (14g sugars, 1g fiber), 2g pro.

QUICK GARLIC TOAST

Mom knew how to easily round out a meal with this crisp, cheesy garlic toast. We gobbled it up when she served it alongside slaw or salad, and used it to soak up gravy from her stew, too.

—*Teresa Ingebrand, Perham, MN*

> TAKES: 10 MIN. • MAKES: 12 PIECES

⅓ cup butter, softened
12 slices bread
½ tsp. garlic salt
3 Tbsp. grated Parmesan cheese

Spread butter on 1 side of each slice of bread. Cut each slice in half; place plain side down on a baking sheet. Sprinkle with garlic salt and Parmesan cheese. Broil 4 in. from the heat until lightly browned, 1-2 minutes.

1 PIECE: 128 cal., 6g fat (4g sat. fat), 15mg chol., 287mg sod., 15g carb. (2g sugars, 1g fiber), 3g pro.

GREEN ONION ROLLS

Better double the batch—these savory, elegant rolls will disappear fast.

—Jane Kroeger, Key Largo, FL

PREP: 30 MIN. + RISING • BAKE: 20 MIN. • MAKES: 1 DOZEN

1 Tbsp. butter
1½ cups chopped
    green onions
½ tsp. pepper
¾ tsp. garlic salt, optional
1 loaf (1 lb.) frozen bread
    dough, thawed
½ cup shredded part-skim
    mozzarella cheese
⅓ cup grated Parmesan
    cheese

1. Preheat oven to 375°. In a large skillet, heat butter over medium-high heat; saute green onions until tender. Stir in pepper and, if desired, garlic salt. Remove from heat.

2. On a lightly floured surface, roll dough into a 12x8-in. rectangle. Spread with onion mixture. Sprinkle with cheeses.

3. Roll up jelly-roll style, starting with a long side; pinch seam to seal. Cut into 12 slices; place in greased muffin cups. Cover; let rise in a warm place until doubled, about 30 minutes. Preheat oven to 375°.

4. Bake until golden brown, 18-20 minutes. Remove from pan to a wire rack. Serve warm.

1 ROLL: 142 cal., 4g fat (1g sat. fat), 7mg chol., 415mg sod., 20g carb. (2g sugars, 2g fiber), 6g pro.

EASY PEASY BISCUITS

I love that I can make these biscuits and have enough left over to freeze for another meal. They are wonderful with homemade peach preserves.

—Amanda West, Shelbyville, TN

PREP: 25 MIN. • BAKE: 10 MIN. • MAKES: 2 DOZEN

4 cups all-purpose flour
4 Tbsp. baking powder
1 Tbsp. sugar
1 Tbsp. ground flaxseed
1 tsp. sea salt
1 cup solid coconut oil
1½ cups 2% milk

1. Preheat oven to 450°. In a large bowl, whisk flour, baking powder, sugar, flaxseed and salt. Add coconut oil and cut in with a pastry blender until mixture resembles coarse crumbs. Add milk; stir just until moistened.

2. Turn onto a lightly floured surface; knead gently 8-10 times. Pat or roll dough into a rectangle ½ in. thick; fold dough into thirds (as you would a letter). Pat or roll dough again into a rectangle ½ in. thick; cut with a pizza cutter or knife into 24 biscuits, each about 2½ in. square. Place 1½ in. apart on ungreased baking sheets. Bake until light brown, 8-10 minutes. Serve warm.

FREEZE OPTION: Freeze cut biscuit dough on waxed paper-lined baking sheets until firm. Transfer to airtight containers; return to freezer. To use, bake biscuits in a preheated 350° oven until light brown, 15-20 minutes.

1 BISCUIT: 167 cal., 10g fat (8g sat. fat), 1mg chol., 328mg sod., 17g carb. (1g sugars, 1g fiber), 3g pro.

ITALIAN RICOTTA EASTER BREAD

I changed our family's traditional Easter bread by adding ricotta and
a few other ingredients. The almond flavoring works wonders!
—*Tina Mirilovich, Johnstown, PA*

PREP: 30 MIN. • **BAKE:** 45 MIN. • **MAKES:** 18 SERVINGS

¾ cup plain or butter-
  flavored shortening,
  room temperature
1½ cups sugar
 3 large eggs, room
   temperature
 3 large egg yolks, room
   temperature
 1 cup whole-milk ricotta
   cheese
 1 tsp. almond extract (or
   flavor of choice)

 6 cups all-purpose flour
 1 Tbsp. baking powder
 1 tsp. salt
 ½ cup 2% milk

GLAZE

1½ cups confectioners' sugar
 3 Tbsp. 2% milk
 ½ tsp. almond extract (or
   flavor of choice)
   Sliced toasted almonds
   or assorted sprinkles

1. Preheat oven to 350°. Cream shortening and sugar until light
and fluffy. Add eggs and egg yolks, 1 at a time, beating well after
each addition. Beat in ricotta and extract. In another bowl, whisk
flour, baking powder and salt; add to creamed mixture alternately
with milk, beating well after each addition, stirring in final 1 cup
flour by hand.

2. Turn onto a lightly floured surface; divide into thirds. Roll each
into an 18-in. rope. Place ropes on a parchment-lined baking
sheet and braid. Pinch ends to seal; tuck under braid. Bake until
a toothpick inserted in center comes out clean, 45-55 minutes
(do not overbake). Remove to wire racks to cool.

3. Meanwhile, beat confectioners' sugar, milk and extract until
smooth. Brush on bread while still warm; top with sliced almonds
or sprinkles.

NOTE: To toast nuts, bake them in a shallow pan in a 350° oven for
5-10 minutes or cook in a skillet over low heat until lightly browned,
stirring occasionally.

1 PIECE: 376 cal., 11g fat (4g sat. fat), 68mg chol., 247mg sod., 60g
carb. (28g sugars, 1g fiber), 8g pro.

HERB & SUN-DRIED TOMATO MUFFINS

Mom often served these muffins instead of bread or buns. Now I bake them to serve with soup or chili.
—*Elizabeth King, Duluth, MN*

PREP: 20 MIN. • **BAKE:** 20 MIN. • **MAKES:** 1 DOZEN

2 **cups all-purpose flour**
2 **tsp. baking powder**
1 **tsp. snipped fresh dill or ¼ tsp. dill weed**
1 **tsp. minced fresh thyme or ¼ tsp. dried thyme**
½ **tsp. baking soda**
½ **tsp. salt**
½ **tsp. pepper**
1 **large egg, room temperature**
1¼ **cups 2% milk**
¼ **cup olive oil**
½ **cup shredded cheddar cheese**
½ **cup oil-packed sun-dried tomatoes, finely chopped**

1. Preheat oven to 375°. In a large bowl, mix first 7 ingredients. In another bowl, whisk egg, milk and oil. Add to flour mixture; stir just until moistened. Fold in cheese and tomatoes.

2. Fill 12 greased muffin cups three-fourths full. Bake for 18-20 minutes or until a toothpick inserted in center comes out clean. Cool 5 minutes before removing from pan to a wire rack. Serve warm.

1 MUFFIN: 161 cal., 8g fat (2g sat. fat), 25mg chol., 277mg sod., 18g carb. (2g sugars, 1g fiber), 5g pro. **DIABETIC EXCHANGES:** 1½ fat, 1 starch.

HAM & BROCCOLI CORNBREAD

Leftovers haunt me. Often nobody wants to eat them, and I hate to see them go to waste. This cornbread is an excellent way to use many combinations of leftover meat and veggies.
—*Fay A Moreland, Wichita Falls, TX*

PREP: 15 MIN. • **BAKE:** 35 MIN. + COOLING • **MAKES:** 12 SERVINGS

5 **Tbsp. butter, divided**
2 **large eggs, room temperature**
1 **cup 2% milk**
½ **cup sour cream**
   Pinch cayenne pepper
2 **pkg. (8½ oz. each) cornbread/muffin mix**
2 **cups chopped fresh broccoli**
1½ **cups shredded sharp cheddar cheese**
1½ **cups cubed fully cooked ham**
3 **green onions, thinly sliced**

1. Preheat oven to 375°. Place 3 Tbsp. butter in a 12-in. cast-iron skillet; place pan in oven until butter is melted, 3-5 minutes. Carefully tilt pan to coat bottom and sides with butter.

2. Melt remaining butter. In a large bowl, whisk together eggs, milk, sour cream, cayenne pepper and melted butter until blended. Add muffin mixes; stir just until moistened. Fold in remaining ingredients. Pour into hot pan.

3. Bake until golden brown and a toothpick inserted in the center comes out clean, 35-40 minutes. Let stand 15 minutes before serving.

1 PIECE: 338 cal., 18g fat (9g sat. fat), 73mg chol., 700mg sod., 31g carb. (10g sugars, 3g fiber), 12g pro.

MOM'S
BUTTERMILK
BISCUITS

MOM'S BUTTERMILK BISCUITS

These fluffy biscuits are so tasty served warm, slathered with butter or used to mop every last drop of gravy off your plate. I can still see Mom pulling these tender biscuits out of the oven.

—Vera Reid, Laramie, WY

TAKES: 30 MIN. • MAKES: 10 SERVINGS

2 cups all-purpose flour
2 tsp. baking powder
½ tsp. baking soda
½ tsp. salt
¼ cup shortening
¾ cup buttermilk

Preheat oven to 450°. In a bowl, combine flour, baking powder, baking soda and salt; cut in shortening until mixture resembles coarse crumbs. Stir in buttermilk; knead dough gently. Roll out to ½-in. thickness. Cut with a 2½-in. biscuit cutter and place on a lightly greased baking sheet. Bake until golden brown, 10-15 minutes.

FREEZE OPTION: Freeze cooled biscuits in a resealable freezer container. To use, heat in a preheated 350° oven 15-20 minutes.

1 BISCUIT: 142 cal., 5g fat (1g sat. fat), 1mg chol., 281mg sod., 20g carb. (1g sugars, 1g fiber), 3g pro.

HERB BISCUITS: To buttermilk, add 2 Tbsp. minced fresh basil and 2 tsp. minced fresh rosemary.

PARMESAN-CHIVE BISCUITS: To buttermilk, add 2 Tbsp. minced fresh chives. Beat 1 egg white with 1 Tbsp. water. Brush over tops of biscuits. Sprinkle with 3-4 tsp. grated Parmesan. Bake at 425° 10-15 minutes.

GRANDMA'S PUMPKIN BREAD

You just can't beat the aroma of pumpkin bread fresh out of the oven. This classic recipe is tender and moist, and it has a sugary crust around the edges.

—Kathleene Baker, Plano, TX

PREP: 25 MIN. • BAKE: 55 MIN. + COOLING • MAKES: 2 LOAVES (16 PIECES EACH)

⅔ cup shortening
2⅔ cups sugar
4 large eggs, room temperature
1 can (15 oz.) solid-pack pumpkin
⅔ cup water
3⅓ cups all-purpose flour
1 tsp. baking soda
1 tsp. ground cinnamon
½ tsp. baking powder
½ tsp. salt
⅛ tsp. ground nutmeg
⅔ cup chopped pecans or walnuts

1. In a large bowl, cream shortening and sugar until light and fluffy, 5-7 minutes. Beat in the eggs, pumpkin and water (mixture will appear curdled). Combine the flour, baking soda, cinnamon, baking powder, salt and nutmeg; gradually beat into pumpkin mixture until blended. Stir in nuts.

2. Transfer to 2 greased 9x5-in. loaf pans. Bake at 350° for 55-65 minutes or until a toothpick inserted in the center comes out clean. Cool for 10 minutes before removing from pans to wire racks.

1 PIECE: 179 cal., 7g fat (1g sat. fat), 26mg chol., 92mg sod., 28g carb. (17g sugars, 1g fiber), 3g pro.

GARLIC FONTINA BREAD

With its golden brown color and soft texture, this bread is a must at any family meal.
It's a modified version of a traditional white bread recipe my brother gave me.
Try it as garlic bread toast, for grilled sandwiches or enjoy it as it as is.
—*Cindy Ryan, St. Johns, MI*

PREP: 30 MIN. + RISING • **BAKE:** 30 MIN. + COOLING • **MAKES:** 2 LOAVES (16 PIECES EACH)

2 pkg. (¼ oz. each) active dry yeast
2 cups warm water (110° to 115°)
3 Tbsp. sugar
2 Tbsp. shortening
1 Tbsp. garlic powder
2 tsp. salt
5 to 5½ cups all-purpose flour
1½ cups plus 2 Tbsp. shredded fontina cheese, divided
1½ tsp. canola oil

1. In a large bowl, dissolve yeast in warm water. Add the sugar, shortening, garlic powder, salt and 3 cups flour. Beat until smooth. Stir in enough remaining flour to form a firm dough. Stir in 1½ cups cheese.

2. Turn onto a floured surface; knead until smooth and elastic, 6-8 minutes. Place in a greased bowl, turning once to grease the top. Cover and let rise in a warm place until doubled, about 1 hour. Preheat oven to 375°.

3. Punch dough down. Shape into 2 loaves. Place in 2 greased 9x5-in. loaf pans. Cover and let rise in a warm place until doubled, about 30 minutes. Brush with oil; sprinkle with remaining cheese. Bake 30-35 minutes or until golden brown. Cool on a wire rack.

1 PIECE: 119 cal., 4g fat (2g sat. fat), 10mg chol., 215mg sod., 17g carb. (2g sugars, 1g fiber), 4g pro.

MONKEY BREAD BISCUITS

Classic monkey bread is a sweetly spiced breakfast treat. I came up with an easy
dinner version featuring garlic and Italian seasoning the crowd will love.
—*Dana Johnson, Scottsdale, AZ*

TAKES: 20 MIN. • **MAKES:** 1 DOZEN

1 tube (16.3 oz.) large refrigerated flaky biscuits
3 Tbsp. butter, melted
1 garlic clove, minced
½ tsp. Italian seasoning
¼ cup grated Parmesan cheese
Additional Italian seasoning

1. Preheat oven to 425°. Separate biscuits; cut each into 6 pieces. In a large bowl, combine butter, garlic and Italian seasoning; add biscuit pieces and toss to coat.

2. Place 4 pieces in each of 12 greased muffin cups. Sprinkle with cheese and additional Italian seasoning. Bake until golden brown, 8-10 minutes. Serve warm.

1 BISCUIT: 159 cal., 9g fat (3g sat. fat), 9mg chol., 418mg sod., 16g carb. (3g sugars, 1g fiber), 3g pro.

HERB & ROMANO CHEESE WREATH

After the wreath is baked and cooled, it can be wrapped in foil, placed in an airtight container and frozen until you are ready to use it yourself or give it away. Add some whipped butter on the side and it's the perfect gift.

—Linda Padia, Wauna, WA

PREP: 30 MIN. + RISING • **BAKE:** 30 MIN. + COOLING
MAKES: 1 LOAF (24 PIECES)

1 pkg. (¼ oz.) active dry yeast
2 Tbsp. honey
1½ cups warm water (110° to 115°)
½ cup nonfat dry milk powder
2 large eggs, room temperature
½ cup butter, softened
4 Tbsp. grated Romano cheese, divided
2 tsp. minced fresh rosemary or ½ tsp. dried rosemary, crushed
2 tsp. minced fresh thyme or ½ tsp. dried thyme
1½ tsp. salt
5½ to 6 cups bread flour
1 Tbsp. butter, melted

1. In a small bowl, dissolve yeast and honey in warm water; stir in milk powder. In a large bowl, combine eggs, softened butter, 2 Tbsp. cheese, rosemary, thyme, salt, yeast mixture and 2 cups flour; beat on medium speed until smooth. Stir in enough remaining flour to form a soft dough (dough will be sticky).

2. Turn dough onto a floured surface; knead until smooth and elastic, 6-8 minutes. Place in a greased bowl, turning once to grease the top. Cover and let rise in a warm place until doubled, about 1 hour.

3. Punch down dough. Turn onto a lightly floured surface; divide into thirds. Roll each into a 30-in. rope. Place ropes on a greased baking sheet and braid. Shape into a wreath and pinch ends to seal.

4. Cover with a kitchen towel; let rise in a warm place until almost doubled, about 45 minutes. Preheat oven to 375°.

5. Brush braid with melted butter; sprinkle with remaining cheese. Bake until golden brown, 30-35 minutes. Remove from pan to a wire rack to cool.

1 PIECE: 174 cal., 6g fat (3g sat. fat), 27mg chol., 215mg sod., 25g carb. (2g sugars, 1g fiber), 5g pro.

DILL BATTER BREAD

Even those who don't consider themselves bakers can make
this bread with success. And your guests will be delighted!
—*Donna Lindecamp, Morganton, NC*

PREP: 15 MIN. + RISING • **BAKE:** 45 MIN. + COOLING • **MAKES:** 1 LOAF (16 PIECES)

¼ **cup sugar**
2 **pkg. (¼ oz. each) active
   dry yeast**
2 **tsp. dill weed**
1½ **tsp. salt**
4½ **cups all-purpose flour**
1 **cup water**
1 **cup 2% milk**
¼ **cup canola oil**
1 **large egg, room
   temperature**
2 **tsp. butter, melted**
½ **tsp. kosher salt**

1. In a large bowl, mix sugar, yeast, dill weed, salt and 2 cups flour. In a small saucepan, heat the water, milk and canola oil to 120°-130°. Add to dry ingredients; beat on medium speed 2 minutes. Add egg; beat on high 2 minutes. Stir in remaining flour to form a stiff batter. Cover and let rise until doubled, about 1 hour.

2. Preheat oven to 375°. Stir down batter. Transfer to a greased 2½-qt. round baking dish. Bake until bread is deep golden brown and sounds hollow when tapped, 45-50 minutes.

3. Cool 5 minutes before removing to a wire rack. Brush with butter; sprinkle with salt. Cool completely.

1 PIECE: 191 cal., 5g fat (1g sat. fat), 14mg chol., 298mg sod., 31g carb. (4g sugars, 1g fiber), 5g pro.

FROM GRANDMA'S KITCHEN: Easy batter bread lets you enjoy homemade yeast bread without the work of kneading. It dirties fewer dishes and leaves your counter clean, since the dough stays in its mixing bowl for the first rise. Since beating the batter with a mixer takes the place of kneading, be sure to beat for the time specified in the recipe. Batter bread dough is more loose and sticky than traditional kneaded doughs.

DILL BATTER
BREAD

CRESCENT DINNER ROLLS

These light, golden rolls have a heavenly homemade flavor and aroma. Mom never hesitates to whip up a batch of these from-scratch rolls, since they round out a meal so satisfyingly.

—*Debra Falkiner, St. Charles, MO*

PREP: 40 MIN. + RISING • **BAKE:** 10 MIN. • **MAKES:** 2 DOZEN

- **1 pkg. (¼ oz.) active dry yeast**
- **¼ cup warm water (110° to 115°)**
- **1 Tbsp. plus ½ cup sugar, divided**
- **¾ cup warm milk (110° to 115°)**
- **3 large eggs, room temperature, lightly beaten**
- **½ cup butter, softened**
- **1 tsp. salt**
- **5 to 5½ cups all-purpose flour**
  Melted butter

1. In a large bowl, dissolve yeast in warm water. Add 1 Tbsp. sugar; let stand for 5 minutes. Add the milk, eggs, butter, salt and remaining sugar. Stir in enough flour to form a stiff dough. Turn onto a floured surface; knead until smooth and elastic, 6-8 minutes. Place in a greased bowl, turning once to grease top. Cover and let rise in a warm place until doubled, about 1½ hours.

2. Punch dough down. Divide into thirds. Roll each into a 12-in. circle; cut each circle into 8 wedges. Brush with melted butter; roll up wedges from the wide end and place, pointed end down, 2 in. apart on greased baking sheets. Cover and let rise in a warm place until doubled, about 30 minutes. Bake at 375° for 10-12 minutes or until golden brown. Remove from pans to wire racks.

1 ROLL: 161 cal., 5g fat (3g sat. fat), 38mg chol., 149mg sod., 25g carb. (5g sugars, 1g fiber), 4g pro.

HONEY OATMEAL LOAVES

There's nothing like the taste and aroma of homemade bread. A friend gave me this recipe for a wedding gift. It was originally a family recipe passed down from her grandmother, and now it's a staple in our house, too. The best part? It contains lots of healthy ingredients.
—*Amy Morrison, Derry, NH*

PREP: 30 MIN. + RISING • **BAKE:** 40 MIN. + COOLING • **MAKES:** 2 LOAVES (16 PIECES EACH)

1¾ cups water
1 cup fat-free milk
½ cup canola oil
¼ cup honey
¼ cup molasses
1¼ cups quick-cooking oats
4 to 5 cups bread flour
2 pkg. (¼ oz. each) quick-rise yeast
2 tsp. salt
3 cups whole grain spelt flour or whole wheat flour

1. In a saucepan, heat water, milk, oil, honey and molasses to a simmer; stir in oats. Remove from heat; cool mixture to 120°-130°. In a large bowl, mix 4 cups bread flour, yeast and salt. Stir in cooled oat mixture. Stir in spelt flour and enough remaining bread flour to form a soft dough (dough will be sticky).

2. Turn dough onto a floured surface; knead until smooth and elastic, 6-8 minutes. Cover and let rest 10 minutes.

3. Divide dough in half. Roll each into a 12x8-in. rectangle. Roll up jelly-roll style, starting with a short side; pinch seam and ends to seal. Place in greased 9x5-in. loaf pans, seam side down.

4. Cover with kitchen towels; let rise in a warm place until almost doubled, about 1 hour. Preheat oven to 350°.

5. Bake until golden brown, 40-45 minutes. Remove from pans to wire racks; cool completely.

FREEZE OPTION: Securely wrap cooled loaves in plastic, then place in resealable plastic freezer bags to freeze. To use, thaw at room temperature.

1 PIECE: 169 cal., 4g fat (0 sat. fat), 0 chol., 153mg sod., 27g carb. (5g sugars, 2g fiber), 4g pro.

GRANDMA'S SECRET

Next time you open a new bag of flour, save yourself some mess with this trick. Slap the top of the bag a couple of times before opening it. This settles the flour so it doesn't spray out when you open the bag.

GRANDMA'S HOLIDAY LEFTOVER ROLLS

Grab that leftover turkey and roll it up with some sausage, cheese and vegetables to make a savory roll. Eat it for dinner, breakfast or just as a snack. To add an over the top touch, drizzle with turkey gravy.
—*Kellie Braddell, West Point, CA*

PREP: 45 MIN. + RISING • BAKE: 25 MIN. • MAKES: 1 DOZEN

1 pkg. (¼ oz.) active dry yeast
1¼ cups warm water (110° to 115°)
1 large egg, room temperature
1 Tbsp. sugar
4 to 4½ cups all-purpose flour

FILLING
½ lb. bulk pork sausage
1 small onion, chopped
1 celery rib, chopped
2 cups shredded cooked turkey
½ tsp. pepper
1 tsp. garlic powder
1 tsp. onion powder
1 tsp. poultry seasoning
½ tsp. celery salt
½ tsp. dried rosemary, crushed
1 cup whole-berry cranberry sauce
2 cups shredded Swiss cheese
1 large egg, beaten

1. In a small bowl, dissolve yeast in warm water. In a large bowl, combine egg, sugar, yeast mixture and 2 cups flour; beat on medium speed until smooth. Stir in enough remaining flour to form a soft dough (dough will be sticky).

2. Turn dough onto a floured surface; knead until smooth and elastic, 6-8 minutes. Place in a greased bowl, turning once to grease the top. Cover and let rise in a warm place until doubled, about 1 hour.

3. In a large skillet, cook the sausage, onion and celery over medium sausage is no longer pink and vegetables are tender, 8-10 minutes, breaking sausage into crumbles; drain if needed. Stir in turkey and seasonings.

4. Punch down dough. Turn onto a lightly floured surface. Roll into an 20x12-in. rectangle. Spread cranberry sauce to within 1 in. of edges; sprinkle with cheese and top with sausage mixture. Roll up jelly-roll style, starting with a long side; pinch seam to seal. Cut into 12 slices.

5. Place 1 in. apart on a parchment-lined baking sheet, cut side down. Cover with a kitchen towel; let rise in a warm place until almost doubled, about 35 minutes.

6. Preheat oven to 350°. Brush rolls with beaten egg. Bake until lightly browned, 25-30 minutes. Remove from pan to a wire rack; serve warm.

1 ROLL: 362 cal., 12g fat (5g sat. fat), 82mg chol., 248mg sod., 44g carb. (7g sugars, 2g fiber), 19g pro.

APPLE & HERB
ROASTED TURKEY,
PAGE 111

GRANDMA'S FAVORITE

MAIN COURSES

———— ✦ ————

Every dinner is special when you're sitting at
Grandma's table. From simple one-pot dishes
for busy days to hearty holiday feasts, these
are the recipes we love to pass down.

MOM'S CHICKEN TETRAZZINI

Rotisserie chicken turns this baked spaghetti into a warm, cozy meal
our family craves. If we have leftover turkey, we use that, too.
—Jennifer Petrino, Newnan, GA

PREP: 35 MIN. • **BAKE:** 25 MIN. + STANDING • **MAKES:** 6 SERVINGS

8 **oz. uncooked spaghetti**
2 **tsp. plus 3 Tbsp. butter,**
  divided
8 **bacon strips, chopped**
2 **cups sliced**
  fresh mushrooms
1 **small onion, chopped**
1 **small green pepper,**
  chopped
⅓ **cup all-purpose flour**
¼ **tsp. salt**
¼ **tsp. pepper**
3 **cups chicken broth**
3 **cups coarsely shredded**
  rotisserie chicken
2 **cups frozen peas**
  (about 8 oz.)
1 **jar (4 oz.) diced**
  pimientos, drained
½ **cup grated Romano or**
  Parmesan cheese

1. Preheat oven to 375°. Cook spaghetti according to package directions for al dente. Drain; transfer to a greased 13x9-in. baking dish. Add 2 tsp. butter and toss to coat.

2. Meanwhile, in a large skillet, cook bacon over medium heat until crisp, stirring occasionally. Remove with a slotted spoon; drain on paper towels. Discard drippings, reserving 1 Tbsp. in pan. Add mushrooms, onion and green pepper to drippings; cook and stir over medium-high heat 5-7 minutes or until tender. Remove from pan.

3. In same pan, heat remaining butter over medium heat. Stir in flour, salt and pepper until smooth; gradually whisk in broth. Bring to a boil, stirring occasionally; cook and stir 3-5 minutes or until slightly thickened. Add chicken, peas, pimientos and mushroom mixture; heat through, stirring occasionally. Spoon over spaghetti. Sprinkle with bacon and cheese.

4. Bake, uncovered, 25-30 minutes or until golden brown. Let stand 10 minutes before serving.

1½ CUPS: 533 cal., 23g fat (10g sat. fat), 107mg chol., 1133mg sod., 44g carb. (6g sugars, 4g fiber), 38g pro.

"My family loved it! I did, however, make one change since I am the only one in my family who likes peas. I substituted a bag of fresh spinach for the peas, and I can't imagine eating it the other way. This is something I will definitely make again."
—ANGIEGILBERT, TASTEOFHOME.COM

SPICED LIME & CILANTRO CHICKEN

As a working mom and home cook, I strive to have fabulous, flavor-packed dinners that make my family smile. Nothing is more awesome than a slow-cooker recipe that makes it seem as though you've been cooking in the kitchen all day!
—*Mari Smith, Ashburn, VA*

PREP: 15 MIN. • COOK: 3 HOURS • MAKES: 6 SERVINGS

2 tsp. chili powder
1 tsp. sea salt
1 tsp. ground cumin
1 tsp. pepper
¼ tsp. cayenne pepper
6 bone-in chicken thighs (about 2¼ lbs.)

⅓ cup lime juice (about 3 limes)
1 Tbsp. olive oil
½ cup fresh cilantro leaves
5 garlic cloves, halved

1. Combine the first 5 ingredients; rub over chicken. Place in a 4- or 5-qt. slow cooker. Combine remaining ingredients in a blender; cover and process until pureed. Pour over chicken.

2. Cook, covered, on low until a thermometer inserted in chicken reads 170°-175°, 3-4 hours.

1 CHICKEN THIGH: 253 cal., 17g fat (4g sat. fat), 81mg chol., 390mg sod., 2g carb. (0 sugars, 0 fiber), 23g pro.

GORGONZOLA & ORANGE CHICKEN TENDERS

My mom likes to make this for family gatherings, and we all like to eat it. Marmalade and Gorgonzola might sound like an unusual combo, but they actually make a marvelous pair.
—*Yvette Gorman, Denver, PA*

TAKES: 25 MIN. • MAKES: 4 SERVINGS

1 large egg
¼ tsp. salt
¾ cup seasoned bread crumbs
1 lb. chicken tenderloins
2 Tbsp. olive oil
¼ cup orange marmalade, warmed
¼ cup crumbled Gorgonzola cheese

1. In a shallow bowl, whisk egg and salt. Place bread crumbs in another shallow bowl. Dip chicken in egg, then in bread crumbs, patting to help coating adhere.

2. In a large skillet, heat oil over medium heat. Add chicken; cook 3-4 minutes on each side or until chicken is no longer pink. Drizzle with warm marmalade; top with cheese. Remove from heat; let stand, covered, until cheese begins to melt.

1 SERVING: 318 cal., 12g fat (3g sat. fat), 108mg chol., 543mg sod., 23g carb. (13g sugars, 1g fiber), 32g pro.

SHRIMP & FETA SKILLET

My friend's feisty Italian grandmother, Gemma, makes a dish similar to my shrimp with tomatoes. When I make this recipe, I think of Gemma and smile while stirring.
—*Celeste Ehrenberg, Topeka, KS*

TAKES: 25 MIN. • MAKES: 4 SERVINGS

2 cans (14½ oz. each) diced tomatoes with basil, oregano and garlic, undrained
2 tsp. garlic powder
2 tsp. dried basil
1¼ lbs. uncooked shrimp (31-40 per lb.), peeled and deveined
1 cup crumbled feta cheese
  Crusty whole grain bread, optional

1. In a large skillet, combine tomatoes, garlic powder and basil; bring to a boil. Reduce heat; simmer, uncovered, 4-6 minutes or until slightly thickened.

2. Add shrimp; cook and stir 3-4 minutes or until shrimp turn pink. Sprinkle feta over shrimp; serve with bread if desired.

1¼ CUPS: 261 cal., 6g fat (3g sat. fat), 187mg chol., 1092mg sod., 15g carb. (7g sugars, 5g fiber), 30g pro.

GRANDMA'S CABBAGE ROLLS

Hearty and heartwarming, these traditional cabbage rolls are nothing short of delicious. Toasted rye bread and polenta make lovely accompaniments.
—*Teodora Cosac, Ottawa, ON*

PREP: 45 MIN. • COOK: 6 HOURS • MAKES: 12 SERVINGS

1 large head cabbage, cored
1 large egg
1 medium onion, finely chopped
½ cup uncooked converted rice
1 Tbsp. snipped fresh dill or 1 tsp. dill weed
1 tsp. paprika
1 tsp. dried savory or thyme
½ tsp. salt
½ tsp. pepper
1½ lbs. lean ground beef (90% lean)
2 cups sauerkraut, rinsed, well drained and chopped
2 cups canned crushed tomatoes
6 bacon strips, chopped
1 can (14½ oz.) vegetable broth

1. Cook cabbage in boiling water just until outer leaves pull away easily from head. Set aside 12 large leaves for rolls. Refrigerate remaining cabbage for another use. Cut out the thick vein from the bottom of each leaf, making a V-shaped cut.

2. In a large bowl, combine the egg, onion, rice, dill, paprika, savory, salt and pepper. Crumble beef over mixture and mix well. Place ⅓ cup meat mixture on a cabbage leaf; overlap cut ends of leaf. Fold in sides. Beginning from the cut end, roll up. Repeat with remaining cabbage leaves and filling.

3. Combine the sauerkraut, tomatoes and bacon. Spoon half into a 6-qt. slow cooker. Arrange 6 cabbage rolls, seam side down, over sauerkraut mixture. Top with remaining sauerkraut mixture and rolls. Add broth to slow cooker. Cover and cook on low for 6-8 hours or until a thermometer inserted in rolls reads 160°.

1 CABBAGE ROLL WITH ⅓ CUP SAUCE: 227 cal., 10g fat (4g sat. fat), 61mg chol., 620mg sod., 18g carb. (5g sugars, 4g fiber), 16g pro.

GRILLED ONION & SKIRT
STEAK TACOS

GRILLED ONION & SKIRT STEAK TACOS

I grew up watching my grandmother and mother in the kitchen. My grandparents came from Mexico, and this steak marinated in beer and lime juice honors their passion for cooking.
—*Adan Franco, Milwaukee, WI*

PREP: 15 MIN. + MARINATING • **GRILL:** 5 MIN. • **MAKES:** 8 SERVINGS

2 beef skirt or flank steaks (1 lb. each)
1 bottle (12 oz.) beer
¼ cup lime juice
3 Tbsp. olive oil, divided
8 spring onions or green onions
1¼ tsp. salt, divided
¾ tsp. pepper, divided
Corn tortillas, minced fresh cilantro and lime wedges

1. Pound beef with a meat mallet to tenderize. In a large bowl, mix beer, lime juice and 2 Tbsp. oil until blended. Add beef to marinade; turn to coat. Refrigerate, covered, at least 30 minutes.

2. Meanwhile, cut partially through the onions, leaving tops intact. Drizzle with remaining oil; sprinkle with ¼ tsp. salt and ¼ tsp. pepper.

3. Drain beef, discarding marinade; sprinkle with the remaining salt and pepper. On a greased grill rack, grill steaks and onions, covered, over medium heat or broil 4 in. from heat until meat reaches desired doneness (for medium-rare, a thermometer should read 135°; medium, 140°; medium-well, 145°) and onions are crisp-tender, 2-4 minutes on each side. Cut steak diagonally across the grain into thin slices. Serve steak slices with tortillas, onions, cilantro and lime wedges.

1 SERVING: 288 cal., 14g fat (5g sat. fat), 67mg chol., 458mg sod., 7g carb. (3g sugars, 1g fiber), 31g pro.

SPEEDY SALMON PATTIES

When I was a girl growing up on the farm, my mom often fixed these salmon patties when we were working late in the field. They're tasty with chopped green peppers added to the mixture, too.
—*Bonnie Evans, Cameron, NC*

TAKES: 25 MIN. • **MAKES:** 3 SERVINGS

⅓ cup finely chopped onion
1 large egg, beaten
5 saltines, crushed
½ tsp. Worcestershire sauce
¼ tsp. salt
⅛ tsp. pepper
1 can (14¾ oz.) salmon, drained, bones and skin removed
2 tsp. butter

1. In a large bowl, combine the first 6 ingredients. Crumble salmon over mixture and mix well. Shape into 6 patties.

2. In a large skillet over medium heat, fry patties in butter for 3-4 minutes on each side or until set and golden brown.

2 PATTIES: 288 cal., 15g fat (4g sat. fat), 139mg chol., 1063mg sod., 5g carb. (1g sugars, 0 fiber), 31g pro.

GERMAN-STYLE BEEF ROAST

My grandmother used to make this, and I adapted it for the slow cooker.
You'll love its convenience and terrific taste.
—*Lois Stanley, Myrtle Beach, SC*

PREP: 10 MIN. • COOK: 8 HOURS • MAKES: 10 SERVINGS

1 boneless beef chuck
   roast (4 lbs.), trimmed
1 tsp. pepper
1 large onion, thinly sliced
1 bottle (12 oz.) beer or
   nonalcoholic beer
1 cup ketchup
¼ cup packed brown sugar
¼ cup all-purpose flour
¼ cup cold water

1. Cut roast in half; sprinkle with pepper. Place onion and roast in a 5-qt. slow cooker. In a small bowl, combine the beer, ketchup and brown sugar; pour over top. Cover and cook on low for 8-10 hours or until meat is tender.

2. Remove meat to a serving platter; keep warm. Skim fat from cooking juices; transfer to a small saucepan. Bring liquid to a boil.

3. Combine flour and water until smooth; gradually stir into the pan. Bring to a boil; cook and stir for 2 minutes or until thickened. Serve with roast.

1 SERVING: 376 cal., 17g fat (7g sat. fat), 118mg chol., 382mg sod., 16g carb. (13g sugars, 0 fiber), 36g pro.

FETTUCCINE CARBONARA

When a man at church found out how much my family likes fettuccine carbonara,
he shared his Italian grandmother's recipe with us. I've made it my own over the
last 25 years. Grated Parmesan cheese works just as well as Romano.
—*Kristine Chayes, Smithtown, NY*

TAKES: 30 MIN. • MAKES: 6 SERVINGS

½ lb. bacon strips, chopped
1 pkg. (16 oz.) fettuccine
1 small onion,
   finely chopped
2 garlic cloves, minced
1 cup half-and-half cream
4 large eggs, lightly beaten
½ cup grated
   Romano cheese
½ tsp. salt
¼ tsp. pepper
1 Tbsp. minced
   fresh parsley
   Additional grated
   Romano cheese, optional

1. In a large skillet, cook bacon over medium heat until crisp, stirring occasionally. Remove with a slotted spoon; drain on paper towels. Discard drippings, reserving 1 Tbsp. in skillet.

2. Meanwhile, in a Dutch oven, cook fettuccine according to package directions. Drain; return to pan.

3. Add onion to drippings in skillet; cook and stir over medium heat 2-3 minutes or until tender. Add garlic; cook 1 minute longer. Reduce heat to medium-low. Stir in cream. In a small bowl, whisk a small amount of warm cream into eggs; return all to skillet, whisking constantly. Cook 8-10 minutes or until a thermometer reads 160°, stirring constantly.

4. Stir cheese, salt, pepper and bacon into sauce. Add to the fettuccine and toss to combine. Sprinkle with parsley and, if desired, additional cheese. Serve immediately.

1 CUP: 495 cal., 19g fat (9g sat. fat), 162mg chol., 684mg sod., 56g carb. (4g sugars, 3g fiber), 25g pro.

SUNDAY'S BEST CHICKEN

I am a busy mom of four and a nursing student,
so weeknight dinners are often rushed. Sunday dinners
are very important to our family, and everyone loves
when I make this old-fashioned chicken recipe.

—*Amy Jenkins, Mesa, AZ*

PREP: 40 MIN. • **BAKE:** 2¼ HOURS + STANDING • **MAKES:** 10 SERVINGS

2 to 3 medium lemons
2 fresh rosemary sprigs
1 roasting chicken
  (6 to 7 lbs.)
1 Tbsp. olive oil
2 Tbsp. minced
  fresh rosemary
1 Tbsp. coarsely ground
  pepper
1½ tsp. salt

1. Finely grate enough zest from the lemons to measure 2 Tbsp.;
set aside. Coarsely chop 2 lemons; place chopped lemons and
rosemary sprigs in the chicken cavity. Save the remaining lemon
for another use.

2. Place chicken on a rack in a shallow roasting pan; brush with
oil. Combine the minced rosemary, pepper, salt and lemon zest;
rub over chicken.

3. Bake chicken, uncovered, at 350° for 2¼-2¾ hours or until a
thermometer inserted in thickest part of thigh reads 170°-175°,
basting occasionally with drippings. (Cover loosely with foil if
chicken browns too quickly.)

4. Let stand for 15 minutes before carving. Discard lemons and
rosemary sprigs.

5 OZ. COOKED CHICKEN: 334 cal., 20g fat (6g sat. fat), 108mg chol.,
458mg sod., 2g carb. (0 sugars, 1g fiber), 34g pro.

*"The recipe is fairly easy, and the chicken turned out
wonderful. The rosemary and lemon are a really nice flavor
combination and go so nicely with chicken. Be sure to let
it rest as directed prior to carving/slicing. This truly is an
excellent Sunday dinner chicken recipe."*
—LVARNER, TASTEOFHOME.COM

SHRIMP MOZAMBIQUE

This recipe was passed down from my grandma and is one that is frequently made in our Portuguese culture. Variations include adding other seafood, such as clams, muscles or scallops. I've also made it with chicken since my kids will not eat seafood.
—*Christina Souza, Brooksville, FL*

PREP: 20 MIN. • COOK: 20 MIN. • MAKES: 6 SERVINGS

3 Tbsp. olive oil
1 medium onion, finely chopped
6 garlic cloves, minced
2 lbs. uncooked shell-on shrimp (16-20 per lb.)
2 envelopes sazon with coriander and annatto
2 tsp. garlic salt
2 tsp. garlic powder
2 tsp. onion powder
1 tsp. paprika
1 bay leaf
1 bottle (12 oz.) beer or 1½ cups chicken broth
1 tsp. lemon juice
¼ cup ketchup
3 Tbsp. chopped fresh parsley
  Hot cooked rice

In a Dutch oven, heat oil over medium-high heat. Add onion; cook and stir until tender, 4-5 minutes. Add garlic and shrimp; cook 1 minute longer. Stir in seasonings. Add beer and lemon juice; bring to a boil. Reduce heat. Simmer, uncovered, until shrimp turn pink, 10-15 minutes. Stir in ketchup and parsley; discard bay leaf. Serve with rice.

1 SERVING: 223 cal., 9g fat (1g sat. fat), 184mg chol., 1190mg sod., 9g carb. (4g sugars, 1g fiber), 25g pro.

"We halved this recipe for two and served it with brown rice. It was delicious with a very unusual (to us) spice palate. Highly recommended!"
—JANIECEMURPHY, TASTEOFHOME.COM

MOM'S MEAT LOAF

Mom made the best meat loaf, and now I do, too. When I first met my husband, he wasn't a meat loaf guy, but this recipe won him over.
—*Michelle Beran, Claflin, KS*

PREP: 15 MIN. • BAKE: 1 HOUR + STANDING • MAKES: 6 SERVINGS

2 large eggs, lightly beaten
¾ cup 2% milk
⅔ cup finely crushed saltines
½ cup chopped onion
1 tsp. salt
½ tsp. rubbed sage
  Dash pepper
1½ lbs. lean ground beef (90% lean)
1 cup ketchup
½ cup packed brown sugar
1 tsp. Worcestershire sauce

1. Preheat oven to 350°. In a large bowl, combine the first 7 ingredients. Add beef; mix lightly but thoroughly. Shape into an 8x4-in. loaf in an ungreased 15x10x1-in. baking pan.

2. In a small bowl, combine remaining ingredients, stirring to dissolve sugar; remove ½ cup for sauce. Spread remaining mixture over meat loaf.

3. Bake 60-65 minutes or until a thermometer reads 160°. Let stand 10 minutes before slicing. Serve with reserved sauce.

1 SLICE: 366 cal., 12g fat (5g sat. fat), 135mg chol., 1092mg sod., 38g carb. (31g sugars, 0 fiber), 26g pro.

SHRIMP
MOZAMBIQUE

MOM'S ROAST BEEF

Everyone loves slices of this fork-tender roast beef with its savory gravy. The well-seasoned roast is Mom's specialty. People always ask about the secret ingredients. Now you have the delicious recipe for our favorite meat dish!
—*Linda Gaido, New Brighton, PA*

PREP: 20 MIN. • COOK: 2½ HOURS + STANDING • MAKES: 8 SERVINGS

1 **Tbsp. canola oil**	1 **medium onion, chopped**
1 **beef eye round roast** **(about 2½ lbs.)**	1 **tsp. beef bouillon** **granules**
1 **garlic clove, minced**	1 **cup brewed coffee**
2 **tsp. dried basil**	¾ **cup water**
1 **tsp. salt**	
1 **tsp. dried rosemary,** **crushed**	GRAVY
	¼ **cup all-purpose flour**
½ **tsp. pepper**	¼ **cup cold water**

1. In a Dutch oven, heat oil over medium heat; brown roast on all sides. Remove from pan. Mix garlic and seasonings; sprinkle over the roast.

2. Add onion to same pan; cook and stir over medium heat until tender. Stir in bouillon, coffee and ¾ cup water. Add roast; bring to a boil. Reduce heat; simmer, covered, until meat is tender, about 2½ hours.

3. Remove roast from pan, reserving cooking juices. Tent with foil; let stand 10 minutes before slicing.

4. Mix flour and cold water until smooth; stir into cooking juices. Bring to a boil, stirring constantly. Cook and stir until thickened, 1-2 minutes. Serve with roast.

1 SERVING: 198 cal., 6g fat (2g sat. fat), 65mg chol., 453mg sod., 5g carb. (1g sugars, 1g fiber), 28g pro.

MEAT & POTATO POT ROAST: Prepare roast as directed in step 1. Simmer 1¾ hours. Cut 16 small red potatoes in half and 5 carrots into chunks. Quarter 2 onions. Add to pan; cover and simmer 45 minutes or until meat and vegetables are tender. Remove meat and vegetables; keep warm. Make gravy as directed in step 4.

HEAVENLY CITRUS HAM

This recipe is special because it's based on the ham my grandma and mom used to make for holidays. Leftovers can be frozen up to 3 months and thawed before using. You'll want to remember this recipe for Easter!
—*Penny Hawkins, Mebane, NC*

PREP: 15 MIN. • BAKE: 1¾ HOURS + STANDING • MAKES: 12 SERVINGS

1 **fully cooked**
  bone-in ham (6 to 8 lbs.)
  Whole cloves
1¼ **cups orange soda**
1¼ **cups orange marmalade**
½ **cup packed brown sugar**
¼ **cup Dijon mustard**

1. Place ham on a rack in a shallow roasting pan. Score the surface of the ham, making diamond shapes ½ in. deep; insert a clove in the center of each diamond. Loosely cover ham with foil. Bake at 325° for 1½ hours.

2. In a small saucepan, combine the soda, marmalade and brown sugar. Bring to a boil; cook until liquid is reduced by half, about 15 minutes. Stir in mustard.

3. Brush ham with some of the glaze; bake 15-30 minutes longer or until a thermometer reads 140°, basting occasionally with remaining glaze. Let stand 10 minutes before slicing.

4 OZ. COOKED HAM: 345 cal., 6g fat (2g sat. fat), 106mg chol., 1422mg sod., 38g carb. (35g sugars, 0 fiber), 36g pro.

APPLE & HERB ROASTED TURKEY

PICTURED ON PAGE 98

My daughter loves to help me make this moist roasted turkey with herbs. Her job is to hand Mommy the ingredients—if she doesn't eat the apples first!
—*Kimberly Jackson, Gay, GA*

PREP: 20 MIN. • BAKE: 3 HOURS + STANDING • MAKES: 14 SERVINGS

¼ **cup minced fresh sage**
¼ **cup minced**
  fresh rosemary
1 **turkey (14 lbs.)**
1 **medium apple, quartered**
1 **medium onion, halved**
1 **celery rib, halved**
½ **cup butter, melted**
½ **cup apple jelly, warmed**

1. Preheat oven to 325°. Combine sage and rosemary. With fingers, carefully loosen skin from the turkey breast; rub herbs under the skin. Secure skin to underside of breast with toothpicks.

2. Place breast side up on a rack in a roasting pan. Place apple, onion and celery in turkey cavity. Brush turkey with butter.

3. Roast, uncovered, until a thermometer inserted in thickest part of thigh reads 170°-175°, 3-3½ hours. (Cover loosely with foil if turkey browns too quickly.) Remove turkey from oven; brush with apple jelly. Tent with foil and let stand 15 minutes before removing toothpicks and carving.

8 OZ. COOKED TURKEY: 626 cal., 31g fat (11g sat. fat), 262mg chol., 222mg sod., 10g carb. (9g sugars, 0 fiber), 72g pro.

BREADED
PORK CHOPS

GRANDMA'S SECRET

The saltine-cracker coating is a classic. You can also prepare this recipe with chicken breasts or cubed steaks.

BREADED PORK CHOPS

These traditional pork chops have a wonderful home-cooked
flavor like the ones Mom used to make. The breading makes them crispy outside
and tender and juicy inside. Why not treat your family to them tonight?
—*Deborah Amrine, Fort Myers, FL*

TAKES: 20 MIN. • MAKES: 6 SERVINGS

1　large egg, lightly beaten
½　cup 2% milk
1½　cups crushed
　　saltine crackers
6　boneless pork loin chops
　　(1 in. thick)
¼　cup canola oil

1. In a shallow bowl, combine egg and milk. Place cracker crumbs in another shallow bowl. Dip each pork chop in egg mixture, then coat with cracker crumbs, patting to make a thick coating.

2. In a large skillet, cook chops in oil for 4-5 minutes on each side or until a thermometer reads 145°. Let meat stand for 5 minutes before serving.

1 PORK CHOP: 405 cal., 22g fat (5g sat. fat), 115mg chol., 233mg sod., 14g carb. (1g sugars, 0 fiber), 36g pro.

ONE-POT MEATY SPAGHETTI

I used to help my mom make this when I was growing up, and the recipe stuck.
It was a beloved comfort food at college and is now a weeknight staple for my fiance and me.
—*Kristin Michalenko, Seattle, WA*

TAKES: 30 MIN. • MAKES: 6 SERVINGS

1　lb. extra-lean ground
　　beef (95% lean)
2　garlic cloves, minced
1　tsp. sugar
1　tsp. dried basil
½　tsp. dried oregano
¼　tsp. salt
¼　tsp. paprika
¼　tsp. pepper
1　can (28 oz.) diced
　　tomatoes, undrained
1　can (15 oz.) tomato sauce
2　cups water
¼　cup chopped fresh
　　parsley
8　oz. uncooked whole
　　wheat spaghetti, broken
　　in half
¼　cup grated Parmesan
　　cheese
　　Additional chopped
　　parsley

1. In a 6-qt. stockpot, cook and crumble beef with garlic over medium heat until no longer pink, 5-7 minutes. Stir in sugar and seasonings. Add tomatoes, tomato sauce, water and ¼ cup parsley; bring to a boil. Reduce heat; simmer, covered, 5 minutes.

2. Stir in spaghetti, a little at a time; return to a boil. Reduce heat to medium-low; cook, uncovered, until spaghetti is al dente, 8-10 minutes, stirring occasionally. Stir in cheese. Sprinkle with additional parsley.

1⅓ CUPS: 292 cal., 6g fat (2g sat. fat), 46mg chol., 737mg sod., 40g carb. (6g sugars, 8g fiber), 24g pro. **DIABETIC EXCHANGES:** 3 starch, 2 lean meat.

EASY TEXAS BBQ BRISKET

My mom tried my brisket and said it was even better than the version we used to have back in Texas.
What a compliment! Jazz up your sandwiches and tacos with the leftovers.
—*Audra Rorick, Lyons, KS*

PREP: 15 MIN. + CHILLING • BAKE: 4 HOURS + STANDING • MAKES: 10 SERVINGS

2 **Tbsp. packed
   brown sugar**
1 **Tbsp. salt**
1 **Tbsp. onion powder**
1 **Tbsp. garlic powder**
1 **Tbsp. ground mustard**
1 **Tbsp. smoked paprika**
1 **Tbsp. pepper**
2 **fresh beef briskets
   (3½ lbs. each)**
1 **bottle (10 oz.)
   Heinz 57 steak sauce**
½ **cup liquid smoke**
¼ **cup Worcestershire
   sauce**

1. In a small bowl, combine the first 7 ingredients. With a fork or sharp knife, prick holes in briskets. Rub meat with seasoning mixture. Cover and refrigerate overnight.

2. Preheat oven to 325°. Place briskets, fat sides up, in a roasting pan. In a small bowl, combine steak sauce, liquid smoke and Worcestershire sauce; pour over meat.

3. Cover tightly with foil; bake 4-5 hours or until tender. Let stand in juices 15 minutes. To serve, thinly slice across the grain. Skim fat from pan juices; spoon over meat.

NOTE: This is a fresh beef brisket, not corned beef.

6 OZ. COOKED BEEF WITH ABOUT 2 TBSP. JUICES: 456 cal., 14g fat (5g sat. fat), 135mg chol., 1283mg sod., 13g carb. (11g sugars, 1g fiber), 66g pro.

MY MOTHER'S LEMONY CHICKEN WITH BROCCOLI

My mom used to make super succulent chicken with broccoli for our family in Montana.
The few lucky guests invited for supper could never stop raving.
—*Jessy Drummond, Springfield, TN*

PREP: 15 MIN. • COOK: 20 MIN. • MAKES: 4 SERVINGS

1 **lb. boneless skinless
   chicken breasts,
   cut into 1-in. strips**
½ **tsp. salt**
¼ **tsp. pepper**
½ **cup all-purpose flour**
¼ **tsp. garlic powder**
¼ **tsp. paprika**
1 **large egg**
3 **Tbsp. lemon juice, divided**
¼ **cup butter, cubed**
1 **cup chicken broth**
½ **tsp. grated lemon zest**
4 **cups fresh
   broccoli florets
   Lemon wedges
   Hot cooked rice, optional**

1. Sprinkle chicken with salt and pepper. In a shallow bowl, mix flour, garlic powder and paprika. In another shallow bowl, whisk egg and 1 Tbsp. lemon juice. Dip chicken in egg mixture, then in flour mixture; shake off excess.

2. In a large skillet, heat butter over medium heat. Add chicken; cook, stirring occasionally, for 8-12 minutes or until no longer pink. Remove and keep warm. Add the broth, lemon zest and remaining lemon juice to skillet; bring to a boil. Stir in broccoli. Reduce heat; simmer, covered, 8-10 minutes or until broccoli is tender. Serve with chicken, lemon wedges and, if desired, rice.

3 OZ. COOKED CHICKEN WITH ¾ CUP BROCCOLI: 304 cal., 15g fat (8g sat. fat), 122mg chol., 716mg sod., 14g carb. (1g sugars, 3g fiber), 28g pro.

GRANDMA'S RICE DISH

My grandmother often made this casserole when I was young. I forgot about it until one day I found myself adding the same ingredients to leftover rice. The memories came flooding back.
—*Lorna Moore, Glendora, CA*

PREP: 20 MIN. • **BAKE:** 15 MIN. • **MAKES:** 4 SERVINGS

1 **lb. ground beef**
⅓ **cup chopped onion**
½ **cup chopped green pepper**
2 **cups cooked long grain rice**
1 **can (14½ oz.) diced tomatoes, undrained**
1 **can (11 oz.) whole kernel corn, drained**
1 **can (2¼ oz.) sliced ripe olives, drained**

6 **bacon strips, cooked and crumbled**
2 **tsp. chili powder**
1 **tsp. garlic powder**
½ **tsp. salt**
1½ **cups shredded cheddar cheese, divided**
½ **cup dry bread crumbs**
1 **Tbsp. butter, melted**

1. Preheat oven to 350°. In a large skillet, cook beef, onion and green pepper over medium heat until meat is no longer pink, breaking it into crumbles; drain.

2. Stir in rice, tomatoes, corn, olives, bacon and seasonings; heat through. Stir in 1 cup cheese until melted.

3. Transfer to a greased 11x7-in. baking dish. Sprinkle with remaining cheese. Toss bread crumbs with butter; sprinkle over top.

4. Bake, uncovered, 15-20 minutes or until cheese is melted.

1½ CUPS: 719 cal., 37g fat (18g sat. fat), 136mg chol., 1397mg sod., 52g carb. (9g sugars, 5g fiber), 41g pro.

"I love this recipe. It is a good family favorite. I generally also add 1 can rinsed black beans to the mix. It is delicious! It tastes like the dishes I was served in Brazil."
—SILLYMAN1, TASTEOFHOME.COM

COUNTRY PORK & SAUERKRAUT

The secret ingredient in this recipe is the applesauce. When everything is cooked, you wouldn't know it's in there—yet the taste is just a bit sweeter. My mother and grandmother once ran a beanery for a train crew. That inspired a lot of my cooking. In fact, I adapted this recipe from one of theirs. Luckily for me, my husband likes to eat what I fix as much as I like to cook it!
—*Donna Hellendrung, Minneapolis, MN*

PREP: 15 MIN. • BAKE: 1½ HOURS • MAKES: 4 SERVINGS

2 lbs. bone-in country-style pork ribs
1 medium onion, chopped
1 Tbsp. canola oil
1 can (14 oz.) sauerkraut, undrained
1 cup unsweetened applesauce
2 Tbsp. brown sugar
2 tsp. caraway seeds
1 tsp. garlic powder
½ tsp. pepper

1. In a Dutch oven, cook ribs and onion in oil until ribs are browned and onion is tender. Remove from the heat. Combine remaining ingredients and pour over ribs.

2. Cover and bake at 350° until ribs are tender, 1½-2 hours.

1 SERVING: 477 cal., 24g fat (8g sat. fat), 130mg chol., 757mg sod., 23g carb. (15g sugars, 5g fiber), 41g pro.

TOMATO-ARTICHOKE TILAPIA

My mom and I really like tomatoes, capers and artichokes, so I use them together in this one-pan meal. The best part is that, on a busy night, all of the ingredients are ready and waiting.
—*Denise Klibert, Shreveport, LA*

TAKES: 15 MIN. • MAKES: 4 SERVINGS

1 Tbsp. olive oil
1 can (14½ oz.) diced tomatoes with roasted garlic, drained
1 can (14 oz.) water-packed quartered artichoke hearts, drained
2 Tbsp. drained capers
4 tilapia fillets (6 oz. each)

1. In a large skillet, heat oil over medium heat. Add the tomatoes, artichoke hearts and capers; cook until heated through, 3-5 minutes, stirring occasionally.

2. Arrange tilapia over tomato mixture. Cook, covered, until fish begins to flake easily with a fork, 6-8 minutes.

1 FILLET WITH ¾ CUP SAUCE: 246 cal., 5g fat (1g sat. fat), 83mg chol., 886mg sod., 15g carb. (6g sugars, 1g fiber), 35g pro.

ITALIAN FISH FILLETS: Substitute 1 medium julienned green pepper, 1 small julienned onion, ½ cup Italian salad dressing and ½ tsp. Italian seasoning for first 4 ingredients. Cook 5 minutes or until vegetables are tender. Add 2 cans (14½ oz. each) diced tomatoes; bring to a boil. Add fish and cook as directed.

COUNTRY PORK
& SAUERKRAUT

DANISH MEATBALLS WITH PAN GRAVY

My great-grandmother made these meatballs, and I'm sure her mother must have taught her. Six generations have enjoyed them, and one of my daughters even served them at her wedding.
—*Kallee Krong-Mccreery, Escondido, CA*

PREP: 25 MIN. • COOK: 20 MIN. • MAKES: 8 SERVINGS

1 cup soft bread crumbs	2 Tbsp. canola oil
½ cup finely chopped onion	1 to 3 Tbsp. butter, divided
⅓ cup 2% milk	
1 large egg, lightly beaten	**GRAVY**
3 Tbsp. minced fresh parsley	3 Tbsp. all-purpose flour
1 tsp. salt	¾ tsp. beef bouillon granules
½ tsp. pepper	½ tsp. pepper
1 lb. ground beef	¼ tsp. salt
1 lb. bulk pork sausage	1¾ cups 2% milk

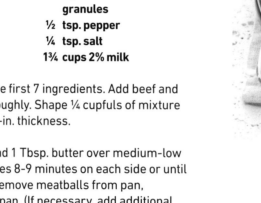

1. In a large bowl, combine the first 7 ingredients. Add beef and sausage; mix lightly but thoroughly. Shape ¼ cupfuls of mixture into 18 meatballs; flatten to 1-in. thickness.

2. In a large skillet, heat oil and 1 Tbsp. butter over medium-low heat; cook meatballs in batches 8-9 minutes on each side or until a thermometer reads 160°. Remove meatballs from pan, reserving ¼ cup drippings in pan. (If necessary, add additional butter to the drippings to reach ¼ cup.)

3. For gravy, stir flour, bouillon granules, pepper and salt into drippings until smooth; gradually whisk in milk. Bring to a boil, stirring constantly; cook and stir 1-2 minutes or until thickened. Serve with meatballs.

NOTE: To make soft bread crumbs, tear bread into pieces and place in a food processor or blender. Cover and pulse until crumbs form. Just 1 slice of bread yields ½-¾ cup crumbs.

2 MEATBALLS WITH 3 TBSP. GRAVY: 333 cal., 24g fat (8g sat. fat), 88mg chol., 786mg sod., 10g carb. (5g sugars, 1g fiber), 18g pro.

"My mother-in-law in Sweden makes this dish, and it's so delicious. I compared this recipe to hers and it's almost exact. She uses pork and ox, or ground sirloin instead of ox. She doesn't use the bouillon, either, but that's a matter of taste. Either way, the cream sauce totally makes the dish sing! Serve with boiled potatoes and you'll be on your way to heaven!"
—ORFELINA, TASTEOFHOME.COM

MAPLE-ROASTED CHICKEN & ACORN SQUASH

When I became a new mother, my mom helped me find comforting and simple recipes to have on hand. This terrific roast chicken is a happy discovery.
—*Sara Eilers, Surprise, AZ*

PREP: 15 MIN. • BAKE: 35 MIN. • MAKES: 6 SERVINGS

1 medium acorn squash
4 medium carrots, chopped (about 2 cups)
1 medium onion, cut into 1-in. pieces
6 bone-in chicken thighs (about 2¼ lbs.)
½ cup maple syrup
1 tsp. salt
½ tsp. coarsely ground pepper

1. Preheat oven to 450°. Cut squash lengthwise in half; remove and discard seeds. Cut each half crosswise into ½-in. slices; discard ends. Place squash, carrots and onion in a greased 13x9-in. baking pan; top with chicken, skin side down. Roast 10 minutes.

2. Turn chicken over; drizzle with maple syrup and sprinkle with salt and pepper. Roast 25-30 minutes longer or until a thermometer inserted in chicken reads 170°-175° and the vegetables are tender.

1 SERVING: 363 cal., 14g fat (4g sat. fat), 81mg chol., 497mg sod., 36g carb. (23g sugars, 3g fiber), 24g pro. DIABETIC EXCHANGES: 3 lean meat, 2 starch, 1 vegetable.

PORK TENDERLOIN WITH PEACH HONEY MUSTARD

My grandmother used to make a beef tenderloin stuffed with peaches and basil when I was young, so I altered that recipe and came up with my own unique version for my husband and me. It's a household favorite!
—*Mary Beth Harris-Murphree, Tyler, TX*

PREP: 15 MIN. • GRILL: 20 MIN. • MAKES: 2 SERVINGS

½ medium peach, peeled
2 Tbsp. Dijon mustard
1 Tbsp. honey
1 Tbsp. brown sugar
1 tsp. salt
½ tsp. pepper
⅛ tsp. cayenne pepper
1 pork tenderloin (¾ lb.)

1. Place the peach, mustard and honey in a blender; cover and process until blended. Set aside.

2. Combine the brown sugar, salt, pepper and cayenne; rub over pork. Place pork on an oiled grill rack.

3. Grill pork, covered, over indirect medium-hot heat for 20-25 minutes or until a thermometer reads 160°. Let stand for 5 minutes before slicing. Serve with peach sauce.

1 SERVING: 281 cal., 6g fat (2g sat. fat), 95mg chol., 1611mg sod., 21g carb. (17g sugars, 1g fiber), 34g pro.

PARMESAN
BAKED COD

PARMESAN BAKED COD

This is a goof-proof way to keep oven-baked cod moist and flavorful.
My mom shared this recipe with me years ago, and I've been loving it ever since.
—*Mary Jo Hoppe, Pewaukee, WI*

TAKES: 25 MIN. • MAKES: 4 SERVINGS

4 **cod fillets (4 oz. each)**
⅔ **cup mayonnaise**
4 **green onions, chopped**
¼ **cup grated**
   Parmesan cheese
1 **tsp. Worcestershire**
   sauce

1. Preheat oven to 400°. Place cod in an 8-in. square baking dish coated with cooking spray. Mix remaining ingredients; spread over fillets.

2. Bake, uncovered, until fish just begins to flake easily with a fork, 15-20 minutes.

1 FILLET: 247 cal., 15g fat (2g sat. fat), 57mg chol., 500mg sod., 7g carb. (2g sugars, 0 fiber), 20g pro. **DIABETIC EXCHANGES:** 3 lean meat, 3 fat.

EASY BREEZY TURKEY LOAF

If you think you can't make meat loaf the way Mom does, try this super easy recipe. Your favorite store-bought spaghetti sauce flavors the tender loaf, and the ground turkey saves on calories.
—*Jo Ann Shappard, Vincennes, IN*

PREP: 10 MIN. • BAKE: 65 MIN. • MAKES: 6 SERVINGS

1 **cup seasoned**
   bread crumbs
1 **cup garden-style**
   spaghetti sauce, divided
1 **medium onion, chopped**
1 **large egg**
1 **tsp. salt**
1 **tsp. pepper**
1½ **lbs. ground turkey**

1. In a large bowl, combine the bread crumbs, ½ cup spaghetti sauce, onion, egg, salt and pepper. Crumble turkey over mixture and mix well. Pat into an ungreased 9x5-in. loaf pan.

2. Bake, uncovered, at 350° for 1 hour. Spread remaining spaghetti sauce over loaf. Bake 5-10 minutes longer or until a thermometer reads 165° and juices run clear.

FREEZE OPTION: Securely wrap individual portions of cooled meat loaf in foil. To use, partially thaw in refrigerator overnight. Unwrap meat loaf; reheat on a greased shallow baking pan in a preheated 350° oven until heated through and a thermometer inserted in center reads 165°.

1 SLICE: 354 cal., 20g fat (6g sat. fat), 114mg chol., 973mg sod., 22g carb. (6g sugars, 2g fiber), 23g pro.

BROWN SUGAR SALMON WITH STRAWBERRIES

*I first tasted strawberries and cucumber together when living
in the UK; now they make a delicious relish for salmon.*
—Judith Foreman, Alexandria, VA

PREP: 20 MIN. + CHILLING • GRILL: 10 MIN. • MAKES: 4 SERVINGS (2 CUPS RELISH)

⅓ cup packed brown sugar
1 Tbsp. canola oil
1 tsp. ground mustard
1 tsp. ground allspice
½ tsp. salt
4 salmon fillets (5 oz. each)

RELISH

1 Tbsp. minced fresh mint
1 Tbsp. canola oil
1 Tbsp. lemon juice
2 tsp. grated lemon zest
⅛ tsp. sugar
1 cup finely chopped
   fresh strawberries
1 small cucumber,
   finely chopped

1. In a small bowl, mix the first 5 ingredients; rub over flesh side of salmon. Refrigerate, covered, 1 hour.

2. For relish, in another bowl, mix mint, oil, lemon juice, lemon zest and sugar. Add strawberries and cucumber; toss to coat.

3. Lightly oil grill rack. Place salmon on grill rack, skin side down. Grill, covered, over medium heat 8-10 minutes or until fish flakes easily with a fork. Serve with relish.

1 FILLET WITH ½ CUP RELISH: 375 cal., 20g fat (3g sat. fat), 71mg chol., 375mg sod., 23g carb. (20g sugars, 1g fiber), 25g pro. DIABETIC EXCHANGES: 3 lean meat, 1½ starch, 1½ fat.

SAUCY RASPBERRY CHICKEN

*I first had this dish as a teenage babysitter, when the children's mom prepared it for
us to eat while she was out. The kids loved it, and so did I! Now I make it for my own kids.*
—Melissa Wales, Elephant Butte, NM

PREP: 15 MIN. • COOK: 5 HOURS • MAKES: 5 SERVINGS

5 chicken leg quarters,
   skin removed
⅓ cup seedless raspberry
   spreadable fruit
3 Tbsp. reduced-sodium
   soy sauce
1 tsp. spicy brown mustard
¼ tsp. pepper
2 Tbsp. cornstarch
2 Tbsp. cold water

1. Place chicken in a 3-qt. slow cooker. In a small bowl, combine the spreadable fruit, soy sauce, mustard and pepper; pour over chicken. Cover and cook on low for 5-6 hours or until the meat is tender.

2. Remove chicken to a serving platter; keep warm. Skim fat from cooking juices; transfer to a small saucepan. Bring to a boil. Combine cornstarch and water until smooth; gradually stir into the pan. Bring to a boil; cook and stir for 2 minutes or until thickened. Serve with chicken.

1 CHICKEN LEG QUARTER WITH ⅓ CUP SAUCE: 337 cal., 16g fat (4g sat. fat), 105mg chol., 468mg sod., 14g carb. (9g sugars, 0 fiber), 31g pro.

FRENCH MEAT & VEGETABLE PIE

Some time ago, a co-worker brought a meat pie for lunch. The aroma was familiar—and after one taste, I was amazed to discover it was the same pie my grandmother used to serve when I was a youngster! My co-worker shared the recipe, and I've been enjoying it ever since.

—*Rita Winterberger, Huson, MT*

PREP: 20 MIN. • BAKE: 30 MIN. • MAKES: 8 SERVINGS

- 2 Tbsp. canola oil
- 1 large onion, thinly sliced
- 1 lb. ground beef
- 1 lb. ground pork
- 1 cup mashed potatoes (with added milk and butter)
- 1 can (8 oz.) mixed vegetables, drained
- 2 tsp. ground allspice
- 1 tsp. salt
- ¼ tsp. pepper
  Dough for double-crust pie
- 1 large egg, lightly beaten, optional

1. Preheat oven to 375°. In a skillet, heat oil over medium heat. Saute onion until tender, 1-2 minutes. Remove and set aside. In the same skillet, brown beef and pork together until no longer pink, breaking meat into crumbles; drain. Combine onion, meat, potatoes, vegetables and seasonings.

2. On a lightly floured surface, roll half the dough to a ⅛-in.-thick circle; transfer to a 9-in. pie plate. Trim crust even with rim. Roll remaining dough to a ⅛-in.-thick circle. Fill bottom crust with meat mixture. Place crust over filling; trim, seal and flute edges. Cut slits in top. If desired, brush with egg.

3. Bake until golden brown, 30-35 minutes.

DOUGH FOR DOUBLE-CRUST PIE: Combine 2½ cups all-purpose flour and ½ tsp. salt; cut in 1 cup cold butter until crumbly. Gradually add ⅓-⅔ cup ice water, tossing with a fork until dough holds together when pressed. Divide dough in half. Shape each half into a disk; wrap and refrigerate 1 hour.

1 SERVING: 531 cal., 32g fat (12g sat. fat), 103mg chol., 724mg sod., 35g carb. (4g sugars, 1g fiber), 25g pro.

GRANDMA'S SECRET

This pie is a French Canadian favorite known as a tourtiere. Tourtieres vary, but each contains a blend of meats, vegetables, potatoes and sweet spices.

BACON-COLBY LASAGNA

My grandmother added bacon to her cheesy lasagna—something
she borrowed from carbonara-style pasta. I learned so much by her side.
—*Cathy McCartney, Davenport, IA*

PREP: 30 MIN. • BAKE: 45 MIN. + STANDING • MAKES: 2 LASAGNAS (12 SERVINGS EACH)

24 **uncooked**
   lasagna noodles
 2 **lbs. lean ground beef**
   (90% lean)
 2 **medium onions, chopped**
1½ **lbs. bacon strips, cooked**
   and crumbled
 2 **cans (15 oz. each)**
   tomato sauce
 2 **cans (14½ oz. each) diced**
   tomatoes, undrained
 2 **Tbsp. sugar**
 1 **tsp. salt**
 8 **cups shredded Colby-**
   Monterey Jack cheese

1. Preheat oven to 350°. Cook noodles according to package
directions for al dente; drain.

2. In a 6-qt. stockpot, cook beef and onions over medium-high
heat until beef is no longer pink, 10-12 minutes, breaking beef into
crumbles; drain. Stir in bacon, tomato sauce, tomatoes, sugar and
salt; heat through.

3. Spread 1 cup sauce into each of 2 greased 13x9-in. baking
dishes. Layer each with 4 noodles, overlapping as needed,
1⅔ cups sauce and 1⅓ cups cheese. Repeat layers twice.

4. Bake, covered, 40 minutes. Uncover; bake until bubbly,
5-10 minutes longer. Let stand 15 minutes before serving.

FREEZE OPTION: Cool unbaked lasagnas; cover and freeze. To use,
partially thaw in refrigerator overnight. Remove from refrigerator
30 minutes before baking. Preheat oven to 350°. Bake the lasagna
as directed, increasing time as necessary to heat through and for
a thermometer inserted in center to read 165°.

1 PIECE: 357 cal., 18g fat (11g sat. fat), 67mg chol., 744mg sod.,
25g carb. (4g sugars, 2g fiber), 23g pro.

FROM GRANDMA'S KITCHEN: Lasagna is lovable, but the boiled
noodles can be a pain to work with. Here's a trick to try when
making this big batch of 2 lasagnas. Place 12 noodles each in
two 13x9-in. baking dishes and cover with hot water warmed on
the stove. Swish noodles a bit to ensure they're covered. Then,
cover the dishes to trap in heat and let stand for 20-25 minutes,
or until noodles are pliable and ready to work with. Drain and use.
Say goodbye to fall-apart lasagna noodles!

ALL-AMERICAN TURKEY POTPIE

Ever since my sister-in-law shared this recipe with me, I haven't
made any other kind of potpie. The crust is very easy to work with.

—*Laureen Naylor, Factoryville, PA*

PREP: 30 MIN. + CHILLING • **BAKE:** 35 MIN. • **MAKES:** 6 SERVINGS

- 2 **cups all-purpose flour**
- ½ **tsp. salt**
- ½ **cup finely shredded cheddar cheese**
- ⅔ **cup shortening**
- 1 **Tbsp. cold butter**
- 3 **to 4 Tbsp. cold water**

FILLING
- 1 **cup cubed peeled potatoes**
- ½ **cup thinly sliced carrots**
- ⅓ **cup chopped celery**
- ¼ **cup chopped onion**
- 1 **Tbsp. butter**
- 1 **garlic clove, minced**
- 1 **cup chicken broth**
- 2 **Tbsp. all-purpose flour**
- ½ **cup 2% milk**
- 1½ **cups cubed cooked turkey**
- ½ **cup frozen peas, thawed**
- ½ **cup frozen corn, thawed**
- ½ **tsp. salt**
- ¼ **tsp. dried tarragon**
- ¼ **tsp. pepper**

1. In a food processor, combine flour and salt; cover and pulse to blend. Add cheese; pulse until fine crumbs form. Add shortening and butter; pulse until coarse crumbs form. While processing, gradually add water until dough forms a ball.

2. Divide dough in half with 1 ball slightly larger than the other; wrap both halves and refrigerate for 30 minutes.

3. For filling, in a large saucepan, saute the potatoes, carrots, celery and onion in butter for 5 minutes. Add the garlic; cook 1 minute longer. Stir in broth; cover and cook for 10 minutes or until vegetables are tender.

4. Combine flour and milk until smooth; gradually add to the vegetable mixture. Bring to a boil; cook and stir for 2 minutes or until thickened. Add the remaining ingredients; simmer 5 minutes longer.

5. Roll out larger pastry ball to fit a 9-in. pie plate; transfer to pie plate. Trim crust even with edge. Pour hot turkey filling into crust. Roll out remaining pastry to fit top of pie; place over filling. Trim, seal and flute edges. Cut slits in top or make decorative cutouts in top crust.

6. Bake at 350° for 35-45 minutes or until the crust is light golden brown.

1 SERVING: 551 cal., 31g fat (11g sat. fat), 50mg chol., 704mg sod., 47g carb. (4g sugars, 3g fiber), 20g pro.

CHICKEN-FRIED STEAK & GRAVY

As a child, I learned from my grandmother how to make these chicken-fried steaks.
I taught my daughters, and when my granddaughters are older, I'll show them, too.
—Donna Cater, Fort Ann, NY

TAKES: 30 MIN. • MAKES: 4 SERVINGS

1¼ cups all-purpose flour,
    divided
 2 large eggs
1½ cups 2% milk, divided
 4 beef cubed steaks
    (6 oz. each)
1¼ tsp. salt, divided
 1 tsp. pepper, divided
    Oil for frying
 1 cup water

1. Place 1 cup flour in a shallow bowl. In a separate shallow bowl, whisk eggs and ½ cup milk until blended. Sprinkle steaks with ¾ tsp. each salt and pepper. Dip in flour to coat both sides; shake off excess. Dip in egg mixture, then again in flour.

2. In a large cast-iron or other heavy skillet, heat ¼ in. oil over medium heat. Add the steaks; cook until golden brown and a thermometer reads 160°, 4-6 minutes on each side. Remove from pan; drain on paper towels. Keep warm.

3. Remove all but 2 Tbsp. oil from pan. Stir in remaining ¼ cup flour, ½ tsp. salt and ¼ tsp. pepper until smooth; cook and stir over medium heat until golden brown, 3-4 minutes. Gradually whisk in water and remaining milk. Bring to a boil, stirring constantly; cook and stir until thickened, 1-2 minutes. Serve with steaks.

1 STEAK WITH ⅓ CUP GRAVY: 563 cal., 28g fat (5g sat. fat), 148mg chol., 839mg sod., 29g carb. (4g sugars, 1g fiber), 46g pro.

FROM GRANDMA'S KITCHEN: Some Southerners differentiate chicken-fried steak from country-fried steak by the former's milk-based gravy. Country-fried steak often has a beef-based gravy (or a gravy made with both beef broth and dairy) instead of milk gravy.

MOM'S MOLASSES HAM & BEANS

This is a recipe my mom made frequently while I was growing up. It's perfect for a cold day when you don't want to bother with lots of cooking. My mother actually used lima beans, but not many people are into those, so I tweaked this dish to make it more enjoyable for my own family.
—*Nancy Heishman, Las Vegas, NV*

PREP: 15 MIN. • **COOK:** 7 HOURS • **MAKES:** 8 SERVINGS

4 **cans (15½ oz. each) navy or cannellini beans, rinsed and drained**
2 **smoked ham hocks (about 1 lb.)**
1 **can (15 oz.) tomato sauce**
1 **large onion, chopped**
¾ **cup packed brown sugar**
¾ **cup molasses**
¼ **cup cider vinegar**
1 **Tbsp. Worcestershire sauce**
2½ **tsp. ground mustard**
1 **tsp. salt**
½ **tsp. pepper**
12 **bacon strips, cooked and crumbled**
Optional: Pickled jalapeno peppers and pickled red onions

1. In a greased 5-qt. slow cooker, combine first 11 ingredients. Cook, covered, on low 7-9 hours.

2. Remove ham hocks. When cool enough to handle, remove meat from bones; discard bones. Cut meat into small cubes; return to slow cooker. Stir in crumbled bacon. If desired, serve with pickled jalapeno peppers and pickled red onions.

FREEZE OPTION: Freeze cooled beans in freezer containers. To use, partially thaw in refrigerator overnight. Heat through in a saucepan, stirring occasionally; add a little water or broth if necessary.

¾ CUP: 521 cal., 7g fat (2g sat. fat), 19mg chol., 1543mg sod., 93g carb. (45g sugars, 13g fiber), 24g pro.

FROM GRANDMA'S KITCHEN: Molasses is a byproduct of refining cane or beets into sugar. Light and dark molasses are made from the first and second refining processes, respectively. Blackstrap, made from the third procedure, is the strongest, darkest and most intensely flavored of the three. Dark molasses works well in most recipes.

SO-TENDER SWISS STEAK

When I was little, my mother's Swiss steak was the dinner I requested the most.
Now it's a favorite with my own family, too.
—*Linda McGinty, Parma, OH*

PREP: 30 MIN. • BAKE: 2 HOURS • MAKES: 8 SERVINGS

¼ cup all-purpose flour
½ tsp. salt
¼ tsp. pepper
2 lbs. beef top
round steak, cut into
serving-size pieces
2 Tbsp. canola oil
1 medium onion,
thinly sliced
2 cups water
2 Tbsp. Worcestershire
sauce

GRAVY
¼ cup all-purpose flour
¼ tsp. salt
⅛ tsp. pepper
1¼ cups beef broth or water
Optional: Hot cooked
noodles or mashed
potatoes

1. Preheat oven to 325°. In a large shallow dish, combine flour, salt and pepper. Pound steak with a mallet to tenderize. Add meat, a few pieces at a time, and toss to coat.

2. In an ovenproof Dutch oven, brown steak in oil on both sides. Arrange onion slices between layers of meat. Add water and Worcestershire sauce.

3. Cover and bake 2-2½ hours or until meat is very tender. Remove to a serving platter and keep warm.

4. In a small bowl, combine flour, salt, pepper and broth until smooth; stir into pan juices. Bring to a boil over medium heat; cook and stir 2 minutes or until thickened. Serve steak and gravy with noodles or mashed potatoes, if desired.

FREEZE OPTION: Freeze cooled beef mixture in freezer containers. To use, partially thaw in refrigerator overnight. Heat through in a covered saucepan, stirring occasionally; add a little broth or water if necessary.

1 SERVING: 213 cal., 7g fat (2g sat. fat), 64mg chol., 424mg sod., 9g carb. (1g sugars, 1g fiber), 27g pro.

CAESAR FISH FILLETS

I'm so thankful that my mother, a fantastic cook, taught me the ropes in the kitchen when I was fairly young. Mom won several cooking contests over the years, and this is one of my favorite recipes of hers.
—*Mary Lou Boyce, Wilmington, DE*

TAKES: 25 MIN. • MAKES: 8 SERVINGS

8 flounder or sole fillets
(4 oz. each)
1 cup creamy Caesar
salad dressing
2 cups crushed
butter-flavored crackers
(about 50 crackers)
1 cup shredded
cheddar cheese

1. Preheat oven to 400°. Place fillets in an ungreased 13x9-in. baking dish. Drizzle with salad dressing and sprinkle with crushed crackers.

2. Bake, uncovered, 10 minutes. Sprinkle with cheese. Bake 3-5 minutes longer or until fish flakes easily with a fork and cheese is melted.

1 SERVING: 421 cal., 28g fat (6g sat. fat), 93mg chol., 716mg sod., 17g carb. (3g sugars, 1g fiber), 24g pro.

GERMAN SAUERBRATEN

Our family loves it when Mom prepares this wonderful old-world dish. The tender beef has a bold blend of mouthwatering seasonings. It smells so good while its cooking in the oven and tastes even better!

—*Cathy Eland, Highstown, NJ*

PREP: 10 MIN. + MARINATING • COOK: 3 HOURS • MAKES: 14 SERVINGS

2 tsp. salt
1 tsp. ground ginger
1 beef top round roast (4 lbs.)
2½ cups water
2 cups cider vinegar
⅓ cup sugar
2 medium onions, sliced, divided

2 Tbsp. mixed pickling spices, divided
1 tsp. whole peppercorns, divided
8 whole cloves, divided
2 bay leaves, divided
2 Tbsp. canola oil
14 to 16 gingersnaps, crushed

1. In a small bowl, combine salt and ginger; rub over roast. Place in a deep glass bowl. In a large bowl, combine the water, vinegar and sugar. Pour half the marinade into a large saucepan; add half the onions, pickling spices, peppercorns, cloves and bay leaves. Bring to a boil. Pour over roast; turn to coat. Cover and refrigerate for 2 days, turning twice a day.

2. To the remaining marinade, add the remaining onions, pickling spices, peppercorns, cloves and bay leaves. Cover and refrigerate.

3. Drain roast, discarding marinade; pat roast dry. In a Dutch oven over medium-high heat, brown roast in oil on all sides. Pour 1 cup reserved marinade with all the onions and seasonings over roast (cover and refrigerate remaining marinade). Bring to a boil. Reduce heat; cover and simmer for 3 hours or until meat is tender.

4. Strain cooking juices, discarding the onions and seasonings. Add enough reserved marinade to the cooking juices to measure 3 cups. Pour liquid into a large saucepan; bring to a boil. Add gingersnaps; reduce heat and simmer until gravy is thickened. Slice roast and serve with gravy.

4 OZ. COOKED BEEF WITH GRAVY: 233 cal., 7g fat (2g sat. fat), 72mg chol., 410mg sod., 11g carb. (6g sugars, 0 fiber), 30g pro.

GRANDMA'S SECRET

Serve the sauerbraten with a starchy side dish to soak up the flavorful liquid. Potatoes, noodles, spaetzle or dumplings would all make tasty accompaniments.

HUNGARIAN GOULASH

Talk about your heirloom recipes! My grandmother made this for my mother
when she was a child, and then my mom made it for us to enjoy. Paprika and caraway add
wonderful flavor, and sour cream gives it a creamy richness. It's simply scrumptious!

—*Marcia Doyle, Pompano, FL*

PREP: 20 MIN. • COOK: 7 HOURS • MAKES: 12 SERVINGS

3 medium onions, chopped
2 medium carrots, chopped
2 medium green peppers,
　chopped
3 lbs. beef stew meat
¾ tsp. salt, divided
¾ tsp. pepper, divided
2 Tbsp. olive oil
1½ cups reduced-sodium
　beef broth
¼ cup all-purpose flour
3 Tbsp. paprika
2 Tbsp. tomato paste
1 tsp. caraway seeds
1 garlic clove, minced
　Dash sugar
12 cups uncooked
　whole wheat egg noodles
1 cup reduced-fat
　sour cream

1. Place the onions, carrots and green peppers in a 5-qt. slow cooker. Sprinkle meat with ½ tsp. salt and ½ tsp. pepper. In a large skillet, brown meat in oil in batches. Transfer to slow cooker.

2. Add broth to skillet, stirring to loosen browned bits from pan. Combine the flour, paprika, tomato paste, caraway seeds, garlic, sugar and remaining salt and pepper; stir into skillet. Bring to a boil; cook and stir for 2 minutes or until thickened. Pour over meat. Cover and cook on low for 7-9 hours or until meat is tender.

3. Cook noodles according to package directions. Stir sour cream into slow cooker. Drain noodles; serve with goulash.

⅔ CUP GOULASH WITH 1 CUP NOODLES: 388 cal., 13g fat (4g sat. fat), 78mg chol., 285mg sod., 41g carb. (5g sugars, 7g fiber), 31g pro. DIABETIC EXCHANGES: 3 lean meat, 2 starch, 1 vegetable, 1 fat.

FROM GRANDMA'S KITCHEN: To keep pasta from sticking together while cooking, use a large pot with plenty of water. Add a little cooking oil if desired (this also prevents boiling over).

TURKEY SPAGHETTI CASSEROLE

My mom made this creamy and comforting dish while I was growing up. Whenever I have leftover chicken or turkey, I look forward to making this simple yet tasty meal.
—*Casandra Hetrick, Lindsey, OH*

PREP: 30 MIN. • **BAKE:** 1¼ HOURS • **MAKES:** 6 SERVINGS

1 **medium onion, chopped**	¼ **tsp. salt**
1 **medium carrot, chopped**	¼ **tsp. pepper**
1 **celery rib, chopped**	2½ **cups cubed cooked**
⅓ **cup sliced fresh**	**turkey breast**
mushrooms	6 **oz. uncooked spaghetti,**
1 **Tbsp. butter**	**broken into 2-in. pieces**
2½ **cups reduced-sodium**	½ **cup shredded**
chicken broth	**reduced-fat Colby-**
1 **can (10¾ oz.) reduced-fat**	**Monterey Jack cheese**
reduced-sodium	½ **tsp. paprika**
condensed	
cream of mushroom	
soup, undiluted	

1. In a small skillet, saute the vegetables in butter until tender. In a large bowl, combine the broth, soup, salt and pepper.

2. In a 2½-qt. baking dish coated with cooking spray, layer the turkey, spaghetti and vegetable mixture. Pour broth mixture over the top.

3. Cover and bake at 350° for 70-80 minutes or until spaghetti is tender, stirring once. Uncover; sprinkle with cheese and paprika. Bake 5-10 minutes longer or until cheese is melted.

1 CUP: 284 cal., 6g fat (3g sat. fat), 62mg chol., 702mg sod., 30g carb. (4g sugars, 3g fiber), 26g pro. **DIABETIC EXCHANGES:** 3 lean meat, 1½ starch, 1 vegetable, ½ fat.

ROSEMARY-ORANGE ROASTED CHICKEN

When your guests see this impressive citrus-and-herb roasted chicken, it will
be love at first sight. My best friend's mom raved about it when she came for a visit.

—Sarah Vasques, Milford, NH

PREP: 30 MIN. • BAKE: 1¼ HOURS + STANDING • MAKES: 4 SERVINGS

¼ cup butter, softened
1 Tbsp. minced
   fresh rosemary or 1 tsp.
   dried rosemary, crushed
2 tsp. grated orange zest
½ tsp. pepper, divided
1 broiler/fryer chicken
   (3 to 4 lbs.)
⅓ cup orange juice
½ tsp. salt
2 medium onions,
   quartered
1 medium apple, quartered
1 large carrot, chopped
1 celery rib, chopped
4 fresh thyme sprigs
4 sprigs fresh parsley
2 bay leaves
1 fresh rosemary sprig
2 cups white wine or
   chicken broth

GRAVY
   Chicken broth
3 Tbsp. butter
2 Tbsp. all-purpose flour
⅛ tsp. ground nutmeg,
   optional

1. Preheat oven to 350°. In a small bowl, combine butter, minced rosemary, orange zest and ⅛ tsp. pepper. With fingers, carefully loosen skin from the chicken; rub butter mixture under the skin. Brush chicken with orange juice. Sprinkle salt and remaining pepper over chicken and inside cavity.

2. Place 1 onion and half the apple inside the cavity. Tuck wings under chicken; tie drumsticks together. Place breast side up on a rack in a roasting pan. Arrange carrot, celery, thyme, parsley, bay leaves, rosemary sprig, and remaining onion and apple around chicken. Pour wine into pan.

3. Roast 1¼-1½ hours or until a thermometer inserted in thickest part of thigh reads 170°-175°, basting occasionally with drippings. Cover loosely with foil if chicken browns too quickly. Cover and let stand 15 minutes before carving.

4. For gravy, pour drippings and loosened browned bits into a measuring cup. Skim fat. Add enough broth to the drippings to measure 1 cup. In a small saucepan, melt butter. Stir in flour until smooth; gradually add broth mixture and nutmeg if desired. Bring to a boil; cook and stir 2 minutes or until thickened. Serve with chicken.

7 OZ. COOKED CHICKEN WITH ¼ CUP GRAVY: 635 cal., 41g fat (19g sat. fat), 185mg chol., 695mg sod., 20g carb. (11g sugars, 3g fiber), 44g pro.

HERB ROASTED CHICKEN: Omit first 4 ingredients, orange juice and salt. Mix 2 Tbsp. canola oil, 2 tsp. minced fresh parsley, 2 minced garlic cloves, 1 tsp. dried tarragon, 1 tsp. dried basil, 1 tsp. garlic powder, ½ tsp. salt and ¼ tsp. pepper. Rub mixture over chicken and inside cavities. Proceed as recipe directs. Omit nutmeg in gravy.

DREAMY POLENTA,
PAGE 140

GRANDMA'S FAVORITE

SIDE DISHES

We don't even mind eating our vegetables
at Grandma's house! Oh, and please
pass the polenta, potatoes, grains,
beans and pretty salads.

ORANGE & OLIVES SALAD

My grandmother made sure this salad was on our holiday table every year. We always celebrated the rustic Italian way and she made lots of delicious food. This is so light and simple to make, and it didn't fill you up before one of her fantastic meals. It looks pretty on the table.
—*Angela David, Lakeland, FL*

TAKES: 10 MIN. • MAKES: 16 SERVINGS

4 large navel oranges, peeled and sliced
2 cans (6 oz. each) pitted ripe olives, drained
1 Tbsp. canola oil
⅛ tsp. pepper

Arrange orange slices along outer edge of a serving dish, leaving center open. Place olives in center of dish. Drizzle with oil; sprinkle with pepper.

1 SERVING: 54 cal., 3g fat (0 sat. fat), 0 chol., 185mg sod., 7g carb. (4g sugars, 2g fiber), 1g pro. DIABETIC EXCHANGES: ½ fruit, ½ fat.

ZUCCHINI PANZANELLA SALAD

I learned how to make panzanella from a dear friend's grandmother. This is a version I crave during the summer. It's a tasty way to use day-old bread and your garden's bounty of zucchini.
—*Felicity Wolf, Kansas City, MO*

PREP: 20 MIN. • BAKE: 40 MIN. • MAKES: 14 CUPS

3 medium zucchini, cut into ¼-in. slices
¼ cup olive oil, divided
1 French bread baguette (10½ oz.), cubed
1½ cups heirloom mini or cherry tomatoes, halved
1 medium green pepper, coarsely chopped
½ medium red onion, thinly sliced
¼ cup balsamic vinegar
1 tsp. jarred roasted minced garlic
1 tsp. Italian seasoning
½ tsp. crushed red pepper flakes
1 tsp. kosher salt
½ tsp. coarsely ground pepper
1½ cups fresh mozzarella cheese pearls

1. Place zucchini in a 15x10x1-in. baking pan. Toss with 1 Tbsp. olive oil. Bake, uncovered, at 400° until tender and lightly browned, 25-30 minutes, stirring halfway. Remove from oven and cool.

2. Meanwhile, in a large bowl, toss bread cubes with 1 Tbsp. olive oil. Transfer to a baking sheet. Bake at 400° until lightly browned, 12-14 minutes, stirring occasionally.

3. Place the cooled zucchini, toasted bread, tomatoes, green pepper and red onion in a large bowl. In a small bowl, whisk together vinegar, garlic, seasonings and remaining oil. Drizzle over salad; toss gently to combine. Add the mozzarella and stir to combine. Serve immediately.

1 CUP: 152 cal., 8g fat (3g sat. fat), 13mg chol., 301mg sod., 16g carb. (4g sugars, 1g fiber), 5g pro. DIABETIC EXCHANGES: 1½ fat, 1 starch.

FROM GRANDMA'S KITCHEN: If the raw onion is too pungent for you, roast it with the zucchini. Or use sweet onion, such as Vidalia.

ORANGE &
OLIVES SALAD

OKTOBERFEST RED CABBAGE

Four generations of our family celebrate Oktoberfest.
We love this dish of red cabbage and apples,
known as *rotkohl,* for its tart and sweet flavors.
—*Diana Likes, Chandler, AZ*

PREP: 20 MIN. • COOK: 50 MIN. • MAKES: 6 SERVINGS

3 Tbsp. bacon drippings or
   canola oil
1 small head red cabbage
   (about 1½ lbs.), shredded
2 medium tart apples,
   peeled and chopped

1 cup water
¼ cup sugar
¾ tsp. salt
¼ tsp. pepper
⅛ tsp. ground cloves
¼ cup white vinegar

1. In a Dutch oven, heat bacon drippings over medium heat. Add cabbage and apples; cook and stir 2-3 minutes. Stir in water, sugar, salt, pepper and cloves.

2. Bring to a boil. Reduce heat; simmer, covered, 40-45 minutes or until cabbage is tender, stirring occasionally. Stir in vinegar.

¾ CUP: 146 cal., 7g fat (3g sat. fat), 6mg chol., 331mg sod., 22g carb. (17g sugars, 3g fiber), 1g pro.

DREAMY POLENTA

PICTURED ON PAGE 136

I grew up eating polenta, so it's a must at my holiday gatherings.
Traditional recipes require constant stirring, but using my handy slow cooker
allows me to turn my attention to the lineup of other foods on my spread.
—*Ann Voccola, Milford, CT*

PREP: 10 MIN. • COOK: 5 HOURS • MAKES: 12 SERVINGS

1 Tbsp. butter
5 cups whole milk
4 cups half-and-half cream
12 Tbsp. butter, divided
2 cups yellow cornmeal
¾ tsp. salt
½ tsp. minced fresh
   rosemary
¼ tsp. pepper
2 cups shredded
   Asiago cheese

1. Generously grease a 5-qt. slow cooker with 1 Tbsp. butter. Add milk, cream, 6 Tbsp. butter, cornmeal, salt, rosemary and pepper; stir to combine.

2. Cook, covered, on low 5-6 hours or until polenta is thickened, whisking every hour. Just before serving, whisk again; stir in cheese and remaining butter. Garnish with additional rosemary if desired.

¾ CUP: 444 cal., 29g fat (18g sat. fat), 100mg chol., 379mg sod., 29g carb. (9g sugars, 1g fiber), 13g pro.

FESTIVE RICE

My mom and I transformed plain rice by adding feta, cranberries, pumpkin seeds and cayenne. We wound up with a sweet and spicy crowd-pleaser.
—*Lisa de Perio, Dallas, TX*

PREP: 20 MIN. • BAKE: 30 MIN. • MAKES: 6 SERVINGS

2¼ cups water
¼ cup butter, cubed
1 tsp. salt
1 tsp. white vinegar
½ tsp. garlic powder
1 cup uncooked jasmine rice
¼ cup salted pumpkin seeds or pepitas
2 tsp. brown sugar
¼ to ½ tsp. cayenne pepper
¼ cup crumbled feta cheese
¼ cup chopped fresh mint
¼ cup dried cranberries

1. Preheat oven to 325°. In a small saucepan, bring first 5 ingredients to a boil. Remove from heat. Pour over rice in a greased 8-in. square baking dish. Bake, covered, until all liquid is absorbed, 30-35 minutes.

2. Meanwhile, in a small nonstick skillet over medium-high heat, cook pumpkin seeds, brown sugar and cayenne pepper, stirring constantly until sugar melts and cayenne coats pumpkin seeds, 4-5 minutes. Remove from heat; transfer to a plate, spreading out seeds to cool.

3. Sprinkle cooked rice with feta, mint, cranberries and spiced pumpkin seeds.

⅔ CUP: 244 cal., 11g fat (6g sat. fat), 23mg chol., 514mg sod., 32g carb. (5g sugars, 1g fiber), 5g pro.

BRENDA'S BAKED BEANS

When I was a kid, my mom made baked beans all the time. Sometimes we'd turn this side into a main dish by adding sliced hot dogs.
—*Brenda Brooks, Bowie, MD*

PREP: 15 MIN. + SOAKING • COOK: 10 HOURS • MAKES: 6 SERVINGS

1 lb. dried navy beans
1½ cups water
½ cup packed brown sugar
½ cup chopped sweet onion
½ cup apple juice
6 bacon strips, cooked and crumbled
¼ cup maple syrup
½ tsp. ground mustard
¼ tsp. ground cinnamon
1 tsp. salt

1. Rinse and sort beans; soak according to package directions.

2. Drain and rinse beans, discarding liquid. Transfer beans to a 3-qt. slow cooker. Stir in water, brown sugar, onion, apple juice, bacon, maple syrup, mustard and cinnamon. Cook, covered, on low 10-12 hours or until beans are tender. Stir in salt.

¾ CUP: 416 cal., 4g fat (1g sat. fat), 8mg chol., 551mg sod., 77g carb. (31g sugars, 12g fiber), 20g pro.

GRANDMA'S SECRET

Lighten this salad by leaving off the walnuts and blue cheese. You'll save 150 calories per serving, but the grilled apples and homemade dressing will still make it taste like it came from a restaurant.

GRILLED APPLE TOSSED SALAD

The grilled apples in this salad combine so well with the blue cheese, walnuts and balsamic dressing.
I like to serve it on pink Depression glass dessert plates from my great-grandmother.
—Paul Soska, Toledo, OH

PREP: 15 MIN. + MARINATING • GRILL: 10 MIN. • MAKES: 6 SERVINGS

6 Tbsp. olive oil
¼ cup minced fresh cilantro
¼ cup orange juice
¼ cup white or regular
   balsamic vinegar
2 Tbsp. honey
1 garlic clove, minced
½ tsp. salt
½ tsp. Sriracha chili sauce
2 large apples, cut into ½-
   in. wedges
1 pkg. (5 oz.) spring mix
   salad greens
1 cup walnut halves,
   toasted
½ cup crumbled blue
   cheese

1. For dressing, whisk together first 8 ingredients. In a bowl, toss apples with ¼ cup dressing. Let stand 10 minutes.

2. Place apple slices on a grill rack over medium heat; reserve marinade left in bowl. Grill apples, covered, until tender and lightly browned, 3-4 minutes per side, brushing with reserved marinade.

3. To serve, toss greens with remaining dressing. Top with grilled apples, walnuts and cheese.

NOTE: To toast nuts, bake in a shallow pan in a 350° oven for 5-10 minutes or cook in a skillet over low heat until lightly browned, stirring occasionally.,

1 SERVING: 341 cal., 28g fat (5g sat. fat), 8mg chol., 360mg sod., 22g carb. (16g sugars, 3g fiber), 6g pro.

SPAETZLE DUMPLINGS

These tender homemade spaetzle noodles take only minutes to make and are a natural accompaniment
to chicken. You can serve them with chicken gravy or simply butter them and sprinkle with parsley.
—Pamela Eaton, Monclova, OH

TAKES: 15 MIN. • MAKES: 6 SERVINGS

2 cups all-purpose flour
4 large eggs, lightly beaten
⅓ cup 2% milk
2 tsp. salt
8 cups water
1 Tbsp. butter
   Minced fresh parsley,
   optional

1. In a large bowl, stir the flour, eggs, milk and salt until smooth (dough will be sticky). In a large saucepan over high heat, bring water to a boil. Pour dough into a colander or spaetzle maker coated with cooking spray; place over boiling water.

2. With a wooden spoon, press dough until small pieces drop into boiling water. Cook for 2 minutes or until dumplings are tender and float. Remove with a slotted spoon; toss with butter. If desired, sprinkle with parsley.

1 CUP: 223 cal., 6g fat (2g sat. fat), 130mg chol., 856mg sod., 33g carb. (1g sugars, 1g fiber), 9g pro.

MOM'S GINGERED APPLE SALAD

For a refreshing twist on the classic Waldorf salad, try this version that's seasoned
with ginger, dried cranberries and water chestnuts. The combo is quick and delicious.
—*Rebekah Radewahn, Wauwatosa, WI*

TAKES: 15 MIN. • MAKES: 6 SERVINGS

3 medium apples, chopped
1 can (8 oz.) water
   chestnuts, drained
   and finely chopped
2 celery ribs, finely
   chopped
½ cup dried cranberries
3 Tbsp. crystallized ginger,
   finely chopped
½ cup vanilla yogurt
¼ cup reduced-fat
   mayonnaise
2 Tbsp. sugar
¼ to ½ tsp. ground ginger
⅛ tsp. salt
¼ cup chopped pecans,
   toasted

1. In a large bowl, combine the first 5 ingredients. Combine
the yogurt, mayonnaise, sugar, ginger and salt; pour over apple
mixture and toss to coat. Chill until serving.

2. Just before serving, sprinkle with pecans.

¾ CUP: 213 cal., 7g fat (1g sat. fat), 5mg chol., 161mg sod., 38g carb.
(25g sugars, 4g fiber), 2g pro.

GREEN BEAN SALAD WITH CREAMY DRESSING

My grandmother passed this refreshing side dish recipe on to me. It's always devoured at my house.
—*Jodi Galanis, Murray, UT*

PREP: 15 MIN. + CHILLING • MAKES: 2 SERVINGS

1 cup cut fresh
   green beans (2 in.)
½ medium cucumber,
   halved lengthwise
   and sliced
⅓ cup julienned sweet
   red pepper
¼ cup thinly sliced onion

DRESSING
2 Tbsp. cream cheese,
   softened
1 Tbsp. 2% milk
1 Tbsp. tarragon vinegar
2 tsp. sugar
¼ tsp. salt
¼ tsp. pepper

1. In a saucepan of boiling water, cook green beans, uncovered,
until crisp-tender, 3-5 minutes. Remove beans with a slotted
spoon; drop immediately into ice water. Drain and pat dry.

2. Place cucumber, red pepper, onion and beans in a large bowl.
Whisk together dressing ingredients; toss with vegetables.
Refrigerate, covered, until cold.

1 CUP: 107 cal., 5g fat (3g sat. fat), 15mg chol., 349mg sod.,
13g carb. (9g sugars, 3g fiber), 3g pro. DIABETIC EXCHANGES:
1 vegetable, 1 fat.

*"Refreshing summer salad. However, I boiled the beans
only about 1 minute, as I like them crispy in salads. Drain
the beans on paper towels. Also, I used sweet onion instead
of regular, as raw regular onion can be overwhelming."*
—CWBUFF, TASTEOFHOME.COM

CAULIFLOWER AU GRATIN

This is a lower-carb side dish that pairs well with pork, ham or beef. It's so creamy and delicious that even the kids will ask for seconds! If you like a little crunch, sprinkle buttered bread crumbs over the top after 30 minutes of baking.
—*Mary Zinchiak, Boardman, OH*

PREP: 25 MIN. • **BAKE:** 45 MIN. • **MAKES:** 8 SERVINGS

1 **large head cauliflower, cut into florets**
2 **Tbsp. olive oil**
1 **tsp. salt, divided**
1 **tsp. pepper, divided**
4 **Tbsp. butter, cubed**
3 **Tbsp. all-purpose flour**
2 **cups 2% milk**
1 **cup shredded Swiss cheese**
½ **cup grated Parmesan cheese**
½ **tsp. onion powder**
½ **tsp. ground mustard**
½ **tsp. Worcestershire sauce**
⅛ **tsp. cayenne pepper**
Chopped fresh thyme, optional

1. Preheat oven to 375°. Place cauliflower on a rimmed baking sheet. Drizzle with oil; sprinkle with ½ tsp. salt and ½ tsp. pepper. Toss to coat. Bake 8 minutes. Stir; bake until crisp-tender and lightly browned, 7-8 minutes longer.

2. In a large saucepan, melt butter over medium heat. Stir in flour until smooth; gradually whisk in milk. Bring to a simmer, stirring constantly; cook and stir until thickened, 2-3 minutes. Remove from heat. Stir in next 6 ingredients and remaining ½ tsp. salt and ½ tsp. pepper until smooth.

3. Pour ¾ cup cheese sauce into a greased 2-qt. baking dish. Top with cauliflower and remaining cheese sauce. Bake, uncovered, until bubbly and lightly browned, 30-35 minutes. If desired, top with chopped fresh thyme.

¾ **CUP:** 196 cal., 14g fat (7g sat. fat), 34mg chol., 291mg sod., 11g carb. (5g sugars, 2g fiber), 9g pro.

FROM GRANDMA'S KITCHEN: Freshly shredded Parmesan cheese works best in this recipe. Canned, grated Parmesan cheese will make the texture grainy.

SWEET POTATO, ORANGE & PINEAPPLE CRUNCH

I combined my two absolute favorite sweet potato casseroles
in the world to create my own version for the holiday table.
—Lisa Varner, El Paso, TX

PREP: 35 MIN. • BAKE: 40 MIN. • MAKES: 12 SERVINGS

2 **lbs. sweet potatoes,**
  peeled and cubed
  (about 6 cups)
¾ **cup sugar**
1 **can (8 oz.) crushed**
  pineapple, drained
2 **large eggs, lightly beaten**
½ **cup sour cream or**
  plain yogurt
½ **tsp. grated orange zest**
¼ **cup orange juice**
¼ **cup butter, melted**
1 **tsp. vanilla extract**

TOPPING
1 **cup sweetened**
  shredded coconut
1 **cup chopped pecans**
1 **cup packed brown sugar**
½ **cup all-purpose flour**
¼ **cup butter, melted**

1. Preheat oven to 350°. Place sweet potatoes in a large saucepan; add water to cover. Bring to a boil over high heat. Reduce heat to medium; cook, uncovered, until tender, 10-15 minutes. Drain.

2. Place sweet potatoes in a large bowl; mash potatoes. Stir in sugar, pineapple, eggs, sour cream, orange zest, juice, butter and vanilla; transfer to a greased 13x9-in. baking dish. For topping, in a large bowl, mix coconut, pecans, brown sugar and flour. Add butter; mix until crumbly. Sprinkle over top.

3. Bake, uncovered, until heated through and topping is golden brown, 40-45 minutes.

½ CUP: 432 cal., 20g fat (9g sat. fat), 58mg chol., 110mg sod., 62g carb. (45g sugars, 4g fiber), 4g pro.

GRANDMA'S SECRET

Some cooks like to boil, then mash, a strip or two of fresh orange zest right along with their vegetables when preparing mashed sweet potatoes.

LEMON-GARLIC LIMA BEANS

When I was growing up on Cyprus, my mother would
often make this side dish to have with roast lamb.
Although I hated lima beans when I was a kid (who didn't?),
I love them now. They always remind me of home.
—*Paris Paraskeva, San Francisco, CA*

PREP: 15 MIN. + SOAKING • COOK: 1¼ HOURS • MAKES: 6 SERVINGS

1 lb. dried lima beans	2 Tbsp. lemon juice
2 bay leaves	1 Tbsp. chopped fresh oregano
3 Tbsp. extra virgin olive oil, divided	2 tsp. grated lemon zest
1 medium onion, chopped	½ tsp. salt
4 garlic cloves, thinly sliced	¼ tsp. pepper
¼ cup chopped fresh parsley	Additional chopped fresh parsley

1. Rinse and sort beans; soak according to package directions.
Drain and rinse beans, discarding liquid.

2. Place beans in a large saucepan; add bay leaves and water to
cover by 2 in. Bring to a boil. Reduce heat; simmer, covered, until
beans are tender, 1¼-1½ hours. Drain.

3. In a large skillet, heat 1 Tbsp. oil over medium heat. Add onion;
cook and stir until tender, 3-4 minutes. Add garlic; cook 1 minute
longer. Add next 6 ingredients. Stir in the drained beans and
remaining oil; toss to combine. Sprinkle with additional parsley.

½ CUP: 326 cal., 8g fat (1g sat. fat), 0 chol., 209mg sod., 51g carb.
(7g sugars, 16g fiber), 16g pro.

ELECTRIC PRESSURE COOKER OPTION: Rinse and sort beans; place
in a large bowl. Add 2 qt. water and 1 Tbsp. salt; stir to combine.
Soak, covered, at room temperature overnight. Drain and rinse
beans, discarding liquid. Transfer to a 6-qt. electric pressure
cooker. Add enough water to cover and 1 tsp. canola oil. Lock
lid; close pressure-release valve. Adjust to pressure-cook on low
for 8 minutes. Allow pressure to naturally release for 5 minutes,
then quick-release any remaining pressure. Drain and proceed
as directed.

FROM GRANDMA'S KITCHEN: Eat these as a warm salad, or pulse
them in a food processor to make a hummus-like dip.

GREENS WITH HOT BACON DRESSING

Growing up in a German community, I ate this salad often. It's an old traditional dish—I recall my grandmother talking about her mother making this recipe. As a variation, the old-timers in my family cut up some boiled potatoes on dinner plates, then serve the warm salad mixture on top.
—*Robert Enigk, Canastota, NY*

TAKES: 20 MIN. • MAKES: 8 SERVINGS

4 **cups torn fresh spinach**
4 **cups torn iceberg lettuce**
3 **celery ribs, sliced**
½ **cup chopped red onion**
4 **bacon strips, diced**
1 **large egg**
⅔ **cup water**
⅓ **cup cider vinegar**
2 **tsp. sugar**
2 **tsp. cornstarch**
½ **tsp. salt**
¼ **tsp. pepper**

In a salad bowl, toss spinach, lettuce, celery and onion; set aside. In a large skillet, cook bacon until crisp; remove with a slotted spoon to paper towels to drain. Discard all but 2 Tbsp. drippings. In a small bowl, beat egg; add water and mix well. Add to the drippings. Combine vinegar, sugar, cornstarch, salt and pepper; add to skillet. Bring to a boil; stirring constantly. Remove from the heat; pour over salad. Add bacon. Toss and serve immediately.

1 SERVING: 93 cal., 7g fat (3g sat. fat), 34mg chol., 266mg sod., 5g carb. (3g sugars, 1g fiber), 3g pro.

VEGETABLE & BARLEY PILAF

Hearty, colorful, easy and fast were the reviews we gave this good-for-you dish. Barley has a healthy amount of soluble fiber, which aids digestion. And it can help to lower cholesterol, too! You can easily substitute other fresh veggies you have on hand.
—*Jesse Klausmeier, Burbank, CA*

TAKES: 30 MIN. • MAKES: 4 SERVINGS

1 **large zucchini, quartered and sliced**
1 **large carrot, chopped**
1 **Tbsp. butter**
2 **cups reduced-sodium chicken broth**
1 **cup quick-cooking barley**
2 **green onions, chopped**
½ **tsp. dried marjoram**
¼ **tsp. salt**
⅛ **tsp. pepper**

1. In a large saucepan, saute zucchini and carrot in butter until crisp-tender. Add broth; bring to a boil. Stir in barley. Reduce heat; cover and simmer until barley is tender, 10-12 minutes.

2. Stir in the onions, marjoram, salt and pepper. Remove from the heat; cover and let stand for 5 minutes.

¾ CUP: 219 cal., 4g fat (2g sat. fat), 8mg chol., 480mg sod., 39g carb. (3g sugars, 10g fiber), 9g pro.

SPINACH BARLEY PILAF: With the onions, stir in 1 cup chopped fresh spinach.

FROM GRANDMA'S KITCHEN: Not sure how to incorporate grains into your menu plans? Try serving brown rice, barley or quinoa as a side instead of potatoes or white rice. To dress grains up a little, add some sauteed onion, garlic, and green or sweet red pepper, or cooked beans, snow peas or peas. Use leftover cooked grains in soups and stews.

ORANGE-PISTACHIO
QUINOA SALAD

ORANGE-PISTACHIO QUINOA SALAD

Add this fresh and healthy salad to your holiday spread. Its citrusy, nutty taste is simply delicious.

—*Jean Greenfield, San Anselmo, CA*

PREP: 15 MIN. • COOK: 15 MIN. + COOLING • MAKES: 8 SERVINGS

1⅓ cups water

⅔ cup quinoa, rinsed

2 cups chopped romaine lettuce

1 can (15 oz.) garbanzo beans or chickpeas, rinsed and drained

1 can (15 oz.) mandarin oranges, drained

1 medium cucumber, halved and sliced

1 cup shelled pistachios, toasted

½ cup finely chopped red onion

1 medium navel orange

2 Tbsp. olive oil

½ tsp. salt

Pinch pepper

1. In a large saucepan, bring water to a boil. Add quinoa. Reduce heat; simmer, covered, 12-14 minutes or until liquid is absorbed. Remove from heat; fluff with a fork. Cool.

2. In a large bowl, combine romaine, beans, mandarin oranges, cucumber, pistachios, onion and cooled quinoa. In a small bowl, finely grate zest from orange. Cut orange crosswise in half; squeeze juice from orange and add to zest. Whisk in oil, salt and pepper. Drizzle over salad; toss to coat.

1 CUP: 257 cal., 12g fat (1g sat. fat), 0 chol., 287mg sod., 31g carb. (10g sugars, 6g fiber), 8g pro. DIABETIC EXCHANGES: 2 starch, 2 fat.

"This salad was really good. We loved the orange dressing. I used sliced almonds instead of pistachios, and I cooked the quinoa in chicken broth. I think fresh avocado slices would be good with this, too."
—ORANGELOBSTER, TASTEOFHOME.COM

SEASONED MASHED POTATOES

Simply seasoned, these creamy mashed potatoes go so well with Mom's meat loaf. They've always been a favorite at our house. You can make the potatoes ahead and keep them warm, covered, in the baking pan in the oven.

—*Emily Dennis, Hancock, MI*

PREP: 15 MIN. • COOK: 20 MIN. • MAKES: 6 SERVINGS

3 lbs. potatoes, peeled and quartered (about 9 medium)

6 oz. cream cheese, softened

6 Tbsp. butter, softened

¼ cup 2% milk

¾ tsp. seasoned salt

¾ tsp. pepper

¼ tsp. onion salt

1. Place potatoes in a large saucepan and cover with water. Bring to a boil. Reduce heat; cover and cook for 15-20 minutes or until tender. Drain.

2. In a large bowl, mash potatoes. Add the remaining ingredients; beat until fluffy.

1 CUP: 354 cal., 22g fat (14g sat. fat), 62mg chol., 479mg sod., 31g carb. (1g sugars, 6g fiber), 6g pro.

MOM'S MACARONI & CHEESE

The wonderful homemade goodness of this creamy macaroni and cheese
makes it a staple dish in my mother's kitchen and in mine as well.
It has tender noodles and a crowd-pleasing golden crumb topping.

—*Maria Costello, Monroe, NC*

PREP: 30 MIN. • **BAKE:** 30 MIN. • **MAKES:** 6 SERVINGS

1½ **cups uncooked elbow
macaroni**
5 **Tbsp. butter, divided**
3 **Tbsp. all-purpose flour**
½ **tsp. salt**
¼ **tsp. pepper**
1½ **cups whole milk**
1 **cup shredded cheddar
cheese**
2 **oz. cubed Velveeta**
2 **Tbsp. dry bread crumbs**

1. Cook macaroni according to package directions. Meanwhile, in a saucepan, melt 4 Tbsp. butter over medium heat. Stir in flour, salt and pepper until smooth. Gradually add milk. Bring to a boil; cook and stir for 2 minutes or until thickened. Reduce heat. Add the cheeses, stirring until cheese is melted. Drain macaroni.

2. Transfer macaroni to a greased 1½-qt. baking dish. Pour cheese sauce over macaroni; mix well. Melt the remaining butter; add the bread crumbs. Sprinkle over top. Bake, uncovered, at 375° for 30 minutes or until heated through and topping is golden brown.

1 SERVING: 309 cal., 20g fat (13g sat. fat), 60mg chol., 569mg sod., 22g carb. (4g sugars, 1g fiber), 11g pro.

FROM GRANDMA'S KITCHEN: It's usually cheaper to buy cheese in blocks rather than already shredded. So purchase large quantities of cheddar, Monterey Jack and mozzarella, then use a food processor to shred it. Store the shredded cheese in the freezer so you have it when you need it.

LEMON COUSCOUS WITH BROCCOLI

I combined two recipes to create this side with broccoli and pasta. The splash of lemon adds nice flavor. Instead of toasted almonds, you could also sprinkle servings with grated Parmesan cheese.

—*Beth Dauenhauer, Pueblo, CO*

TAKES: 25 MIN. • **MAKES:** 6 SERVINGS

1 Tbsp. olive oil
4 cups fresh broccoli florets, cut into small pieces
1 cup uncooked whole wheat couscous
2 garlic cloves, minced
1¼ cups reduced-sodium chicken broth
1 tsp. grated lemon zest
1 tsp. lemon juice
½ tsp. salt
½ tsp. dried basil
¼ tsp. coarsely ground pepper
1 Tbsp. slivered almonds, toasted

1. In a large cast-iron or other heavy skillet, heat oil over medium-high heat. Add broccoli; cook and stir until crisp-tender.

2. Add couscous and garlic; cook and stir 1-2 minutes longer. Stir in broth, lemon zest, lemon juice and seasonings; bring to a boil. Remove from heat; let stand, covered, until broth is absorbed, 5-10 minutes. Fluff with a fork. Sprinkle with almonds.

⅔ CUP: 115 cal., 3g fat (0 sat. fat), 0 chol., 328mg sod., 18g carb. (1g sugars, 4g fiber), 5g pro. **DIABETIC EXCHANGES:** 1 starch, ½ fat.

YELLOW SQUASH & ZUCCHINI GRATIN

This gratin is the perfect way to use up an abundance of summer squash. It's easy to prepare, takes just 10 minutes in the oven, and serves up bubbly and delicious.

—*Jonathan Lawler, Greenfield, IN*

PREP: 25 MIN. • BAKE: 10 MIN. • MAKES: 6 SERVINGS

2 Tbsp. butter
2 medium zucchini, cut into ¼-in. slices
2 medium yellow summer squash, cut into ¼-in. slices
2 shallots, minced
½ tsp. sea salt
¼ tsp. coarsely ground pepper
4 garlic cloves, minced
½ cup heavy whipping cream
1 cup panko bread crumbs, divided
½ cup grated Parmesan cheese, divided

1. Preheat oven to 450°. In a large skillet, melt butter over medium heat; add zucchini, yellow squash and shallots. Sprinkle with salt and pepper. Cook, stirring occasionally, until vegetables are crisp-tender, 4-6 minutes. Add garlic; cook 1 minute more.

2. Add the cream; cook until thickened, 3-5 minutes. Remove from heat; stir in ½ cup bread crumbs and ¼ cup cheese. Spoon mixture into a greased 11x7-in. or 2-qt. baking dish. Sprinkle with remaining bread crumbs and cheese. Bake until golden brown, 8-10 minutes.

1 CUP: 203 cal., 14g fat (8g sat. fat), 39mg chol., 357mg sod., 15g carb. (4g sugars, 2g fiber), 6g pro.

GRANDMA'S FRUIT SALAD

I can't believe how easy this pretty salad is to make. The colorful blend of bananas, pineapple, pears, peaches and grapes is tossed with a creamy pudding sauce. People of all ages enjoy this dish.

—*Carolyn Tomatz, Jackson, WI*

PREP: 25 MIN. + CHILLING • MAKES: 12 SERVINGS

1 can (20 oz.) unsweetened pineapple chunks
1 can (15 oz.) reduced-sugar sliced pears, drained
1 can (15 oz.) sliced peaches in juice, drained
1½ cups seedless red grapes
1 pkg. (3 oz.) cook-and-serve vanilla pudding mix
2 medium firm bananas
3 Tbsp. lemon juice
1 jar (10 oz.) maraschino cherries, well drained

1. Drain pineapple, reserving juice in a 1-cup measuring cup. In a large bowl, combine the pineapple, pears, peaches and grapes. Refrigerate until chilled.

2. Add enough water to pineapple juice to measure 1 cup. Pour into a small saucepan. Whisk in pudding mix. Bring to a boil over medium heat, stirring constantly. Remove from heat; set aside to cool to room temperature.

3. Slice bananas into a small bowl. Drizzle with lemon juice; gently toss to coast. Let stand for 5 minutes; drain. Add bananas and cherries to chilled fruit. Add cooled pudding; toss gently to combine. Refrigerate until serving.

½ CUP: 140 cal., 0 fat (0 sat. fat), 0 chol., 53mg sod., 37g carb. (33g sugars, 2g fiber), 0 pro.

YELLOW SQUASH
& ZUCCHINI GRATIN

CRANBERRY AMBROSIA SALAD

My paternal grandmother used to make this for Christmas dinner. I'm not sure how many batches she made, as there were nearly 50 aunts, uncles and cousins in our family. I still make the recipe in memory of her, and it's always as good as I remember.
—*Janet Hurley, Shell Rock, IA*

PREP: 20 MIN. + CHILLING • MAKES: 9 SERVINGS

1 lb. fresh or frozen cranberries	2 cups miniature marshmallows
1 can (20 oz.) crushed pineapple, drained	1 cup heavy whipping cream, whipped
1 cup sugar	½ cup chopped pecans

1. In a food processor, cover and process cranberries until coarsely chopped. Transfer to a large bowl; stir in pineapple and sugar. Cover and refrigerate overnight.

2. Just before serving, fold in marshmallows, whipped cream and pecans. If desired, top with additional chopped pecans.

¾ CUP: 331 cal., 15g fat (7g sat. fat), 36mg chol., 17mg sod., 52g carb. (43g sugars, 3g fiber), 2g pro.

BACON & BROCCOLI SALAD

You'll want to serve this family-friendly side dish year-round. The broccoli gets a big-time flavor boost from bacon, toasted pecans, dried berries and a mayo dressing.
—*Cindi Read, Hendersonville, TN*

TAKES: 30 MIN. • MAKES: 16 SERVINGS

3 bunches broccoli, cut into florets (about 10 cups)

1 lb. bacon strips, cooked and crumbled

1 cup chopped pecans, toasted

1 cup dried blueberries

1 cup dried cherries

¼ cup finely chopped red onion

DRESSING

1 cup mayonnaise

¼ cup sugar

¼ cup cider vinegar

In a large bowl, combine the first 6 ingredients. For dressing, in a small bowl, whisk mayonnaise, sugar and vinegar. Pour over broccoli mixture; toss to coat.

¾ CUP: 300 cal., 19g fat (3g sat. fat), 11mg chol., 290mg sod., 26g carb. (15g sugars, 5g fiber), 8g pro.

GRANDPA'S PARTY POTATOES

My grandpa, who gave me this recipe, liked the way the cream cheese and onion dip created a wonderful velvety texture. I often assemble these potatoes the night before, then pop them in the oven the next day.
—*Mary Kay Elert, St. Paul Park, MN*

PREP: 20 MIN. + CHILLING • **BAKE:** 50 MIN. • **MAKES:** 14 SERVINGS

12 **medium potatoes, peeled and quartered**
2 **Tbsp. butter**
2 **Tbsp. 2% milk**
¾ **tsp. salt**
¼ **tsp. pepper**
1 **pkg. (8 oz.) cream cheese, softened**
1 **carton (8 oz.) French onion dip**
   Paprika

1. Place potatoes in a large saucepan and cover with water. Bring to a boil. Reduce heat; cover and cook for 15-20 minutes or until tender. Drain. Mash the potatoes with butter, milk, salt and pepper until smooth. Add cream cheese and onion dip; mix well.

2. Spread in a greased 2½-qt. baking dish. Sprinkle with paprika. Cover and refrigerate for 8 hours or overnight.

3. Remove from the refrigerator 30 minutes before baking. Bake, uncovered, at 350° for 50-60 minutes or until heated through.

1 CUP: 181 cal., 10g fat (6g sat. fat), 22mg chol., 316mg sod., 21g carb. (2g sugars, 2g fiber), 4g pro.

OLD-FASHIONED WILTED LETTUCE

I remember my grandmother making this wonderful wilted salad with leaf lettuce from her garden and serving it with a creamy dressing.
—*Rose Shawyer, Otterbein, IN*

TAKES: 20 MIN. • **MAKES:** 8 SERVINGS

2 **large eggs**
½ **cup 2% milk**
¼ **cup cider vinegar**
½ **tsp. salt**
¼ **tsp. pepper**
8 **bacon strips, cut into 1-in. pieces**
1 **head medium head iceberg lettuce or 1 bunch leaf lettuce, torn**
1 **large onion, sliced into rings**

1. In a small bowl, beat the eggs, milk, vinegar, salt and pepper until smooth; set aside. In a large skillet, cook bacon over medium heat until crisp. Remove bacon to paper towels to drain, reserving the drippings.

2. Whisk egg mixture into drippings. Cook and stir over medium heat until mixture reaches 160° or is thick enough to coat the back of a metal spoon.

3. In a large salad bowl, combine the lettuce, onion and bacon. Pour dressing over salad; toss to coat. Serve immediately.

1 CUP: 163 cal., 13g fat (4g sat. fat), 67mg chol., 365mg sod., 5g carb. (3g sugars, 1g fiber), 6g pro.

SLICED
TOMATO
SALAD

SLICED TOMATO SALAD

This treasured recipe is from my grandmother.
It's a perfect platter to serve with burgers or hot sandwiches.
—*Kendal Tangedal, Plentywood, MT*

TAKES: 25 MIN. • MAKES: 12 SERVINGS

8 **large tomatoes, cut into ¼-in. slices**
2 **large sweet onions, halved and thinly sliced**
⅓ **cup olive oil**
2 **Tbsp. lemon juice**
1 **tsp. dried oregano**
¾ **tsp. salt**
¼ **tsp. pepper**
2 **Tbsp. minced fresh parsley**

Arrange tomatoes and onions on a large rimmed serving platter. In a small bowl, whisk the oil, lemon juice, oregano, salt and pepper. Drizzle over top. Sprinkle with parsley.

1 SERVING: 94 cal., 6g fat (1g sat. fat), 0 chol., 159mg sod., 9g carb. (6g sugars, 2g fiber), 2g pro. DIABETIC EXCHANGES: 2 vegetable, 1 fat.

CAULIFLOWER-BROCCOLI CHEESE BAKE

One of the first dishes my mom taught me is a tasty pairing of broccoli and cauliflower in a thick, comforting cheese sauce. It's absolutely my best side.
—*Devin Mulertt, Cedarburg, WI*

PREP: 15 MIN. • BAKE: 50 MIN. + STANDING • MAKES: 9 SERVINGS

2 **Tbsp. butter**
1 **small onion, chopped**
2 **Tbsp. all-purpose flour**
½ **cup 2% milk**
1 **pkg. (8 oz.) Velveeta, cubed**
¼ **tsp. salt**
3 **large eggs, lightly beaten**
2 **pkg. (12 oz. each) frozen broccoli-cauliflower blend, thawed**

1. Preheat the oven to 325°. In a Dutch oven, heat the butter over medium-high heat. Add onion; cook and stir until tender, 2-3 minutes. Stir in flour until blended; gradually whisk in milk. Bring to a boil, stirring constantly; cook and stir until thickened, 1-2 minutes. Stir in cheese and salt until cheese is melted.

2. Remove from heat. Gradually whisk in eggs. Stir in vegetable blend. Transfer to a greased 8-in.-square baking dish. Bake, uncovered, until set, 50-60 minutes. Let stand 10 minutes before serving.

1 PIECE: 170 cal., 11g fat (6g sat. fat), 95mg chol., 461mg sod., 8g carb. (2g sugars, 1g fiber), 8g pro.

FROM GRANDMA'S KITCHEN: Try this casserole as a side dish with dinner, or pop it onto your brunch buffet. Feel free to use all broccoli or all cauliflower if you're not a fan of one of them.

SIDE DISHES

GRANDMA'S GELATIN FRUIT SALAD

Whenever I'm hosting a family dinner, my sons and grandchildren ask me to make this lovely layered fruit salad. The taste doesn't just run in my family—the salad is always popular at potluck gatherings, too.
—*Wilma McLean, Medford, OR*

PREP: 25 MIN. + CHILLING • **MAKES:** 15 SERVINGS

2 **cups boiling water, divided**
1 **pkg. (3 oz.) lemon gelatin**
2 **cups ice cubes, divided**
1 **can (20 oz.) crushed pineapple, liquid drained and reserved**
1 **pkg. (3 oz.) orange gelatin**
2 **cups miniature marshmallows**
½ **cup sugar**
2 **Tbsp. cornstarch**
1 **cup reserved pineapple juice**
1 **large egg, lightly beaten**
1 **Tbsp. butter**
3 **large bananas, sliced**
1 **cup whipped topping**
½ **cup finely shredded cheddar cheese**

1. In a large bowl, combine 1 cup water and lemon gelatin. Add 1 cup ice cubes, stirring until melted. Stir in pineapple. Pour into a 13x9-in. dish coated with cooking spray; refrigerate until set but not firm.

2. Repeat with the orange gelatin, remaining water and ice. Stir in marshmallows. Pour over lemon layer; refrigerate until firm.

3. Meanwhile, in a small saucepan, combine sugar and cornstarch. Stir in reserved pineapple juice until smooth. Cook and stir over medium-high heat until thickened and bubbly. Reduce heat; cook and stir 2 minutes longer. Remove from the heat.

4. Stir a small amount of hot filling into egg; return all to the pan, stirring constantly. Bring to a gentle boil; cook and stir 2 minutes longer. Remove from the heat; stir in butter. Cool to room temperature without stirring. Refrigerate for 1 hour or until chilled.

5. Arrange bananas over gelatin. Stir whipped topping into dressing. Spread over bananas. Sprinkle with cheese.

1 PIECE: 194 cal., 3g fat (2g sat. fat), 20mg chol., 64mg sod., 40g carb. (35g sugars, 1g fiber), 3g pro.

ZUCCHINI ONION PIE

We have a lot of zucchini on hand when it's in season. This is a good and different way to use the large amounts that we have.
—*Lucia Johnson, Massena, NY*

TAKES: 30 MIN. • MAKES: 6 SERVINGS

3	large eggs	1	garlic clove, minced
1	cup grated Parmesan cheese	¼	tsp. salt
½	cup canola oil	⅛	tsp. pepper
1	Tbsp. minced fresh parsley	3	cups sliced zucchini
		1	cup biscuit/baking mix
		1	small onion, chopped

In a large bowl, whisk the first 7 ingredients. Stir in zucchini, baking mix and onion. Pour into a greased 9-in. deep-dish pie plate. Bake at 350° for 25-35 minutes or until lightly browned.

1 PIECE: 353 cal., 27g fat (5g sat. fat), 104mg chol., 627mg sod., 18g carb. (2g sugars, 1g fiber), 9g pro.

FROM GRANDMA'S KITCHEN: If you don't have a deep-dish pie plate, feel free to use a small baking dish (8-in. square) or a souffle dish (1½ to 2 qt.). Reduce oven time as needed, baking until lightly browned and eggs have reached an internal temperature of 160°. For an easy swap, use fresh basil or dill in place of the parsley. Dill packs a punch, so you need only 1 tsp.

RAINBOW FRUIT SALAD

When my children were young, I would often dress up fresh fruit in this easy-to-fix salad.
Decades later, my grandchildren and great-grandchildren still love digging into the fruity layers.
The salad goes well with barbecued meats or cold sandwiches.
—*Jonnie Adams Sisler, Stevensville, MT*

TAKES: 20 MIN. • MAKES: 20 SERVINGS

2 large firm bananas, sliced
2 Tbsp. lemon juice
2 cups seeded cubed watermelon
2 cups fresh or canned pineapple chunks
1 pint fresh blueberries
3 kiwifruit, peeled, halved and sliced
1 pint fresh strawberries, halved
6 oz. cream cheese, softened
⅓ cup confectioners' sugar
2 Tbsp. fresh lime juice
½ tsp. grated lime zest
1 cup heavy whipping cream, whipped

1. Toss bananas in lemon juice; place in a 4-qt. glass serving bowl. Add remaining fruit in layers.

2. In a bowl, beat cream cheese until smooth. Gradually add sugar and the lime juice and zest. Stir in a small amount of whipped cream; mix well. Fold in remaining whipped cream. Spread over fruit. Chill until serving.

¾ CUP: 123 cal., 7g fat (5g sat. fat), 22mg chol., 31mg sod., 14g carb. (10g sugars, 2g fiber), 1g pro.

MY MOTHER'S MAC & CHEESE

I remember my mother sending me to the store for 15 cents' worth of cheese. The butcher
would cut off a slice from a gigantic wheel covered with a wax-coated cloth. Mother would then
blend that cheese into this tasty dish. Today, the memory of her cooking is like food for my soul.
—*Phyllis Burkland, Portland, OR*

PREP: 10 MIN. • BAKE: 1 HOUR • MAKES: 4 SERVINGS

2 cups elbow macaroni, cooked and drained
1 can (28 oz.) diced tomatoes, undrained
½ tsp. onion salt, optional
¼ tsp. pepper
2 cups shredded cheddar cheese, divided
2 Tbsp. butter

In a bowl, combine macaroni, tomatoes, onion salt, pepper and 1½ cups cheddar cheese. Pour into a greased 2-qt. baking dish. Dot with butter. Bake, uncovered, at 350° for 45 minutes. Sprinkle with remaining cheese; bake 15 minutes longer.

1 CUP: 373 cal., 22g fat (16g sat. fat), 75mg chol., 759mg sod., 27g carb. (6g sugars, 2g fiber), 16g pro.

RAINBOW
FRUIT SALAD

BEET & SWEET POTATO FRIES

Instead of offering traditional French fries, try these
oven-baked root vegetables as a flavorful side dish.

—*Marie Rizzio, Interlochen, MI*

PREP: 15 MIN. • **BAKE:** 20 MIN. • **MAKES:** 5 SERVINGS (½ CUP SAUCE)

½ cup reduced-fat
  mayonnaise
1 tsp. pink peppercorns,
  crushed
½ tsp. green peppercorns,
  crushed
½ tsp. coarsely ground
  pepper, divided

1 large sweet potato
  (about 1 lb.)
2 Tbsp. olive oil, divided
½ tsp. sea salt, divided
2 large fresh beets
  (about 1 lb.)

1. In a small bowl, combine the mayonnaise, peppercorns and
¼ tsp. ground pepper. Cover and refrigerate until serving.

2. Peel and cut sweet potato in half widthwise; cut each half into
½-in. strips. Place in a small bowl. Add 1 Tbsp. oil, ¼ tsp. salt and
⅛ tsp. pepper; toss to coat. Spread mixture onto a parchment-
lined baking sheet.

3. Peel and cut beets in half; cut into ½-in. strips. Transfer to the
same bowl; add the remaining oil, salt and pepper. Toss to coat.
Spread onto another parchment-lined baking sheet.

4. Bake vegetables, uncovered, at 425° for 20-30 minutes or until
tender, turning once. Serve with peppercorn mayonnaise.

1 SERVING: 226 cal., 14g fat (2g sat. fat), 8mg chol., 455mg sod., 25g
carb. (14g sugars, 4g fiber), 3g pro. **DIABETIC EXCHANGES:** 2 starch,
2 fat.

*"Such an easy and absolutely delicious recipe! I added
a little rosemary when I roasted the veggies, which my
husband and I enjoyed. The peppercorn sauce really
complements the beets and sweet potatoes, and I'll
definitely be making these fries again!"*

—SGRONHOLZ, TASTEOFHOME.COM

WENDY'S APPLE POMEGRANATE SALAD

My grandparents grew pomegranates, pecans and walnuts and would send us some each year. Some of my best memories are the days I used to spend with my grandmother learning how to cook with them. Whenever I make this it's like having lunch with my grandmother again.
—*Wendy G. Ball, Battle Creek, MI*

TAKES: 20 MIN. • **MAKES:** 8 SERVINGS

1 **bunch romaine, torn (about 8 cups)**
½ **cup pomegranate seeds**
½ **cup chopped pecans or walnuts, toasted**
½ **cup shredded Parmesan cheese**
1 **large Granny Smith apple, chopped**
1 **Tbsp. lemon juice**
¼ **cup olive oil**
¼ **cup white wine vinegar**
2 **Tbsp. sugar**
¼ **tsp. salt**

1. In a large bowl, combine romaine, pomegranate seeds, pecans and cheese. Toss apple with lemon juice and add to salad.

2. In a small bowl, whisk remaining ingredients until blended. Drizzle over salad; toss to coat. Serve immediately.

NOTE: To toast nuts, bake in a shallow pan in a 350° oven for 5-10 minutes or cook in a skillet over low heat until lightly browned, stirring occasionally.

1 CUP: 165 cal., 13g fat (2g sat. fat), 4mg chol., 163mg sod., 10g carb. (8g sugars, 2g fiber), 3g pro. **DIABETIC EXCHANGES:** 2½ fat, 1 vegetable.

MOM'S CHOPPED COLESLAW

For our Friday fish dinners, my mother treated us to her homemade coleslaw on the side. That creamy, tangy flavor is still a family tradition.
—*Cynthia McDowell, Banning, CA*

TAKES: 20 MIN. • **MAKES:** 6 SERVINGS

½ **medium head cabbage (about 1¼ lbs.)**
½ **cup finely chopped celery**
½ **cup finely chopped sweet red or green pepper**
⅓ **cup finely chopped sweet onion**

DRESSING
½ **cup mayonnaise**
¼ **cup sugar**
¼ **cup 2% milk**
¼ **cup buttermilk**
2 **tsp. white vinegar**
¼ **tsp. hot pepper sauce**
Dash pepper

1. Cut cabbage into 1½-2-in. pieces. Place half of the cabbage in a food processor; pulse until chopped. Transfer to a large bowl; repeat with remaining cabbage.

2. Add remaining vegetables to cabbage. In a small bowl, whisk dressing ingredients until blended. Pour over coleslaw and toss to coat. Refrigerate until serving.

¾ CUP: 203 cal., 15g fat (2g sat. fat), 8mg chol., 147mg sod., 16g carb. (13g sugars, 2g fiber), 2g pro.

RED POTATOES
WITH BEANS

RED POTATOES WITH BEANS

You can serve this homey blend of fresh green beans, potato wedges and chopped red onion hot or cold. Either way, this easy side dish makes a pleasing accompaniment to Mom's meat loaf or almost any other meat.

—Daria Burcar, Rochester, MI

TAKES: 20 MIN. • MAKES: 6 SERVINGS

6 small red potatoes, cut into wedges
1⅓ lbs. fresh green beans, trimmed
½ cup chopped red onion
½ cup Italian salad dressing

1. Place potatoes in a large saucepan and cover with water. Bring to a boil. Reduce heat; cover and cook until tender, 10-15 minutes.

2. Meanwhile, place green beans and ⅓ cup water in a 2-qt. microwave-safe dish. Cover and microwave on high until tender, 6-8 minutes.

3. Drain potatoes and beans; place in a bowl. Add onion and dressing; toss to coat.

NOTE: This recipe was tested in a 1,100-watt microwave.

¾ CUP: 138 cal., 3g fat (0 sat. fat), 0 chol., 212mg sod., 23g carb. (5g sugars, 5g fiber), 4g pro. DIABETIC EXCHANGES: 1 starch, 1 vegetable, ½ fat.

SLOW-COOKED WILD RICE

This recipe has become such a family heirloom that I asked permission from my mother before passing it along. It has traveled to weddings, baptisms, landmark birthdays and wedding anniversaries—and it always makes people happy.

—Janet Mahowald, Rice Lake, WI

PREP: 15 MIN. • COOK: 4 HOURS • MAKES: 10 SERVINGS

1 lb. bulk pork sausage
4 celery ribs, chopped
1 small onion, chopped
1 can (10¾ oz.) condensed cream of mushroom soup, undiluted
1 can (10¾ oz.) condensed cream of chicken soup, undiluted
1 cup uncooked wild rice
1 can (4 oz.) mushroom stems and pieces, drained
3 cups chicken broth

1. In a large skillet, cook and crumble sausage with celery and onion over medium heat until sausage is no longer pink and vegetables are tender, 6-8 minutes; drain. Transfer to a 3-qt. slow cooker. Add soups, rice and mushrooms. Stir in broth.

2. Cook, covered, on low until rice is tender, 4-5 hours.

¾ CUP: 236 cal., 14g fat (4g sat. fat), 30mg chol., 1059mg sod., 19g carb. (2g sugars, 2g fiber), 9g pro.

CORN ON THE COB WITH LEMON-PEPPER BUTTER

Roasting fresh-picked corn is as old as the Ozark hills where I was raised. My Grandpa Mitchell always salted and peppered his butter on the edge of his plate before spreading it on his corn, and I did the same as a kid. Today, I continue the tradition by serving lemon-pepper butter with roasted corn—it's a favorite!

—*Allene Bary-Cooper, Wichita Falls, TX*

PREP: 10 MIN. + SOAKING • **GRILL:** 25 MIN. • **MAKES:** 8 SERVINGS

8 **medium ears sweet corn**
1 **cup butter, softened**
2 **Tbsp. lemon-pepper seasoning**

1. Carefully peel back corn husks to within 1 in. of bottoms; remove silk. Rewrap corn in husks; secure with kitchen string. Place in a stockpot; cover with cold water. Soak 20 minutes; drain.

2. Meanwhile, in a small bowl, mix butter and lemon pepper. Grill corn, covered, over medium heat 20-25 minutes or until tender, turning often.

3. Cut string and peel back husks. Serve corn with butter mixture.

1 EAR OF CORN WITH 2 TBSP. BUTTER: 280 cal., 24g fat (15g sat. fat), 60mg chol., 520mg sod., 17g carb. (3g sugars, 3g fiber), 3g pro.

OODLES OF NOODLES

My mother made the most delicious noodles from scratch using our own farm-fresh eggs, flour and salt. I remember her rolling out the dough paper-thin on our big dining room table.

—*Karen Ann Bland, Gove, KS*

PREP: 50 MIN. + STANDING • **COOK:** 15 MIN. • **MAKES:** 9 SERVINGS

3¼ **to 3½ cups all-purpose flour**
¾ **tsp. salt**
6 **eggs, beaten**

1. In a small bowl, combine 3¼ cups flour and salt. Make a well in the center. Pour eggs into well. Stir together, forming a dough. Turn dough onto a floured surface; knead for 3-4 minutes or until smooth, adding remaining flour if necessary.

2. Divide into 9 portions; cover and let rest for 15 minutes. Roll each portion into a 12-in. x 5-in. rectangle. Roll up jelly-roll style, starting with a short side; cut into ¼-in.-thick strips. Unroll noodles and allow to dry on kitchen towels for 1 hour before cooking.

3. To cook, fill a Dutch oven three-fourths full with water. Bring to a boil. Add noodles; cook for 9-12 minutes or until tender. Drain.

¾ CUP: 212 cal., 4g fat (1g sat. fat), 141mg chol., 244mg sod., 35g carb. (1g sugars, 1g fiber), 9g pro.:

GRANDMA'S SECRET

After drying, noodles may be stored in the freezer for up to 2 months if desired. Using waxed paper, store noodles in layers in an airtight container. Frozen noodles are ready to cook.

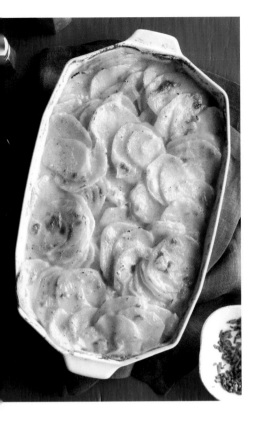

EASY SCALLOPED POTATOES

We all loved my mom's super-rich scalloped potatoes.
I tweaked her recipe to keep all the flavor, but cut the fat.
The cheese blend is the clincher. It's all about experimenting.
—Diane Bramlett, Stockton, CA

PREP: 30 MIN. • BAKE: 20 MIN. • MAKES: 12 SERVINGS (½ CUP EACH)

3 lbs. Yukon Gold potatoes (about 11 medium), peeled and thinly sliced
¼ cup water
¼ cup butter, cubed
1 large sweet onion, chopped
4 garlic cloves, chopped
¼ cup all-purpose flour
1 tsp. salt
1 tsp. pepper
⅛ tsp. cayenne pepper
2 cups chicken broth
⅓ cup half-and-half cream
1 cup shredded Gruyere or Swiss cheese
1 cup shredded Monterey Jack or cheddar cheese
Minced fresh chives, optional

1. Preheat oven to 400°. Place potatoes and water in a large microwave-safe bowl; microwave, covered, on high until almost tender, 12-14 minutes.

2. In a 6-qt. stockpot, heat butter over medium-high heat; saute onion and garlic until tender, 5-7 minutes. Stir in flour and seasonings until blended; gradually stir in broth and cream. Bring to a boil, stirring occasionally; cook and stir until slightly thickened, 2-3 minutes. Stir in cheeses until melted.

3. Drain potatoes; add to sauce, stirring gently. Transfer to a greased 13x9-in. baking dish. Bake, uncovered, until lightly browned, about 20 minutes. If desired, sprinkle with chives.

NOTE: This recipe was tested in a 1,100-watt microwave.

½ CUP: 245 cal., 11g fat (7g sat. fat), 33mg chol., 526mg sod., 29g carb. (4g sugars, 2g fiber), 8g pro.

ROASTED CAULIFLOWER WITH TAHINI YOGURT SAUCE

I created my own cauliflower recipe in honor of my grandma, who taught me to love this delicious and healthy vegetable. She cooked with it all the time.
—*Lidia Haddadian, Pasadena, CA*

PREP: 15 MIN. • **BAKE:** 40 MIN. • **MAKES:** 4 SERVINGS

¼ cup grated Parmesan cheese
3 Tbsp. olive oil
2 garlic cloves, minced
¼ tsp. salt
¼ tsp. pepper
1 small head cauliflower (about 1½ lbs.), cut into 4 wedges

SAUCE
½ cup fat-free plain Greek yogurt
1 Tbsp. lemon juice
1 Tbsp. tahini
¼ tsp. salt
Dash paprika
Dash cayenne pepper
Minced fresh parsley

1. Preheat oven to 375°. In a small bowl, mix first 5 ingredients. Rub over cauliflower; place in a foil-lined 15x10x1-in. baking pan coated with cooking spray, cut sides up. Roast for 40-45 minutes or until golden brown and tender.

2. For sauce, in a small bowl, mix yogurt, lemon juice, salt, paprika and cayenne; serve over cauliflower. Sprinkle with parsley.

1 CAULIFLOWER WEDGE WITH ABOUT 2 TBSP. SAUCE: 177 cal., 14g fat (3g sat. fat), 4mg chol., 421mg sod., 7g carb. (3g sugars, 2g fiber), 7g pro.

GRANDMA'S SCALLOPED CORN

This is a recipe near and dear to my heart. Even today, it's a favorite with our grown children.
—*Connie Hoffa, Okatie, SC*

PREP: 20 MIN. • **BAKE:** 45 MIN. • **MAKES:** 6 SERVINGS

1 celery rib, chopped
½ small onion, chopped
2 Tbsp. butter
1 can (14¾ oz.) cream-style corn
1 cup 2% milk
1 cup crushed saltines (about 20 crackers)
⅔ cup cubed Velveeta
2 large eggs, lightly beaten
1 tsp. salt
¼ tsp. paprika

1. In a small skillet, saute celery and onion in butter until tender. Transfer to a large bowl; cool to room temperature. Stir in the corn, milk, saltines, cheese, eggs and salt.

2. Transfer to a greased 1½-qt. baking dish. Sprinkle with paprika. Cover and bake at 350° for 45-55 minutes or until golden brown.

¾ CUP: 219 cal., 11g fat (6g sat. fat), 95mg chol., 952mg sod., 24g carb. (6g sugars, 1g fiber), 8g pro.

ROASTED CAULIFLOWER
WITH TAHINI YOGURT SAUCE

HERBED RICE PILAF

This savory side dish has been a family favorite for years.
Our 12-year-old daughter, Jennifer, is an expert with this recipe,
which is a wonderful help for a busy working mom like me.
We sure enjoy this rice dish in the summer with a grilled entree.

—*Jeri Dobrowski, Beach, ND*

PREP: 15 MIN. • **COOK:** 15 MIN. + STANDING • **MAKES:** 6 SERVINGS

1   **cup uncooked long grain rice**
1   **cup chopped celery**
¾   **cup chopped onion**
¼   **cup butter, cubed**
2½ **cups water**
1   **pkg. (2 to 2½ oz.) chicken noodle soup mix**
1   **tsp. dried thyme**
¼   **tsp. rubbed sage**
¼   **tsp. pepper**
2   **Tbsp. fresh minced parsley**
1   **Tbsp. chopped pimientos, optional**

1. In a large skillet, cook the rice, celery and onion in butter, stirring constantly, until rice is browned. Stir in the next 5 ingredients; bring to a boil. Reduce heat; cover and simmer for 15 minutes. Sprinkle with parsley; stir in pimientos if desired.

2. Remove from heat and let stand, covered, for 10 minutes. Fluff with a fork.

¾ CUP: 226 cal., 8g fat (5g sat. fat), 23mg chol., 426mg sod., 34g carb. (3g sugars, 2g fiber), 4g pro. **DIABETIC EXCHANGES:** 2 starch, 1½ fat.

ROASTED BEET WEDGES

This recipe makes ordinary beets taste tender and delicious
with just a few good-for-you ingredients.

—*Wendy Stenman, Germantown, WI*

PREP: 15 MIN. • **BAKE:** 1 HOUR • **MAKES:** 4 SERVINGS

1   **lb. fresh beets (about 3 medium), peeled**
4   **tsp. olive oil**
½   **tsp. kosher salt**
3   **to 5 fresh rosemary sprigs**

1. Preheat oven to 400°. Cut each beet into 6 wedges; place in a shallow dish. Add olive oil and salt; toss gently to coat.

2. Place a piece 12-in.-long heavy-duty foil in a 15x10x1-in. baking pan. Arrange beets on foil; top with rosemary. Fold foil around beets and seal tightly.

3. Bake until tender, about 1 hour. Open foil carefully to allow steam to escape. Discard rosemary sprigs.

ABOUT 4 WEDGES: 92 cal., 5g fat (1g sat. fat), 0 chol., 328mg sod., 12g carb. (9g sugars, 3g fiber), 2g pro. **DIABETIC EXCHANGES:** 1 vegetable, 1 fat.

GRANDMA'S POTATO SALAD

This salad is a must for the Fourth of July. The red potatoes hold their shape and texture even after they are boiled. It's Grandma's treasured recipe.
—*Sue Gronholz, Beaver Dam, WI*

PREP: 1 HOUR + CHILLING • **MAKES:** 24 SERVINGS

6 **lbs. medium red potatoes**

DRESSING
1 **cup water**
½ **cup butter, cubed**
¼ **cup white vinegar**
2 **large eggs**
½ **cup sugar**
4½ **tsp. cornstarch**
¾ **cup heavy whipping cream**
¾ **cup Miracle Whip**

SALAD
1 **small onion, finely chopped**
2 **green onions, sliced**
1 **tsp. salt**
½ **tsp. pepper**
3 **hard-boiled large eggs, sliced**
 Paprika

1. Place potatoes in a stockpot and cover with water. Bring to a boil. Reduce heat; cover and cook until tender, about 20 minutes. Drain. When cool enough to handle, peel and slice potatoes; cool completely.

2. For the dressing, in the top of a double boiler or metal bowl over barely simmering water, heat 1 cup water, butter and vinegar until butter is melted. In a small bowl, beat eggs; add sugar and cornstarch. Add to butter mixture; cook and stir until thickened, 5-7 minutes. Transfer to a large bowl; cool completely.

3. In a small bowl, beat cream until stiff peaks form. Stir Miracle Whip into cooled dressing mixture; fold in whipped cream. Stir in onion, green onions, salt and pepper. Add potatoes; toss lightly to combine. Refrigerate, covered, until chilled.

4. To serve, top with hard-boiled eggs; sprinkle with paprika.

¾ CUP: 197 cal., 10g fat (5g sat. fat), 58mg chol., 202mg sod., 24g carb. (6g sugars, 2g fiber), 4g pro.

"A must-have at all family gatherings! Very creamy! I used mayo instead of Miracle Whip, and it was amazing. Everyone came back for seconds."
—HKAROW9713, TASTEOFHOME.COM

MOM'S APPLE CORNBREAD STUFFING

My speedy recipe is the be-all and end-all stuffing in our family. Not surprisingly, we never have leftovers.
—*Marie Forte, Raritan, NJ*

PREP: 15 MIN. • **BAKE:** 35 MIN. • **MAKES:** 16 SERVINGS

6 **large Granny Smith apples, peeled and chopped**
1 **pkg. (14 oz.) crushed cornbread stuffing**
½ **cup butter, melted**
1 **can (14½ oz.) chicken broth**

1. Preheat oven to 350°. Combine apples, stuffing and melted butter. Add broth; mix well.

2. Transfer to a greased 13x9-in. baking dish. Bake until golden brown, 35-40 minutes.

¾ CUP: 183 cal., 7g fat (4g sat. fat), 16mg chol., 434mg sod., 28g carb. (8g sugars, 2g fiber), 3g pro. **DIABETIC EXCHANGES:** 2 starch, 1½ fat.

CHEDDAR HAM SOUP,
PAGE 179

SOUPS & STEWS

When you're hungry and it's cold outside, nothing beats a bowl of steaming-hot homemade soup. Grandma knows, it's like a hug in a bowl.

WHITE BEAN CHICKEN CHILI

My sister shared this white bean chili recipe with me. I usually double it and
add one extra can of beans, then serve with cheddar biscuits or warmed tortillas.
The jalapeno adds just enough heat to notice but not too much for my children.
—*Kristine Bowles, Rio Rancho, NM*

PREP: 25 MIN. • **COOK:** 3 HOURS • **MAKES:** 6 SERVINGS (1½ QT.)

¾ **lb. boneless skinless chicken breasts, cut into 1¼-in. pieces**
¼ **tsp. salt**
¼ **tsp. pepper**
2 **Tbsp. olive oil, divided**
1 **medium onion, chopped**
1 **jalapeno pepper, seeded and chopped**
4 **garlic cloves, minced**
2 **tsp. dried oregano**
1 **tsp. ground cumin**
2 **cans (15 oz. each) cannellini beans, rinsed and drained, divided**
2½ **cups chicken broth, divided**
1½ **cups shredded cheddar cheese**
   Optional toppings: Sliced avocado, quartered cherry tomatoes and chopped cilantro

1. Sprinkle chicken with salt and pepper. In a large skillet, heat 1 Tbsp. oil over medium-high heat; saute chicken until browned. Transfer to a 3-qt. slow cooker.

2. In same skillet, heat remaining oil over medium heat; saute onion until tender. Add jalapeno, garlic, oregano and cumin; cook and stir 2 minutes. Add to slow cooker.

3. In a bowl, mash 1 cup beans; stir in ½ cup broth. Stir bean mixture and the remaining whole beans and broth into the chicken mixture.

4. Cook, covered, on low until chicken is tender, 3-3½ hours. Stir before serving. Sprinkle with cheese; add toppings if desired.

FREEZE OPTION: Freeze cooled chili in freezer containers. To use, partially thaw in refrigerator overnight. Heat through in a saucepan, stirring occasionally and adding a little broth or water if necessary.

NOTE: Wear disposable gloves when cutting hot peppers; the oils can burn skin. Avoid touching your face.

1 CUP: 344 cal., 16g fat (6g sat. fat), 62mg chol., 894mg sod., 23g carb. (1g sugars, 6g fiber), 25g pro.

FROM GRANDMA'S KITCHEN: Want a slimmer chili? Leave off the cheese and this winter warmer is just 230 calories and 7g fat per serving. Garnish with flavorful (and virtually calorie-free) cilantro instead!

QUICK MUSHROOM BARLEY SOUP

I surprised my mother with a visit some years ago, and she was preparing this soup when I walked in. It was so wonderful that I asked for the recipe, and I've been fixing it ever since.
—*Edie Irwin, Cornwall, NY*

TAKES: 30 MIN. • MAKES: 6 SERVINGS (1½ QT.)

1 **Tbsp. olive oil**	¾ **cup quick-cooking barley**
1 **cup sliced fresh mushrooms**	2 **Tbsp. all-purpose flour**
½ **cup chopped carrot**	3 **cups whole milk**
⅓ **cup chopped onion**	1½ **tsp. salt**
2 **cups water**	½ **tsp. pepper**

1. In a large saucepan, heat oil over medium heat. Add the mushrooms, carrot and onion; cook and stir 5-6 minutes or until tender. Add water and barley. Bring to a boil. Reduce heat; simmer, uncovered, 12-15 minutes or until barley is tender.

2. In a small bowl, mix flour, milk, salt and pepper until smooth; stir into soup. Return to a boil, stirring constantly; cook and stir 1-2 minutes or until thickened.

1 CUP: 196 cal., 7g fat (3g sat. fat), 12mg chol., 654mg sod., 27g carb. (7g sugars, 5g fiber), 8g pro. **DIABETIC EXCHANGES:** 1½ starch, ½ whole milk, ½ fat.

GRANDMOTHER'S HAMBURGER STEW

My grandmother gave me this recipe, so it always brings back warm memories whenever I prepare it.
—*Julie Kretchman, Meyersdale, PA*

PREP: 10 MIN. • COOK: 55 MIN. • MAKES: 2 SERVINGS

½ **lb. ground beef**
¼ **cup chopped onion**
¼ **cup chopped celery**
1 **cup canned diced tomatoes, undrained**
¾ **cup beef broth**
¾ **cup cubed peeled potato**
¼ **cup thinly sliced carrot**
2 **Tbsp. uncooked long grain rice**
½ **tsp. salt, optional**
⅛ **tsp. pepper**

In a large saucepan, cook the beef, onion and celery over medium heat until meat is no longer pink; drain. Stir in the tomatoes, broth, potato, carrot, rice, salt if desired and pepper. Bring to a boil. Reduce heat; cover and simmer 40-45 minutes or until rice and vegetables are tender.

1 SERVING: 319 cal., 11g fat (5g sat. fat), 56mg chol., 565mg sod., 31g carb. (7g sugars, 4g fiber), 24g pro.

CHEDDAR HAM SOUP
PICTURED ON PAGE 174

I knew this recipe was a keeper when my mother-in-law asked for it! This creamy soup, chock-full of ham, veggies and cheese, is so comforting. Don't expect leftovers!
—*Marty Matthews, Clarksville, TN*

TAKES: 30 MIN. • MAKES: 7 SERVINGS (1¾ QT.)

2 cups diced peeled potatoes
2 cups water
½ cup sliced carrot
¼ cup chopped onion
¼ cup butter, cubed
¼ cup all-purpose flour
2 cups 2% milk
¼ to ½ tsp. salt
¼ tsp. pepper
2 cups shredded cheddar cheese
1½ cups cubed fully cooked ham
1 cup frozen peas

1. In a large saucepan, combine the potatoes, water, carrot and onion. Bring to a boil. Reduce heat; cover and cook until tender, 10-15 minutes.

2. Meanwhile, in another saucepan, melt butter. Stir in flour until smooth. Gradually stir in milk; add salt and pepper. Bring to a boil; cook and stir until thickened, about 2 minutes. Stir in cheese until melted. Stir into undrained potato mixture. Add ham and peas; heat through.

1 CUP: 331 cal., 20g fat (12g sat. fat), 73mg chol., 772mg sod., 19g carb. (5g sugars, 2g fiber), 19g pro.

"Easy and delish. I didn't have peas so I used mixed vegetables, and it turned out perfect."
—LORIBILLINGS, TASTEOFHOME.COM

VEGETABLE DUMPLING SOUP

As a busy working mother, I love this recipe. I can use common pantry items to put a hearty, healthful dinner on the table for my family to enjoy. It takes only melon or fruit salad to round out this meal!
—*Grace Sandvigen, Rochester, NY*

PREP: 25 MIN. • COOK: 20 MIN. • MAKES: 6 SERVINGS (2 QT.)

1 medium onion, chopped
1 Tbsp. canola oil
3 cans (14½ oz. each) chicken broth
1 pkg. (16 oz.) frozen sugar snap stir-fry vegetable blend, thawed
1 can (15½ oz.) great northern beans, rinsed and drained
1 tsp. ground mustard
½ cup uncooked orzo pasta
¾ cup biscuit/baking mix
½ cup cornmeal
¼ tsp. dried oregano
¼ tsp. dried basil
½ cup 2% milk

1. In a Dutch oven, saute onion in oil until tender. Stir in the broth, vegetable blend, beans and mustard. Bring to a boil. Reduce heat; simmer for 6-8 minutes or until heated through. Meanwhile, in a large saucepan, cook orzo according to package directions; drain.

2. For dumplings, in a small bowl, combine baking mix, cornmeal, oregano and basil. Stir in milk just until moistened; set aside.

3. Stir orzo into soup. Drop dumpling batter by tablespoonfuls into simmering soup. Cover and simmer for 20 minutes or until a toothpick inserted in a dumpling comes out clean (do not lift the cover while simmering).

1⅓ CUPS: 307 cal., 5g fat (1g sat. fat), 2mg chol., 1025mg sod., 54g carb. (7g sugars, 6g fiber), 11g pro.

SMOOTH & CREAMY
PUMPKIN SOUP

SMOOTH & CREAMY PUMPKIN SOUP

My mother-in-law doesn't cook anymore, but she shared this recipe with me.
Now I make it for her, and she enjoys eating it as much as I enjoy making it.
The pumpkin flavor brings a little Thanksgiving to any meal.
—*Helen Espinosa, Miami, FL*

TAKES: 30 MIN. • **MAKES:** 10 SERVINGS (2½ QT.)

1 **large pie pumpkin (about 4 lbs.)**
4 **cups water**
1 **large onion, chopped**
¼ **cup butter, cubed**
2 **Tbsp. chicken bouillon granules**
6 **garlic cloves, peeled and halved**
1 **tsp. salt**
½ **tsp. ground nutmeg**
½ **tsp. pepper**
1 **can (7.6 oz.) media crema table cream**
Roasted pumpkin seeds, fried sage leaves, optional

1. Cut a 4-in. circle around pumpkin stem; remove top and discard. Peel pumpkin; cut in half. Remove strings and seeds; discard seeds or save for roasting. Cut pumpkin into 1-in cubes. Place in a 6-qt. stockpot; add water.

2. Stir in onion, butter, bouillon, garlic, salt, nutmeg and pepper. Bring to a boil. Reduce heat to medium-low; cook, uncovered, 10-12 minutes or until pumpkin is tender.

3. Add cream; heat through. Puree soup using an immersion blender. Or, cool soup slightly and puree in batches in a blender; return to pan and heat through. If desired, top with roasted pumpkin seeds and fried sage leaves.

NOTE: This recipe was tested with Nestle media crema table cream; look for it in the international foods section. You may substitute 8 oz. creme fraiche (in the dairy section near the mascarpone). Thin with a little milk if desired.

1 CUP: 150 cal., 11g fat (7g sat. fat), 28mg chol., 794mg sod., 13g carb. (3g sugars, 1g fiber), 2g pro.

LOADED POTATO-LEEK SOUP

When I was growing up, my mother made potato and onion soup because it was
affordable and fast. I've trimmed the calories, and it's still a comforting family favorite.
—*Courtney Stultz, Weir, KS*

PREP: 20 MIN. • **COOK:** 6 HOURS • **MAKES:** 6 SERVINGS (ABOUT 1½ QT.)

1 **medium leek**
1½ **lbs. potatoes (about 2 large), peeled and finely chopped**
2 **cups fresh cauliflowerets**
¾ **tsp. rubbed sage**
½ **tsp. salt**
¼ **tsp. pepper**
4 **cups reduced-sodium chicken or vegetable broth**
2 **tsp. olive oil**
2 **tsp. lemon juice**
Sour cream, optional

1. Finely chop white portion of leek. Cut leek greens into thin strips; reserve for topping. In a 3- or 4-qt. slow cooker, combine potatoes, cauliflowerets, seasonings, broth and chopped leek. Cook, covered, on low 6-8 hours or until vegetables are tender.

2. In a small skillet, heat oil over medium-high heat. Add the reserved leek greens; cook 3-5 minutes. Puree soup using an immersion blender. Or cool soup slightly and puree in batches in a blender. Stir in lemon juice. Top with leek greens and, if desired, sour cream.

1 CUP: 108 cal., 2g fat (0 sat. fat), 0 chol., 593mg sod., 20g carb. (3g sugars, 2g fiber), 4g pro. DIABETIC EXCHANGES: 1 starch, ½ fat.

SPICED LAMB STEW WITH APRICOTS

My family loves lamb, especially my son. During his first year of college,
he claimed to be a vegetarian. When he came home, I had a pot of my lamb stew simmering
in the kitchen. When my husband and I wanted to eat dinner, there were only a few
shreds of meat left floating in the gravy—and my son confessed that he was the culprit!
—*Arlene Erlbach, Morton Grove, IL*

PREP: 30 MIN. • **COOK:** 5 HOURS • **MAKES:** 5 SERVINGS

2 lbs. lamb stew meat,
   cut into ¾-in. cubes
3 Tbsp. butter
1½ cups chopped
   sweet onion
¾ cup dried apricots
½ cup orange juice
½ cup chicken broth
2 tsp. paprika
2 tsp. ground allspice
2 tsp. ground cinnamon
1½ tsp. salt
1 tsp. ground cardamom
   Hot cooked couscous
   Chopped dried apricots,
   optional

1. In a large skillet, brown lamb in butter in batches. With a slotted spoon, transfer to a 3-qt. slow cooker. In the same skillet, saute onion in drippings until tender. Stir in the apricots, orange juice, broth and seasonings; pour over lamb.

2. Cover and cook on high for 5-6 hours or until meat is tender. Serve with couscous. Sprinkle with chopped apricots if desired.

1 CUP: 404 cal., 17g fat (8g sat. fat), 136mg chol., 975mg sod., 24g carb. (15g sugars, 5g fiber), 38g pro.

FROM GRANDMA'S KITCHEN: Not a fan of lamb? That's OK—these flavors meld wonderfully with pork, too. Substitute cubed pork shoulder for the lamb stew meat.

GRANDMA'S TOMATO SOUP

This recipe is my grandmother's. Originally, Gram even made the tomato juice in it from scratch!
Gram had this soup cooking on the stove every time I visited her. She enjoyed making this tomato
soup and other favorite dishes for family and friends, and she made everything with love.
—*Gerri Sysun, Narragansett, RI*

TAKES: 15 MIN. • **MAKES:** 2 SERVINGS

2 Tbsp. butter
1 Tbsp. all-purpose flour
2 cups tomato juice
½ cup water
2 Tbsp. sugar
⅛ tsp. salt
¾ cup cooked wide
   egg noodles
   Chopped fresh parsley,
   optional

In a saucepan over medium heat, melt butter. Add flour; stir to form a smooth paste. Gradually add tomato juice and water, stirring constantly; bring to a boil. Cook and stir until thickened, about 2 minutes. Add sugar and salt. Stir in egg noodles and heat through. If desired, sprinkle with parsley.

1 CUP: 259 cal., 12g fat (7g sat. fat), 44mg chol., 1144mg sod., 36g carb. (20g sugars, 1g fiber), 4g pro.

CHICKEN ESCAROLE SOUP WITH MEATBALLS

This is an old recipe from southern Italy. My mother gave it to me when I was first married. It started out as a holidays-only dish, but my children and grandchildren love it so much that we have it every chance we get!
—*Norma Manna, Hobe Sound, FL*

PREP: 20 MIN. • COOK: 1 HOUR 30 MIN. • MAKES: 24 SERVINGS (6 QT.)

15 **chicken wings**
4 **medium carrots, cut into ½-in. pieces**
1 **large potato, cut into ½-in. cubes**
4 **celery ribs, sliced**
1 **large tomato, seeded and diced**
1 **large onion, diced**
3½ **tsp. salt, divided**
1 **tsp. pepper**
4 **qt. water**

1 **large egg, lightly beaten**
½ **cup dry bread crumbs**
1 **Tbsp. minced fresh parsley**
1 **garlic clove, minced**
1 **tsp. grated Parmesan cheese**
½ **lb. ground beef**
1 **small head (about 5 to 6 oz.) escarole, cored and separated**

1. In a stockpot, combine wings, carrots, potato, celery, tomato, onion, 1 Tbsp. salt, pepper and water. Bring to a boil. Reduce heat; cover and simmer 1 hour or until chicken and vegetables are tender.

2. Meanwhile, for the meatballs, combine egg, bread crumbs, parsley, garlic, cheese and the remaining salt in a large bowl. Crumble beef into mixture and mix lightly but thoroughly. Shape into marble-sized balls.

3. Remove chicken meat from bones and cut into bite-sized pieces. Discard bones. Return chicken to the pot. Add meatballs and escarole; cook until meatballs are no longer pink, about 10 minutes longer.

1 CUP: 115 cal., 6g fat (2g sat. fat), 33mg chol., 402mg sod., 7g carb. (2g sugars, 1g fiber), 9g pro.

ITALIAN SAUSAGE & QUINOA STEW

I like how the sweetness of the orange and yellow peppers blends with the spiciness of the Italian sausage. If you have trouble finding quinoa, substitute rice or tiny pasta in this recipe.
—*Marietta Slater, Justin, TX*

PREP: 20 MIN. • **COOK:** 5 HOURS • **MAKES:** 8 SERVINGS

5 **Italian sausage links (4 oz. each), casings removed**
½ **cup chopped onion**
1 **can (16 oz.) kidney beans, rinsed and drained**
1 **can (15¼ oz.) whole kernel corn, drained**
1 **each medium green, sweet orange and yellow peppers, cut into ¾-in. pieces**
1 **cup quinoa, rinsed**
1 **medium zucchini, cut in half lengthwise and sliced into ¼-in. slices**
3 **garlic cloves, minced**
1 **tsp. ground cumin**
1 **tsp. dried oregano**
¾ **tsp. salt**
½ **tsp. crushed red pepper flakes**
¼ **tsp. pepper**
1 **can (14½ oz.) diced tomatoes, undrained**
1 **(14½ oz.) can beef broth**
Minced fresh cilantro

1. In a large skillet, cook sausage and onion over medium heat 5-7 minutes or until sausage is no longer pink, breaking sausage into large crumbles; drain.

2. Transfer sausage and onion to a 4- or 5-qt. slow cooker. Stir in beans, corn, peppers, quinoa, zucchini, garlic, seasonings, tomatoes and broth. Cook, covered, on low until vegetables and quinoa are tender, 5-6 hours. Sprinkle with cilantro.

1 SERVING: 363 cal., 17g fat (5g sat. fat), 38mg chol., 1188mg sod., 36g carb. (9g sugars, 8g fiber), 17g pro.

"This was amazing and so easy to make. I used an Instant Pot for 45 minutes on pressure-cook and it was delicious."
—BILL, TASTEOFHOME.COM

EMPANADA BEEF CHILI

While I lived in Mexico in the 1960s, a friend's mother gave me her grandmother's empanada recipe. I've made it over the years and passed it down to my grandchildren. Eventually I converted the recipe into a chili.
—*Nancy Heishman, Las Vegas, NV*

PREP: 20 MIN. • **COOK:** 1½ HOURS • **MAKES:** 6 SERVINGS

1½ lbs. boneless beef chuck steak, cut into ¾-in. pieces
½ tsp. salt
½ tsp. pepper
4 tsp. canola oil, divided
1 medium onion, chopped
2 garlic cloves, minced
1 can (6 oz.) tomato paste
2 tsp. ground chipotle pepper
2 tsp. ground cinnamon
2½ cups beef broth
1 can (4 oz.) chopped green chiles
½ cup raisins
3 Tbsp. minced fresh cilantro
1 can (15 oz.) black beans, rinsed and drained
1 can (2¼ oz.) sliced ripe olives, drained
Optional toppings: Shredded Mexican cheese blend, minced fresh cilantro and chopped walnuts

1. Toss beef with salt and pepper. In a Dutch oven, heat 2 tsp. oil over medium heat. Brown beef in batches; remove from pan.

2. Add onion and remaining oil to same pan; cook and stir 2-3 minutes or until onion is tender. Add garlic; cook 1 minute longer. Stir in tomato paste, chipotle pepper and cinnamon; cook and stir 3 minutes. Stir in broth, green chiles, raisins and cilantro. Return beef to pan; bring to a boil. Reduce heat; simmer, covered, 1 hour or until beef is tender.

3. Stir in beans and olives; cook, uncovered, 10 minutes. If desired, serve with toppings.

1 CUP: 373 cal., 16g fat (5g sat. fat), 74mg chol., 957mg sod., 30g carb. (11g sugars, 6g fiber), 29g pro.

GRANDMA'S SECRET

No ground chipotle? You can substitute 1½ tsp. of smoked paprika, plus chili powder and/or cayenne to make 2 tsp.

CHICKPEA & POTATO CURRY

I make chana masala, the classic Indian dish, in my slow cooker.
Browning the onion, ginger and garlic first really makes the sauce amazing.
—*Anjana Devasahayam, San Antonio, TX*

PREP: 25 MIN. • COOK: 6 HOURS • MAKES: 6 SERVINGS

1 Tbsp. canola oil
1 medium onion, chopped
2 garlic cloves, minced
2 tsp. minced fresh gingerroot
2 tsp. ground coriander
1 tsp. garam masala
1 tsp. chili powder
½ tsp. salt
½ tsp. ground cumin
¼ tsp. ground turmeric
1 can (15 oz.) crushed tomatoes
2 cans (15 oz. each) chickpeas or garbanzo beans, rinsed and drained
1 large baking potato, peeled and cut into ¾-in. cubes
2½ cups vegetable stock
1 Tbsp. lime juice
Chopped fresh cilantro
Hot cooked rice
Optional: Sliced red onion and lime wedges

1. In a large skillet, heat oil over medium-high heat; saute onion until tender, 2-4 minutes. Add garlic, ginger and dry seasonings; cook and stir 1 minute. Stir in tomatoes; transfer to a 3- or 4-qt. slow cooker.

2. Stir in chickpeas, potato and stock. Cook, covered, on low until potato is tender and flavors are blended, 6-8 hours.

3. Stir in lime juice; sprinkle with cilantro. Serve with rice and, if desired, red onion and lime wedges.

1¼ CUPS CHICKPEA MIXTURE: 240 cal., 6g fat (0 sat. fat), 0 chol., 767mg sod., 42g carb. (8g sugars, 9g fiber), 8g pro.

FROM GRANDMA'S KITCHEN: Indian curry comprises a diverse range of dishes, but what they all have in common is a sauce that's rich and loaded with spices and seasonings. Different spice blends give each curry its signature taste.

SAUSAGE & KALE
LENTIL STEW

GRANDMA'S SECRET

Lentils are an economical, healthy way to stretch the meat in a recipe. Here, the lentils provide 6g of protein and 3g of fiber per serving!

SAUSAGE & KALE LENTIL STEW

I made a pot of this soup when visiting my sister and her family.
Now I bring it along when I stop by, or I pack up a few containers for my
nephew, who appreciates a home-cooked meal while he's away at college.
—Tiffany Ihle, Bronx, NY

PREP: 20 MIN. • **COOK:** 45 MIN. • **MAKES:** 6 SERVINGS (2 QT.)

1 **lb. bulk pork sausage**
10 **baby carrots, chopped (about ¾ cup)**
1 **small onion, finely chopped**
4 **garlic cloves, minced**
4 **plum tomatoes, halved**
¾ **cup roasted sweet red peppers**
1 **cup dried lentils, rinsed**
2 **cans (14½ oz. each) vegetable broth**
1 **bay leaf**
½ **tsp. ground cumin**
¼ **tsp. pepper**
2 **cups coarsely chopped fresh kale**

1. In a Dutch oven, cook sausage, carrots and onion over medium-high heat until sausage is no longer pink, breaking up sausage into crumbles, 8-10 minutes. Stir in garlic; cook 2 minutes longer. Drain.

2. Place tomatoes and red peppers in a food processor; process until finely chopped. Add to sausage mixture; stir in lentils, broth and seasonings. Bring to a boil. Reduce heat; simmer, covered, 20 minutes, stirring occasionally.

3. Stir in kale; cook until lentils and kale are tender, 10-15 minutes. Remove bay leaf.

FREEZE OPTION: Freeze cooled stew in freezer containers. To use, partially thaw in refrigerator overnight. Heat through in a saucepan, stirring occasionally.

1⅓ CUPS: 339 cal., 17g fat (5g sat. fat), 41mg chol., 1007mg sod., 29g carb. (5g sugars, 5g fiber), 17g pro.

ROCKY FORD CHILI

When my brother and sister were in grade school in little Rocky Ford, Colorado,
this comforting chili dish was served in the school cafeteria. My siblings described it to my
mother so she could duplicate it at home. We all enjoy preparing it for our own families now.
—Karen Sikora, Phoenix, AZ

TAKES: 10 MIN. • **MAKES:** 4 SERVINGS

2 **cans (14.3 oz. each) chili with beans**
1 **pkg. (10 oz.) frozen corn**
4 **cups corn chips**
1 **cup shredded lettuce**
1 **cup shredded Mexican cheese blend**
1 **can (2¼ oz.) sliced ripe olives, drained**
¼ **cup sour cream**
¼ **cup salsa**

In a large microwave-safe bowl, cook chili and corn on high for 2-4 minutes or until heated through. Place corn chips in 4 large soup bowls; top with chili mixture, lettuce, cheese, olives, sour cream and salsa.

1 SERVING: 664 cal., 32g fat (11g sat. fat), 55mg chol., 1522mg sod., 69g carb. (6g sugars, 11g fiber), 26g pro.

ALL-AMERICAN BEEF STEW

My mother was born and raised in Japan and wasn't familiar with many
American dishes when she married my father and moved to the States.
My paternal grandmother gave her this mouthwatering recipe.
—*Frances Aldal, Antelope, CA*

PREP: 40 MIN. • **COOK:** 1¾ HOURS • **MAKES:** 8 SERVINGS (2½ QT.)

¾ cup all-purpose flour,
  divided
½ tsp. seasoned salt
½ tsp. pepper, divided
2 lbs. beef stew meat, cut
  into 1-in. cubes
1 Tbsp. olive oil
4½ cups water, divided
1 large onion, halved
  and sliced
2 Tbsp. Worcestershire
  sauce
1 Tbsp. lemon juice
2 garlic cloves, minced
1 tsp. sugar
½ tsp. salt
½ tsp. paprika
⅛ tsp. ground allspice
1 bay leaf
4 medium potatoes, cubed
6 medium carrots, sliced

1. Place ½ cup flour, seasoned salt and ¼ tsp. pepper in a large resealable plastic bag. Add beef, a few pieces at a time, and shake to coat.

2. In a Dutch oven, brown meat in oil in batches. Remove and set aside. Add 4 cups water to the pan, stirring to loosen browned bits. Add the onion, Worcestershire sauce, lemon juice, garlic, sugar, salt, paprika, allspice, bay leaf and remaining pepper. Return beef to the pan. Bring to a boil. Reduce heat; cover and simmer for 1 hour.

3. Stir in potatoes and carrots. Bring to a boil. Reduce heat; cover and simmer for 30-35 minutes or until meat and vegetables are tender.

4. Combine remaining flour and water until smooth; stir into the pan. Bring to a boil; cook and stir for 2 minutes or until thickened. Discard bay leaf.

1¼ CUPS: 324 cal., 10g fat (3g sat. fat), 70mg chol., 322mg sod., 33g carb. (6g sugars, 4g fiber), 25g pro. **DIABETIC EXCHANGES:** 3 lean meat, 2 starch, 1 vegetable.

"We have made this recipe for years over the campfire for all our friends. There's never any left!"
—BACKSEATRIDER, TASTEOFHOME.COM

GRANDMOTHER'S CHICKEN & DUMPLINGS

While I was growing up, my grandmother could feed our whole big family with a single chicken—and lots of dumplings.
—*Cathy Carroll, Bossier City, LA*

PREP: 45 MIN. + RESTING • **COOK:** 30 MIN. • **MAKES:** 10 SERVINGS (2½ QT.)

1	**large chicken (6 lbs.)**
2	**medium carrots, chopped**
2	**celery ribs, sliced**
1	**large onion, sliced**
4	**qt. water**
2	**Tbsp. white vinegar**
2	**tsp. salt**

DUMPLINGS

2	**cups all-purpose flour**
1½	**tsp. salt**
1	**large egg**
½	**cup reserved chicken broth**
½	**tsp. pepper**

1. Place the chicken, carrots, celery and onion in a large Dutch oven or stockpot. Add water, vinegar and salt (adding more water, if necessary, to cover chicken). Bring to a boil. Reduce heat; cover and simmer until meat nearly falls from the bones. Remove chicken from broth; allow to cool. Strain broth, discarding vegetables and seasonings.

2. Remove meat from bones; discard skin and bones. Cut meat into bite-sized pieces; set aside and keep warm. Set aside 1 cup broth; cool to lukewarm.

3. To make dumplings, combine flour and salt. Make a well in flour; add egg. Gradually stir ¼ cup reserved broth into egg, picking up flour as you go. Continue until flour is used up, adding additional broth as needed until dough is consistency of pie dough. Pour any remaining reserved broth back into stockpot.

4. Turn dough onto a floured surface; knead in additional flour to make a stiff dough. Let dough rest for 15 minutes. On a floured surface, roll out dough into a 17-in. square. Cut into 1-in. square pieces. Dust with additional flour; let dry for 30-60 minutes.

5. Bring broth to a boil (you should have about 4 qt.). Drop dumplings into boiling broth. Reduce heat; cover and simmer until a toothpick inserted into center of a dumpling comes out clean (do not lift the cover while simmering), about 10 minutes. Uncover; add reserved chicken. Stir in pepper.

1 CUP: 310 cal., 9g fat (2g sat. fat), 114mg chol., 981mg sod., 22g carb. (2g sugars, 1g fiber), 34g pro.

CURRIED CHICKEN SOUP

This was one of my favorite recipes that my grandmother used to make. I've added
my own touches to it, such as the chickpeas, coconut milk and fresh cilantro.
—*Deanna Hindenach, Paw Paw, MI*

PREP: 25 MIN. • **COOK:** 45 MIN. • **MAKES:** 8 SERVINGS (2½ QT.)

4 tsp. curry powder
½ tsp. salt
½ tsp. pepper
½ tsp. cayenne pepper
1 lb. boneless skinless
  chicken breasts, cubed
3 medium carrots, chopped
1 medium sweet red
  pepper, chopped
1 small onion, chopped
2 Tbsp. olive oil
1 garlic clove, minced
1 can (15 oz.) garbanzo
  beans or chickpeas,
  rinsed and drained
1 can (14½ oz.) chicken
  broth
1 can (14½ oz.) diced
  tomatoes, drained
1 cup water
1 can (13⅔ oz.)
  coconut milk
¾ cup minced fresh cilantro

1. In a large shallow dish, combine the curry, salt, pepper and cayenne. Add chicken, a few pieces at a time, and turn to coat.

2. In a large saucepan over medium heat, cook the chicken, carrots, red pepper and onion in oil for 4 minutes. Add garlic; cook 1-2 minutes longer or until chicken is browned and vegetables are tender; drain.

3. Stir in the garbanzo beans, broth, tomatoes and water. Bring to a boil. Reduce heat; cover and simmer for 30 minutes. Stir in coconut milk; heat through. Garnish servings with cilantro.

1¼ CUPS: 270 cal., 16g fat (10g sat. fat), 32mg chol., 555mg sod., 17g carb. (5g sugars, 5g fiber), 16g pro.

OLD-FASHIONED TOMATO SOUP

My mother made this soup when I was a child, and it was always one of my favorites. After 75 years,
it still is! Mother's cellar was filled with home-canned vegetables, so the basic ingredient of this
soup was right at hand. It never took her long to make a kettle of this wonderful soup.
—*Wilma Miller, Port Angeles, WA*

TAKES: 20 MIN. • **MAKES:** 6 SERVINGS (1½ QT.)

1 can (14½ oz.) diced
  tomatoes, undrained
½ tsp. baking soda
¼ to ½ tsp. garlic salt
⅛ tsp. pepper
  Salt to taste
1 qt. 2% milk
2 Tbsp. butter
  Minced fresh parsley,
  optional

In a large saucepan, bring tomatoes to a boil. Add baking soda, garlic salt, pepper and salt if desired. Reduce heat; add the milk and butter. Heat through, but do not boil. Garnish with parsley if desired.

NOTE: 2 cups of home-canned or freshly stewed tomatoes with liquid may be substituted for the can of tomatoes.

1 CUP: 148 cal., 9g fat (6g sat. fat), 32mg chol., 423mg sod., 10g carb. (9g sugars, 1g fiber), 6g pro.

CURRIED
CHICKEN
SOUP

MUSHROOM-BEAN BOURGUIGNON

In our family, boeuf bourguignon has been a staple for
generations. I wanted a meatless alternative.
All this dish needs is a French baguette.
—*Sonya Labbe, West Hollywood, CA*

PREP: 15 MIN. • **COOK:** 1¼ HOURS • **MAKES:** 10 SERVINGS (2½ QT.)

4 Tbsp. olive oil, divided
5 medium carrots, cut into
   1-in. pieces
2 medium onions, halved
   and sliced
2 garlic cloves, minced
8 large portobello
   mushrooms, cut into
   1-in. pieces
1 Tbsp. tomato paste
1 bottle (750 ml)
   dry red wine
2 cups mushroom broth or
   vegetable broth, divided
1 tsp. salt
1 tsp. minced fresh thyme
   or ½ tsp. dried thyme
½ tsp. pepper
2 cans (15½ oz. each) navy
   beans, rinsed
   and drained
1 pkg. (14.4 oz.) frozen
   pearl onions
3 Tbsp. all-purpose flour

1. In a Dutch oven, heat 2 Tbsp. oil over medium-high heat. Add
carrots and onions; cook and stir 8-10 minutes or until onions are
tender. Add garlic; cook 1 minute longer. Remove from pan.

2. In same pan, heat 1 Tbsp. oil over medium-high heat. Add half
the mushrooms; cook and stir until lightly browned. Remove from
pan; repeat with remaining 1 Tbsp. oil and mushrooms.

3. Return all mushrooms to pan. Add tomato paste; cook and stir
1 minute. Stir in wine, 1½ cups broth, salt, thyme, pepper and
carrot mixture; bring to a boil. Reduce heat; simmer, covered,
25 minutes.

4. Add beans and pearl onions; cook 30 minutes longer. In a small
bowl, whisk flour and remaining broth until smooth; stir into the
pan. Bring to a boil; cook and stir until slightly thickened, about
2 minutes.

1 CUP: 234 cal., 6g fat (1g sat. fat), 0 chol., 613mg sod., 33g carb.
(6g sugars, 7g fiber), 9g pro. **DIABETIC EXCHANGES:** 2 starch,
2 vegetable, 1 lean meat, 1 fat.

FROM GRANDMA'S KITCHEN: Freeze leftover tomato paste in
tablespoon-sized scoops on a plastic wrap-lined plate, then store
the portions in a freezer container. Or keep a tube of tomato paste
on hand. It's convenient because it keeps a long time in the fridge.

CHICKEN POTPIE SOUP

My grandmother hand-wrote a cookbook; she created this
amazing pie crust, and I added the delicious soup for it.
—*Karen LeMay, Seabrook, TX*

PREP: 20 MIN. + CHILLING • COOK: 20 MIN. • MAKES: 6 SERVINGS (2¼ QT.)

2 **cups all-purpose flour**
1¼ **tsp. salt**
⅔ **cup shortening**
5 **to 6 Tbsp. 2% milk**

SOUP
2 **Tbsp. butter**
1 **cup cubed peeled
    potatoes**
1 **cup chopped sweet onion**
2 **celery ribs, chopped**
2 **medium carrots, chopped**
½ **cup all-purpose flour**
½ **tsp. salt**
¼ **tsp. pepper**
3 **cans (14½ oz. each)
    chicken broth**
2 **cups shredded cooked
    chicken**
1 **cup frozen petite peas**
1 **cup frozen corn**

1. In a large bowl, mix flour and salt; cut in shortening until crumbly. Gradually add milk, tossing with a fork until dough holds together when pressed. Shape into a disk, cover and refrigerate for 30 minutes or overnight.

2. Preheat oven to 425°. On a lightly floured surface, roll dough to ⅛-in. thickness. Using a floured 2½-in. heart-shaped or round cutter, cut 18 shapes. Place 1 in. apart on ungreased baking sheets. Bake for 8-11 minutes or until golden brown. Cool on a wire rack.

3. For soup, heat butter in a Dutch oven over medium-high heat. Add the potatoes, onion, celery and carrots; cook and stir for 5-7 minutes or until onion is tender.

4. Stir in the flour, salt and pepper until blended; gradually whisk in broth. Bring to a boil over medium-high heat, stirring occasionally. Reduce heat; simmer, uncovered, for 8-10 minutes or until potatoes are tender. Stir in remaining ingredients; heat through. Serve with pie crust toppers.

1½ CUPS SOUP WITH 3 TOPPERS: 614 cal., 30g fat (9g sat. fat), 57mg chol., 1706mg sod., 60g carb. (7g sugars, 5g fiber), 23g pro.

GRANDMA'S SECRET

The pastry toppers are cute but time-consuming. Instead, you can steam dumplings on top using the recipe on p. 179. Use ¼ tsp. dried thyme instead of the basil and oregano.

THE BEST BEEF STEW

Our best beef stew recipe has tons of flavor, thanks to its blend of herbs and the addition of red wine and balsamic vinegar. Learn how to make this comforting classic and take it to the next level.

—*James Schend, Pleasant Prairie, WI*

PREP: 30 MIN. • COOK: 2 HOURS • MAKES: 6 SERVINGS (2¼ QT.)

1½ lbs. beef stew meat,
    cut into 1-in. cubes
½ tsp. salt, divided
6 Tbsp. all-purpose flour,
    divided
½ tsp. smoked paprika
1 Tbsp. canola oil
3 Tbsp. tomato paste
2 tsp. herbes de Provence
2 garlic cloves, minced
2 cups dry red wine
2 cups beef broth
1½ tsp. minced fresh
    rosemary, divided
2 bay leaves
3 cups cubed peeled
    potatoes
3 cups coarsely chopped
    onions (about 2 large)
2 cups sliced carrots
2 Tbsp. cold water
2 Tbsp. balsamic or red
    wine vinegar
1 cup fresh or frozen peas
    Additional fresh
    rosemary, optional

1. In a small bowl, toss beef and ¼ tsp. salt. In a large bowl, combine 4 Tbsp. flour and paprika. Add beef, a few pieces at a time, and toss to coat.

2. In a Dutch oven, brown beef in oil over medium heat. Stir in tomato paste, herbes de Provence and garlic; cook until fragrant and the color starts to darken slightly. Add wine; cook until the mixture just comes to a boil. Simmer until reduced by half, about 5 minutes. Stir in broth, 1 tsp. rosemary and bay leaves. Bring to a boil. Reduce heat; cover and simmer until meat is almost tender, about 1½ hours.

3. Add potatoes, onions and carrots. Cover; simmer until meat and vegetables are tender, about 30 minutes longer.

4. Discard bay leaves. In a small bowl, combine remaining ½ tsp. rosemary, remaining ¼ tsp. salt and remaining 2 Tbsp. flour. Add cold water and vinegar; stir until smooth. Stir into stew. Bring to a boil; add peas. Cook, stirring, until thickened, about 2 minutes. If desired, top with additional fresh rosemary.

1½ CUPS: 366 cal., 11g fat (3g sat. fat), 71mg chol., 605mg sod., 40g carb. (9g sugars, 6g fiber), 28g pro. DIABETIC EXCHANGES: 3 lean meat, 2½ starch, ½ fat.

FROM GRANDMA'S KITCHEN: We recommend using chuck, also known as front shoulder meat, for this beef stew. The round, or rear muscle, also works well. While these tough cuts take time to become tender, they release collagen as they cook for a smooth, gelatin-rich broth.

MOROCCAN APPLE BEEF STEW

I love the mix of sweet and savory flavors in this stew. It's the perfect blend of adventurous and comforting, and makes a fun dish to share with guests.

—*Trisha Kruse, Eagle, ID*

PREP: 20 MIN. • **COOK:** 2 HOURS • **MAKES:** 8 SERVINGS (2 QT.)

1¼ tsp. salt
½ tsp. ground cinnamon
½ tsp. pepper
¼ tsp. ground allspice
2½ lbs. beef stew meat, cut into 1-in. pieces
2 to 3 Tbsp. olive oil
1 large onion, chopped (about 2 cups)
3 garlic cloves, minced
1 can (15 oz.) tomato sauce
1 can (14½ oz.) beef broth
1 cup pitted dried plums (prunes), coarsely chopped
1 Tbsp. honey
2 medium Fuji or Gala apples, peeled and cut into 1½-in. pieces
Hot cooked rice or couscous, optional

1. Mix salt, cinnamon, pepper and allspice; sprinkle over beef and toss to coat. In a Dutch oven, heat 2 Tbsp. oil over medium heat.

2. Brown beef in batches, adding more oil as necessary. Remove beef with a slotted spoon.

3. Add onion to same pan; cook and stir until tender, 6-8 minutes. Add garlic; cook 1 minute longer. Stir in tomato sauce, broth, dried plums and honey. Return beef to pan; bring to a boil. Reduce heat; simmer, covered, 1½ hours.

4. Add apples; cook, covered, until beef and apples are tender, 30-45 minutes longer. Skim fat. If desired, serve stew with rice or couscous.

FREEZE OPTION: Freeze cooled stew in freezer containers. To use, partially thaw in refrigerator overnight. Heat through in a saucepan, stirring occasionally; add broth if necessary.

1 CUP: 339 cal., 13g fat (4g sat. fat), 88mg chol., 905mg sod., 24g carb. (14g sugars, 2g fiber), 29g pro.

"I made this exactly as written, and it was fantastic! At first I thought maybe next time I'd add extra prunes, because they seemed to disappear, but the prune flavor survived with this amount. I don't normally like too much sweetness in a main dish—and this was just right. Oh, and the aroma while it was simmering was heavenly!"

—DREJKA, TASTEOFHOME.COM

LOBSTER BISQUE

My grandmother would make lobster bisque all the time, so I always thought of it as comfort food. If you don't care to cook live lobsters, they can usually cook it where you buy them. Just be sure to tell them you want to keep the shells; they are key to the most delicious soup!
—*James Schend, Pleasant Prairie, WI*

PREP: 35 MIN. • COOK: 1¾ HOURS • MAKES: 8 SERVINGS (2 QT).

2 live lobsters
   (about 1 lb. each)
2 medium carrots, peeled
   and chopped
1 medium onion, chopped
3 Tbsp. butter
2 Tbsp. tomato paste
2 garlic cloves, minced
¾ cup white wine or sherry
1 carton (32 oz.) seafood
   stock

⅔ cup uncooked
   long grain rice
2 cups heavy whipping
   cream
1 tsp. minced fresh thyme
1½ tsp. salt
1 tsp. coarsely ground
   pepper
   Minced fresh parsley,
   optional

1. In a Dutch oven, add 2 in. water; bring to a rolling boil. Add lobsters, cover, and steam for 8 minutes. Remove lobsters, reserving liquid. When cool enough to handle, remove meat from claws and tail, reserving any juices; refrigerate meat and juices.

2. In the same Dutch oven, cook carrots and onion in butter over medium-high heat until tender, 5-8 minutes. Stir in tomato paste and cook until it starts to caramelize, about 5 minutes. Add garlic; cook 1 minute. Stir in wine and simmer until reduced by half. Add lobster shells, bodies, reserved cooking liquid, reserved lobster juices and stock. Bring mixture to a simmer; cook 1 hour. Strain mixture, pressing to extract as much liquid as possible; discard shells and solids.

3. Return liquid to Dutch oven. Add rice and cook until extremely soft, 25-30 minutes. Puree in a blender until smooth. Add cream, thyme, salt and pepper. Bring mixture to very low simmer; add reserved lobster meat and cook until heated through. If desired, sprinkle with additional ground pepper and parsley.

1 CUP: 373 cal., 26g fat (17g sat. fat), 127mg chol., 942mg sod., 20g carb. (4g sugars, 1g fiber), 10g pro.

ENGLISH PUB SPLIT PEA SOUP

This family favorite is the same recipe my grandmother used. Now with the magic of the slow cooker, I can spend 15 minutes putting it together, walk away for 5 hours, and come back to soup. Finish it with more milk if you like your soup a bit thinner.

—Judy Batson, Tampa, FL

PREP: 15 MIN. • COOK: 5 HOURS • MAKES: 8 SERVINGS (2 QT.)

1   meaty ham bone
1⅓ cups dried green split
    peas, rinsed
2   celery ribs, chopped
1   large carrot, chopped
1   sweet onion, chopped
4   cups water
1   bottle (12 oz.) light beer
1   Tbsp. prepared English
    mustard
½   cup 2% milk
¼   cup minced fresh parsley
½   tsp. salt
¼   tsp. pepper
¼   tsp. ground nutmeg
    Additional minced fresh
    parsley, optional

1. Place ham bone in a 4-qt. slow cooker. Add peas, celery, carrot and onion. Combine water, beer and mustard; pour over vegetables. Cook, covered, on high 5-6 hours or until the peas are tender.

2. Remove ham bone from soup. Cool slightly, trim away fat and remove meat from bone; discard fat and bone. Cut meat into bite-sized pieces; return to slow cooker. Stir in remaining ingredients. If desired, top with additional minced parsley.

1 CUP: 141 cal., 1g fat (0 sat. fat), 1mg chol., 193mg sod., 25g carb. (6g sugars, 9g fiber), 9g pro. DIABETIC EXCHANGES: 1½ starch, 1 lean meat.

FROM GRANDMA'S KITCHEN: We used Coleman's prepared mustard when testing this recipe. If you can't find English mustard, horseradish mustard is a good substitute.

CORN CHOWDER

My grandmother and mother made this dish to warm their families during the cold winter months. Nothing chased away a chill like this chowder! Now when it's cold and damp outside, I make this dish and think of those days. Everyone in my house enjoys the delicious warmth of a steaming bowl of Corn Chowder.

—Phyllis Watson, Havelock, NC

TAKES: 30 MIN. • MAKES: 6 SERVINGS (1½ QT.)

6   potatoes, peeled and
    diced
    Water
1   can (16 oz.) whole kernel
    corn, drained
4   cups whole milk
1   large onion, diced
4   bacon strips, cooked and
    crumbled
1   tsp. salt
¼   tsp. pepper
¼   tsp. dried thyme

Place potatoes in a Dutch oven and cover with water. Bring to a boil. Reduce heat; cover and cook for 10-15 minutes or until tender. Drain. Add remaining ingredients; bring to a boil. Reduce heat and simmer for 15 minutes or until onion is soft.

1 CUP: 357 cal., 8g fat (4g sat. fat), 26mg chol., 760mg sod., 57g carb. (15g sugars, 5g fiber), 13g pro.

ENGLISH PUB
SPLIT PEA SOUP

EGG YOLK COOKIES,
PAGE 223

COOKIES, BROWNIES & BARS

New cookie-jar treats are always debuting at Grandma's house. These good old-fashioned sweets are made to share. Take two, we won't tell!

MEXICAN CHOCOLATE SUGAR CRISPS

My grandma loved these so much, she would hide them from my grandpa!
I think of her every time I make a batch. Like Mexican spice? Try stirring in a little chili powder.
—*Michele Lovio, Thousand Oaks, CA*

PREP: 30 MIN. • BAKE: 10 MIN./BATCH • MAKES: 4½ DOZEN

¾ **cup shortening**
1¼ **cups sugar, divided**
1 **large egg, room temperature**
¼ **cup light corn syrup**
2 **oz. unsweetened chocolate, melted and cooled**
1¾ **cups all-purpose flour**
1½ **tsp. ground cinnamon**
1 **tsp. baking soda**
¼ **tsp. salt**
1 **cup semisweet chocolate chips**

1. Preheat oven to 350°. In a large bowl, cream shortening and 1 cup sugar until fluffy, 5-7 minutes. Beat in egg, corn syrup and melted chocolate. In another bowl, whisk flour, cinnamon, baking soda and salt; gradually beat into creamed mixture. Stir in chocolate chips.

2. Shape dough into 1-in. balls; roll in remaining sugar. Place cookies 2 in. apart on ungreased baking sheets (do not flatten). Bake until tops are puffed and cracked, 8-10 minutes. Cool on pans 2 minutes. Remove to wire racks to cool.

TO MAKE AHEAD: Dough can be made 2 days in advance. Refrigerate in an airtight container and refrigerate.

FREEZE OPTION: Freeze shaped balls of dough on baking sheets until firm. Transfer to airtight containers; return to freezer. To use, bake cookies as directed.

1 COOKIE: 85 cal., 4g fat (2g sat. fat), 3mg chol., 37mg sod., 11g carb. (8g sugars, 1g fiber), 1g pro.

"I made these last year for a Christmas cookie swap party, and they were the hit of the party."
—JELLYBUG, TASTEOFHOME.COM

FUDGY S'MORES BROWNIES

I combined the perfect, simple summer snack with my favorite brownie recipe to get a treat that's sure to wow at your next big party.
—*Judy Cunningham, Max, ND*

PREP: 15 MIN. • BAKE: 25 MIN. + COOLING • MAKES: 1 DOZEN

1⅓ cups butter, softened
2⅔ cups sugar
4 large eggs, room temperature
1 Tbsp. vanilla extract
2 cups all-purpose flour
1 cup baking cocoa
½ tsp. salt
1 cup Golden Grahams, coarsely crushed
1¾ cups miniature marshmallows
4 oz. milk chocolate, chopped

1. Preheat oven to 350°. In a large bowl, cream butter and sugar until light and fluffy, 5-7 minutes. Beat in eggs and vanilla. Mix flour, cocoa and salt; gradually beat into creamed mixture.

2. Spread into a greased 13x9-in. baking pan. Bake 25-30 minutes or until a toothpick inserted in center comes out with moist crumbs (do not overbake).

3. Preheat broiler. Sprinkle brownies with cereal and marshmallows; broil 5-6 in. from heat until golden brown, 30-45 seconds. Immediately sprinkle with chopped chocolate. Cover with foil and let stand until chocolate begins to melt, about 5 minutes. Remove foil and cool completely in pan on a wire rack.

1 BROWNIE: 560 cal., 26g fat (15g sat. fat), 118mg chol., 321mg sod., 80g carb. (56g sugars, 2g fiber), 7g pro.

GRANDMA'S CHEWY OATMEAL COOKIES

For a large batch of cookies without much time in the kitchen, consider these down-home treats. Ever since my husband's grandmother gave me this special recipe, it's been the only one I use.
—*Donna Trumbauer, Coopersburg, PA*

PREP: 15 MIN. • BAKE: 15 MIN./BATCH • MAKES: 7 DOZEN

2 cups butter, softened
1½ cups packed brown sugar
½ cup sugar
4 large eggs, room temperature
7 cups quick-cooking oats
2½ cups all-purpose flour
1 pkg. (5.1 oz.) instant vanilla pudding mix
2 tsp. baking soda

1. In a large bowl, cream butter and sugars until light and fluffy, 5-7 minutes. Add eggs, 1 at a time, beating well after each addition. Combine the oats, flour, dry pudding mix and baking soda; gradually add to the creamed mixture and mix well.

2. Drop by heaping tablespoonfuls 2 in. apart onto lightly greased baking sheets. Bake at 375° until golden brown, 12-14 minutes. Remove to wire racks to cool.

2 COOKIES: 214 cal., 10g fat (6g sat. fat), 44mg chol., 206mg sod., 28g carb. (13g sugars, 1g fiber), 4g pro.

PECAN SHORTBREAD TEA CAKES

My Grandma Ellis made her shortbread cookies only at Christmas
because the ingredients were so indulgent. The results are, too!
—*Trisha Kruse, Eagle, ID*

PREP: 45 MIN. • **BAKE:** 10 MIN./BATCH + COOLING • **MAKES:** ABOUT 6 DOZEN

2 **cups butter, softened**
½ **cup sugar**
½ **cup packed brown sugar**
2 **tsp. vanilla extract**
4 **cups all-purpose flour**
½ **tsp. salt**
72 **pecan halves, toasted**

CARAMEL GLAZE

½ **cup packed brown sugar**
3 **Tbsp. 2% milk**
2 **Tbsp. butter**
1½ **cups confectioners' sugar**
1 **Tbsp. brandy**

1. Preheat oven to 350°. Cream butter and sugars until light and fluffy, 5-7 minutes. Beat in vanilla. In another bowl, whisk together flour and salt; gradually add to creamed mixture and mix well. Roll into 1-in. balls; place in greased miniature muffin cups. Lightly press a pecan half into the center of each. Bake until edges are lightly browned, 10-12 minutes. Cool for 10 minutes before removing from pans to wire racks.

2. For caramel glaze, combine brown sugar, milk and butter in a small saucepan over medium heat. Bring to a boil; cook and stir 1 minute. Remove from heat; cool 5 minutes. Gradually beat in confectioners' sugar and brandy. Drizzle over cookies.

1 COOKIE: 112 cal., 7g fat (4g sat. fat), 14mg chol., 61mg sod., 12g carb. (7g sugars, 0 fiber), 1g pro.

GRANDMA'S POLISH COOKIES

This traditional *khruchiki* recipe has been handed down through my mother's side from my
great-grandmother. As a child, it was my job to loop the end of each cookie through its hole.
—*Sherine Elise Gilmour, Brooklyn, NY*

PREP: 45 MIN. • **COOK:** 5 MIN./BATCH • **MAKES:** 20 COOKIES

4 **cups all-purpose flour**
1 **tsp. salt**
1 **cup cold butter**
4 **large egg yolks, room temperature**
1 **cup evaporated milk**
2 **tsp. vanilla extract**
Oil for deep-fat frying
Confectioners' sugar

1. In a large bowl, combine flour and salt. Cut in butter until mixture resembles coarse crumbs. In another bowl, beat egg yolks until foamy; add milk and vanilla. Stir into crumb mixture until dough is stiff enough to knead.

2. Turn onto a lightly floured surface; knead 8-10 times. Divide dough into 4 pieces. Roll each portion into a ¼-in.-thick rectangle; cut into 4x1½-in. strips. Cut a 2-in. lengthwise slit down the middle of each strip; pull 1 of the ends through the slit like a bow.

3. In an electric skillet or deep-fat fryer, heat oil to 375°. Fry dough strips, a few at a time, until golden brown on both sides, about 5 minutes. Drain on paper towels. Dust cookies with confectioners' sugar.

1 COOKIE: 246 cal., 16g fat (7g sat. fat), 65mg chol., 205mg sod., 20g carb. (1g sugars, 1g fiber), 4g pro.

POMEGRANATE
MAGIC BARS

POMEGRANATE MAGIC BARS

Pomegranates make dessert festive and bright with a burst of juicy sweetness.
My mom taught me how to easily collect the seeds: Slice the fresh pomegranate into
quarters and submerge the pieces in a bowl of water. Gently separate the seeds from the shells
with your fingers. The seeds will fall to the bottom of the bowl, while the fibrous pieces
will float to the top. I think she was happy not to get the red juice all over her counters.
—*Lisa Keys, Kennet Square, PA*

PREP: 45 MIN. • BAKE: 25 MIN. + COOLING • MAKES: 3 DOZEN

1¼ cups all-purpose flour
¾ cup sugar
¼ cup baking cocoa
¾ cup cold butter, cubed
1 large egg, room temperature
½ tsp. vanilla extract
1 Tbsp. sesame seeds, toasted
1 cup sweetened shredded coconut, toasted
½ cup slivered almonds, toasted
2 cups (12 oz.) semisweet chocolate chips
1 can (14 oz.) sweetened condensed milk
1 cup pomegranate seeds

1. Preheat oven to 350°. Line a 13x9-in. pan with parchment, letting ends extend up the sides. Lightly grease parchment with cooking spray. In a food processor, combine the flour, sugar and cocoa; pulse until combined. Add butter; pulse until mixture appears sandy. Add egg and vanilla; pulse just until combined. Press dough into prepared pan.

2. Sprinkle dough with sesame seeds. Bake until top appears dry and toothpick comes out clean, 20-25 minutes. Remove from oven; sprinkle evenly with coconut, almonds and chocolate chips. Pour condensed milk evenly over top; return to oven. Bake until golden brown, 25-30 minutes. Cool on wire rack 10 minutes.

3. Sprinkle with pomegranate seeds; press gently into warm topping with back of a spoon. Cool completely in pan on wire rack. Lifting with parchment, remove from pan. Cut into bars.

1 BAR: 176 cal., 10g fat (6g sat. fat), 19mg chol., 55mg sod., 22g carb. (17g sugars, 1g fiber), 3g pro.

FROSTED ANISE COOKIES

I love anise flavoring, and my nana loved sugar cookies, so I put them together.
These have a soft, from-scratch texture. It's hard to stop at just one!
—*Rachele Angeloni, North Providence, RI*

PREP: 30 MIN. • BAKE: 10 MIN./BATCH + COOLING • MAKES: 3½ DOZEN

1 cup butter, softened
1½ cups sugar
1 large egg, room temperature
1 tsp. anise extract
2¾ cups all-purpose flour
1 tsp. baking soda
½ tsp. baking powder
1 can (16 oz.) vanilla frosting
Holiday sprinkles

1. Cream butter and sugar in a large bowl until light and fluffy, 5-7 minutes. Beat in egg and extract. Combine flour, baking soda and baking powder; gradually add to creamed mixture; mix well.

2. Drop by tablespoonfuls 2 in. apart onto ungreased baking sheets. Bake at 375° until golden brown, 9-11 minutes. Remove to wire racks to cool completely.

3. Spread cookies with frosting and decorate with sprinkles. Let stand until set. Store in an airtight container.

1 COOKIE: 144 cal., 6g fat (4g sat. fat), 16mg chol., 95mg sod., 21g carb. (13g sugars, 0 fiber), 1g pro.

CREAM FILBERTS

These cookies remind me of mothball candy I used to buy with dimes Grandma gave me. The filbert, which is another name for hazelnut, is a nice crunchy surprise in the middle of the cookie.
—*Deanna Richter, Elmore, MN*

PREP: 25 MIN. • **BAKE:** 15 MIN./BATCH + COOLING • **MAKES:** ABOUT 5 DOZEN

1 cup shortening
¾ cup sugar
1 large egg, room temperature
1 tsp. vanilla extract
2½ cups all-purpose flour
½ tsp. baking powder
⅛ tsp. salt
¾ cup whole hazelnuts

GLAZE
2 cups confectioners' sugar
3 Tbsp. water
2 tsp. vanilla extract
Sugar

1. In a large bowl, cream shortening and sugar until light and fluffy, 5-7 minutes. Beat in egg and vanilla. Combine the dry ingredients and gradually add to creamed mixture.

2. Roll heaping teaspoonfuls of dough into balls; press a hazelnut into each and reshape balls. Place 2 in. apart on ungreased baking sheets.

3. Bake at 375° until lightly browned, 12-15 minutes. Cool on wire racks. In a bowl, combine the confectioners' sugar, water and vanilla until smooth; dip tops of cookies in glaze. Sprinkle with sugar.

1 COOKIE: 84 cal., 4g fat (1g sat. fat), 4mg chol., 9mg sod., 11g carb. (6g sugars, 0 fiber), 1g pro.

GRANDMA'S OATMEAL DATE BARS

While I was growing up, my grandma would fix this dessert at Christmas. This recipe reminds me of her. And now I fix the bars for my family.
—*Nancy Hawkins, Brookville, IN*

PREP: 30 MIN. • **BAKE:** 25 MIN. • **MAKES:** 2 DOZEN

1 lb. pitted dates, quartered
1½ cups water
½ cup sugar
1½ cups all-purpose flour
1½ cups old-fashioned oats
1 cup packed brown sugar
1 tsp. vanilla extract
½ tsp. baking soda
½ tsp. salt
¼ tsp. almond extract
¾ cup shortening
Whipped cream, optional

1. Preheat oven to 350°. In a small saucepan, combine dates, water and sugar. Bring to a boil. Reduce heat; simmer, uncovered, until thickened and dates are tender, stirring constantly, 7-9 minutes. Remove from heat.

2. In a large bowl, combine flour, oats, brown sugar, vanilla, baking soda, salt and almond extract. Cut in shortening until crumbly. Press half onto bottom of a greased 13x9-in. baking dish. Carefully spread with date mixture.

3. Sprinkle remaining crumb mixture over filling; press down gently. Bake until lightly browned, 25-30 minutes. Cool on a wire rack. Cut into bars. If desired, serve with whipped cream.

1 BAR: 207 cal., 7g fat (2g sat. fat), 0 chol., 79mg sod., 37g carb. (25g sugars, 2g fiber), 2g pro.

TRIPLE GINGER COOKIES

My dad loved ginger cookies. I tinkered with the recipe my grandma handed down by using fresh, ground and crystallized ginger for more pizzazz.
—*Trisha Kruse, Eagle, ID*

PREP: 20 MIN. + CHILLING • **BAKE:** 15 MIN./BATCH + COOLING
MAKES: ABOUT 2½ DOZEN

½ cup butter, softened
½ cup packed brown sugar
1 large egg, room temperature
3 Tbsp. molasses
½ tsp. grated fresh gingerroot
2¼ cups all-purpose flour
½ tsp. baking powder

½ tsp. ground ginger
¼ tsp. salt
¼ tsp. baking soda

ICING

½ cup confectioners' sugar
2 to 3 tsp. water
¼ cup finely chopped crystallized ginger

1. Preheat oven to 350°. In a large bowl, cream butter and brown sugar until light and fluffy, 5-7 minutes. Beat in egg, molasses and fresh ginger. In another bowl, whisk flour, baking powder, ground ginger, salt and baking soda; gradually beat into creamed mixture. Refrigerate, covered, 2 hours or until firm enough to handle.

2. Shape dough by tablespoonfuls into balls; place 1 in. apart on ungreased baking sheets. Flatten slightly with the bottom of a glass. Bake until cookies are set and edges begin to brown, 12-14 minutes. Remove to wire racks to cool completely.

3. For icing, in a small bowl, mix confectioners' sugar and enough water to reach desired consistency. Drizzle over cookies; sprinkle with crystallized ginger.

1 COOKIE: 97 cal., 3g fat (2g sat. fat), 15mg chol., 64mg sod., 16g carb. (7g sugars, 0 fiber), 1g pro.

GRANDMA'S SECRET

If you have access to an Asian grocery, you can find crystallized ginger there for far less than the grocery store. You'll save up to 75% on it and other spice-cabinet ingredients.

MOM'S CHOCOLATE CHIP COOKIES

My mom always brightened my lunch with these yummy cookies.
—*Tammy Orr, Wharton, NJ*

PREP: 20 MIN. • BAKE: 10 MIN./BATCH • MAKES: 4 DOZEN

1 cup butter, softened
¾ cup packed brown sugar
¼ cup sugar
1 pkg. (3.4 oz.) instant vanilla pudding mix
2 large eggs, room temperature, lightly beaten
1 tsp. vanilla extract
2¼ cups all-purpose flour
1 tsp. baking soda
2 cups semisweet chocolate chips

Preheat oven to 375°. In a bowl, cream butter and sugars until light and fluffy, 5-7 minutes. Add pudding mix, eggs and vanilla. Combine flour and baking soda; add to creamed mixture and mix well. Fold in chocolate chips. Drop by teaspoonfuls onto ungreased baking sheets. Bake cookies until lightly browned, 10-12 minutes.

1 COOKIE: 117 cal., 5g fat (3g sat. fat), 8mg chol., 45mg sod., 20g carb. (14g sugars, 1g fiber), 1g pro.

"By far the best chocolate chip cookie recipe! I've used this one for years and years. You can use different flavors of Instant pudding mixes and different flavors of chips. I bake mine for only 8 minutes. They're really soft, but I keep them frozen. They taste just like fresh cookies when you take them out of the freezer and you eat them frozen!"
—SHEILA, TASTEOFHOME.COM

SUPER SPUD BROWNIES

These moist and cake-like brownies came from my mom's old cookbook. Mashed potatoes may seem like an unusual ingredient, but this recipe took first place at a local festival.
—*Marlene Gerer, Denton, MT*

PREP: 15 MIN. • BAKE: 25 MIN. • MAKES: 16 SERVINGS

¾ cup mashed potatoes
½ cup sugar
½ cup packed brown sugar
½ cup canola oil
2 large eggs, room temperature, lightly beaten
1 tsp. vanilla extract
½ cup all-purpose flour
⅓ cup cocoa powder
½ tsp. baking powder
⅛ tsp. salt
½ cup chopped pecans, optional
Confectioners' sugar

1. In a large bowl, combine the mashed potatoes, sugars, oil, eggs and vanilla. Combine the flour, cocoa, baking powder and salt; gradually add to potato mixture. Fold in pecans if desired. Transfer to a greased 9-in. square baking pan.

2. Bake at 350° until toothpick inserted in the center comes out clean, 23-27 minutes. Cool on a wire rack. Dust top with confectioners' sugar. Cut into bars.

1 BROWNIE: 150 cal., 8g fat (1g sat. fat), 27mg chol., 68mg sod., 19g carb. (13g sugars, 0 fiber), 2g pro. DIABETIC EXCHANGES: 1½ fat, 1 starch.

MOM'S CHOCOLATE
CHIP COOKIES

BANANA NUT BROWNIES

This recipe comes from my Grandma Schlientz. Anytime there are ripe bananas around our house, it's Banana Nut Brownie time! People are always surprised to learn there are bananas in the brownies.

—*Christine Mol, Grand Rapids, MI*

PREP: 10 MIN. • BAKE: 40 MIN. + COOLING • MAKES: 16 BROWNIES

½ cup butter, melted, cooled
1 cup sugar
3 Tbsp. baking cocoa
2 large eggs, room temperature, lightly beaten
1 Tbsp. whole milk
1 tsp. vanilla extract

½ cup all-purpose flour
1 tsp. baking powder
¼ tsp. salt
1 cup mashed ripe bananas (2½ to 3 medium)
½ cup chopped walnuts
Confectioners' sugar, optional

1. In a bowl, combine butter, sugar and cocoa. Stir in eggs, milk and vanilla. Blend in flour, baking powder and salt. Stir in bananas and nuts.

2. Pour into a greased 9-in. square baking pan. Bake at 350° until a toothpick comes out with moist crumbs, 40-45 minutes. Cool on a wire rack. Just before serving, dust with confectioners' sugar if desired.

1 BROWNIE: 163 cal., 9g fat (4g sat. fat), 42mg chol., 128mg sod., 20g carb. (15g sugars, 1g fiber), 3g pro.

BUTTERY POTATO CHIP COOKIES

Can't decide whether to bring chips or cookies to the tailgate? These crisp and buttery cookies make plenty for the crowd, and will keep people guessing the secret ingredient.

—*Rachel Roberts, Lemoore, CA*

PREP: 15 MIN. • BAKE: 10 MIN./BATCH • MAKES: 4½ DOZEN

2 cups butter, softened
1 cup sugar
1 tsp. vanilla extract
3½ cups all-purpose flour
2 cups crushed potato chips
¾ cup chopped walnuts

1. Preheat oven to 350°. In a large bowl, cream butter and sugar until light and fluffy. Beat in vanilla. Gradually add flour to creamed mixture and mix well. Stir in potato chips and walnuts.

2. Drop by rounded tablespoonfuls 2 in. apart onto ungreased baking sheets. Bake 10-12 minutes or until lightly browned. Cool 2 minutes before removing from pans to wire racks.

1 COOKIE: 126 cal., 9g fat (5g sat. fat), 18mg chol., 67mg sod., 11g carb. (4g sugars, 0 fiber), 1g pro.

LEMON OATMEAL COOKIES

My grandmother always made these cookies for us at Christmas, and now I have inherited that task. With rich cream cheese in the dough and the sugary almond topping, a batch doesn't last long at my house!
—*Michelle Naber, Tonawanda, NY*

PREP: 20 MIN. • BAKE: 10 MIN./BATCH • MAKES: 4½ DOZEN

1 cup butter-flavored shortening
3 oz. cream cheese, softened
1¼ cups sugar
1 large egg yolk
2 tsp. grated lemon zest
1 tsp. lemon extract
1⅓ cups all-purpose flour
1⅓ cups quick-cooking oats
½ tsp. salt

TOPPING
1 large egg
1 large egg white
Sugar
½ cup sliced almonds

1. In a large bowl, cream the shortening, cream cheese and sugar until light and fluffy. Beat in the egg yolk, lemon peel and extract. Combine the flour, oats and salt; gradually add to creamed mixture and mix well.

2. Drop by heaping teaspoonfuls 2 in. apart onto greased baking sheets. Beat egg and egg white; brush over dough. Sprinkle with sugar; top with almonds.

3. Bake at 350° until edges are lightly browned, 10-12 minutes. Remove to wire racks.

1 COOKIE: 83 cal., 5g fat (1g sat. fat), 10mg chol., 29mg sod., 9g carb. (5g sugars, 0 fiber), 1g pro.

APPLE KUCHEN BARS

This recipe is about family, comfort and simplicity. My mom made this delicious sweet treat many a winter's night and served it up warm with some of her famous homemade ice cream. I like to make a double batch and pass on the love!
—*Elizabeth Monfort, Celina, OH*

PREP: 35 MIN. • BAKE: 1 HOUR + COOLING • MAKES: 2 DOZEN

3 cups all-purpose flour, divided
¼ tsp. salt
1½ cups cold butter, divided
4 to 5 Tbsp. ice water
8 cups thinly sliced peeled tart apples (about 8 medium)
2 cups sugar, divided
2 tsp. ground cinnamon

1. Preheat oven to 350°. Place 2 cups flour and salt in a food processor; pulse until blended. Add 1 cup butter; pulse until butter is the size of peas. While pulsing, add just enough ice water to form moist crumbs. Press mixture onto bottom of a greased 13x9-in. baking pan. Bake until the edges are lightly browned, 20-25 minutes. Cool on a wire rack.

2. In a large bowl, combine apples, 1 cup sugar and cinnamon; toss to coat. Spoon over crust. Place remaining flour, butter and sugar in food processor; pulse until coarse crumbs form. Sprinkle over apples. Bake until golden brown and apples are tender, 60-70 minutes. Cool completely on a wire rack. Cut into bars.

1 BAR: 240 cal., 12g fat (7g sat. fat), 30mg chol., 106mg sod., 33g carb. (21g sugars, 1g fiber), 2g pro.

GRANDMA'S SECRET
For a springtime flavor profile, use dried cherries instead of cranberries and almond extract instead of orange. Eliminate the orange zest.

WHITE CHOCOLATE
CRANBERRY-ORANGE BARS

WHITE CHOCOLATE CRANBERRY-ORANGE BARS

Our family is scattered across the country now. Making a recipe inspired by my
mom reminds me of home. No pastry cutter? Just use two sharp knives.
—Erin Powell, Amarillo, TX

PREP: 10 MIN. • BAKE: 20 MIN. + COOLING • MAKES: 2 DOZEN

1½ cups all-purpose flour
½ cup packed brown sugar
½ cup cold butter, cubed

FILLING
1 large egg, room
  temperature
1 can (14 oz.) sweetened
  condensed milk
1 tsp. grated orange zest
1 tsp. orange extract
1½ cups white baking chips
1 cup dried cranberries

1. Preheat oven to 350°. Line a 13x9-in. pan with foil, letting ends extend up sides; grease foil. In a bowl, mix flour and brown sugar; cut in butter until crumbly. Press onto bottom of prepared pan. Bake until light golden brown, 10-12 minutes. Cool on a wire rack.

2. For filling, whisk together egg, milk, orange zest and extract until blended; stir in baking chips and cranberries. Spread evenly over crust. Bake until top is golden brown, 20-25 minutes longer. Cool 15 minutes in pan on a wire rack. Lifting with foil, remove bars from pan. Gently peel off foil. Cut into bars. Refrigerate the leftovers.

FREEZE OPTION: Freeze cooled bars in freezer containers, separating layers with waxed paper. To use, thaw before serving.

1 BAR: 214 cal., 9g fat (5g sat. fat), 26mg chol., 66mg sod., 31g carb. (25g sugars, 1g fiber), 3g pro.

MAPLE PECAN BARS

Baking these bars fills me with warm memories of my Grandma Marie, who
made a similar recipe. The pecan treats are popular at our office cookie exchange.
—Amanda Spearing, Newton, IA

PREP: 30 MIN. • BAKE: 20 MIN. + COOLING • MAKES: 5 DOZEN

3 cups all-purpose flour
¾ cup confectioners' sugar
1½ cups cold butter

TOPPING
1½ cups packed brown sugar
1 cup butter, cubed
½ cup maple syrup
2 tsp. ground cinnamon
¼ tsp. salt
4 cups coarsely chopped
  pecans
2 Tbsp. plus 1 tsp. heavy
  whipping cream
¾ tsp. vanilla extract

1. Preheat oven to 350°. In a large bowl, combine flour and confectioners' sugar. Cut in the butter until crumbly. Press into a greased 15x10x1-in. baking pan. Bake until edges are lightly browned, 12-15 minutes.

2. Meanwhile, in a large heavy saucepan, combine brown sugar, butter, syrup, cinnamon and salt. Bring to a boil. Cook and stir over low heat until butter is melted. Stir in pecans, cream and vanilla. Remove from the heat; spread over crust.

3. Bake until bubbly, 20-25 minutes longer. Cool on a wire rack. Cut into bars.

1 BAR: 180 cal., 14g fat (5g sat. fat), 21mg chol., 66mg sod., 15g carb. (9g sugars, 1g fiber), 1g pro.

APPLE-PEANUT BLONDIES

My family and I love apples any time of year, but in the fall, they are always crisp, juicy and absolutely perfect! I found a blondie recipe similar to this and did a bit of tweaking to make it my own.
—Julie Peterson, Crofton, MD

PREP: 15 MIN. • **BAKE:** 25 MIN. + COOLING • **MAKES:** 9 SERVINGS

1 cup packed brown sugar
½ cup butter, melted
1 large egg, room temperature
1 tsp. vanilla extract
1 cup all-purpose flour
½ tsp. baking powder
¼ tsp. baking soda
¼ tsp. salt
2 small apples (about 9 oz.), peeled and sliced
½ cup chopped salted peanuts

1. Preheat oven to 350°. Beat brown sugar and butter until light and fluffy, 5-7 minutes. Add egg and vanilla; beat until smooth. In a separate bowl, whisk together flour, baking powder, baking soda and salt; gradually beat into brown sugar mixture just until combined (batter will be thick).

2. Spread all but ¼ cup batter into a greased and floured 8-in. square baking dish. Layer with apple slices; dot with remaining batter. Sprinkle with peanuts. Bake until top is golden brown and center is set, 22-28 minutes. Cool on a wire rack.

1 BLONDIE: 302 cal., 15g fat (7g sat. fat), 48mg chol., 256mg sod., 39g carb. (26g sugars, 1g fiber), 4g pro.

OAT & COCONUT ICEBOX COOKIES

This recipe was passed down through my family from Grandma Irene and is a favorite of my dad and cousin Dennis. It's a true cookie lover's cookie: crispy on the outside, chewy on the inside and perfectly dunkable.
—Lori Rowe, Tigerton, WI

PREP: 20 MIN. + CHILLING • **BAKE:** 10 MIN./BATCH • **MAKES:** ABOUT 3½ DOZEN

½ cup butter, softened
½ cup shortening
1 cup sugar
1 cup packed brown sugar
2 large eggs, room temperature
1 tsp. vanilla extract
1½ cups all-purpose flour
1 tsp. baking soda
1 tsp. salt
3 cups old-fashioned oats
½ cup sweetened shredded coconut
½ cup chopped walnuts

1. Cream butter, shortening and sugars until light and fluffy, 5-7 minutes. Beat in eggs and vanilla. In another bowl, whisk flour, baking soda and salt; gradually beat into creamed mixture. Stir in oats, coconut and walnuts.

2. Divide dough in half. Shape each into a 10-in.-long roll. Wrap; refrigerate overnight.

3. Preheat oven to 375°. Unwrap and cut dough crosswise into ½-in. slices. Place 2 in. apart on ungreased baking sheets. Bake until edges begin to brown, 8-10 minutes. Cool 2 minutes before removing from pans to wire racks.

1 COOKIE: 142 cal., 7g fat (3g sat. fat), 15mg chol., 117mg sod., 19g carb. (11g sugars, 1g fiber), 2g pro.

MOM'S BUTTERMILK COOKIES

I treasure my mother's recipe for these comforting cookie pillows. The tender treats are topped with thick frosting and a dainty sprinkle of walnuts.
—*Jane Darling, Simi Valley, CA*

PREP: 20 MIN. • **BAKE:** 10 MIN./BATCH + COOLING • **MAKES:** ABOUT 3 DOZEN

½ cup butter, softened
1 cup sugar
1 large egg, room temperature
1 tsp. vanilla extract
2½ cups all-purpose flour
½ tsp. baking soda
½ tsp. salt
½ cup buttermilk

FROSTING

3 Tbsp. butter, softened
3½ cups confectioners' sugar
¼ cup 2% milk
1 tsp. vanilla extract
½ cup finely chopped walnuts, optional

1. Preheat oven to 375°. Cream butter and sugar until light and fluffy. Beat in egg and vanilla. In a separate bowl, whisk flour, baking soda and salt; add to creamed mixture alternately with buttermilk, beating well after each addition.

2. Drop by rounded tablespoonfuls 2 in. apart onto greased baking sheets. Bake cookies until edges are lightly browned, 10-12 minutes. Remove to wire racks to cool.

3. For frosting, combine butter, confectioners' sugar, milk and vanilla; beat until smooth. Spread over cookies; if desired, sprinkle with chopped walnuts.

NOTE: To substitute for each cup of buttermilk, use 1 Tbsp. white vinegar or lemon juice plus enough milk to measure 1 cup. Stir, then let stand 5 min. Or, use 1 cup plain yogurt or 1¾ tsp. cream of tartar plus 1 cup milk.

1 COOKIE: 135 cal., 4g fat (2g sat. fat), 15mg chol., 88mg sod., 24g carb. (17g sugars, 0 fiber), 1g pro.

CHOCOLATE CHIP COOKIE BROWNIES

It was so fun to experiment with this brownie recipe. When my daughter tasted the final version, she told me they were the best brownies ever! Now that sure makes a mom feel good.
—Dion Frischer, Ann Arbor, MI

PREP: 15 MIN. • **BAKE:** 50 MIN. + COOLING • **MAKES:** 1 DOZEN

¾ **cup butter**
1½ **cups sugar**
½ **cup baking cocoa**
3 **large eggs, room temperature**
¾ **cup all-purpose flour**
½ **cup chopped walnuts**

CHOCOLATE CHIP LAYER

½ **cup butter**
1 **cup packed brown sugar**
1 **large egg, room temperature**
1 **cup all-purpose flour**
½ **tsp. baking soda**
1 **cup semisweet chocolate chips**

1. Preheat oven to 350°. Line a 9-in. square baking pan with foil, letting ends extend up the sides; grease foil.

2. In a microwave, melt butter in a large microwave-safe bowl. Stir in sugar and cocoa. Add eggs, 1 at a time, whisking to blend after each addition. Add flour; stir just until combined. Stir in nuts. Spread into prepared pan. Bake 15 minutes.

3. Meanwhile, for cookie layer, melt butter in another microwave-safe bowl. Stir in brown sugar. Whisk in egg. In a small bowl, whisk flour and baking soda; stir into butter mixture just until combined. Stir in chocolate chips.

4. Spoon mixture over hot brownie layer. Bake until a toothpick inserted in center comes out with moist crumbs, 35-40 minutes longer. Cool completely in pan on a wire rack. Lifting foil, remove brownies from pan. Cut into bars.

1 BROWNIE: 536 cal., 29g fat (15g sat. fat), 113mg chol., 236mg sod., 69g carb. (51g sugars, 2g fiber), 6g pro.

"These came out perfectly and are soooooo good! Very rich and the perfect combo of brownie and cookie. I didn't try it (yet), but a scoop of vanilla ice cream on one of these has to be amazing!"
—KERI DUNCAN, TASTEOFHOME.COM

MOM'S OLD-FASHIONED CUTOUTS

Old family memories rush in as soon as
I make these traditional cutout cookies.
—*Lois Smit, Monee, IL*

PREP: 50 MIN. • **BAKE:** 10 MIN./BATCH + COOLING • **MAKES:** 5 DOZEN

1 cup butter, softened
1½ cups sugar
1 large egg, room temperature
½ cup sour cream
1 tsp. vanilla extract
4 cups all-purpose flour, sifted
1 tsp. baking powder
½ tsp. baking soda
½ tsp. salt
½ tsp. ground cinnamon or ground nutmeg
2 cups confectioners' sugar
1 tsp. vanilla extract
¼ tsp. salt
3 to 4 Tbsp. heavy whipping cream
Food coloring, optional

1. In a large bowl, cream butter and sugar until light and fluffy, 5-7 minutes. Beat in the egg, then sour cream and vanilla. In another bowl, mix the flour, baking powder, baking soda, salt and cinnamon; gradually beat into creamed mixture.

2. Divide dough into 3 portions. Shape each into a disk; wrap and refrigerate for 30 minutes or until easy to handle.

3. On a lightly floured surface, roll each portion of dough to ¼-in. thickness. Cut with a floured 3-in. cookie cutter. Place 2 in. apart on greased baking sheets.

4. Bake at 350° until lightly browned, 10-12 minutes. Remove to wire racks to cool completely.

5. In a small bowl, mix the confectioners' sugar, vanilla, salt and enough cream to reach desired consistency. If desired, tint with food coloring. Decorate cookies as desired.

1 COOKIE: 101 cal., 4g fat (2g sat. fat), 13mg chol., 75mg sod., 16g carb. (9g sugars, 0 fiber), 1g pro.

EGG YOLK COOKIES

PICTURED ON PAGE 202

These simple cookies truly melt in your mouth, due to the hard-boiled eggs used.
These are not a thick cookie, but thin, just like my grandma used to make.
—*Kathy Gagliardi, Holmdel, NJ*

PREP: 20 MIN. + CHILLING • BAKE: 15 MIN./BATCH + COOLING • MAKES: ABOUT 6 DOZEN

4 hard-boiled large egg
yolks
1 cup unsalted butter,
softened
½ cup sugar
1 Tbsp. vanilla extract
2½ cups all-purpose flour
Dash salt
1 raw large egg yolk, lightly
beaten

1. Press hard-boiled yolks through a fine-mesh strainer into a bowl. In a large bowl, cream butter and sugar until light and fluffy, 5-7 minutes. Beat in the yolks and vanilla. In another bowl, whisk flour and salt; gradually beat into creamed mixture. Divide dough in half. Shape each into a disk; wrap. Refrigerate 30 minutes or until firm enough to roll.

2. Preheat oven to 350°. On a lightly floured surface, roll each portion of dough to ¼-in. thickness. Cut with a floured 2-in. fluted cookie cutter. Place 1 in. apart on parchment-lined baking sheets. Brush with egg yolk.

3. Bake until lightly browned, 12-14 minutes. Remove from pans to wire racks to cool completely.

1 COOKIE: 46 cal., 3g fat (2g sat. fat), 19mg chol., 3mg sod., 5g carb. (1g sugars, 0 fiber), 1g pro.

FROM GRANDMA'S KITCHEN: Use the leftover cooked egg whites to make a thrifty (but fancy-sounding and delicious) side dish *Polonaise.* Toss chopped egg whites and 1 whole chopped egg with toasted bread crumbs or crushed crackers, parsley, butter, and, if desired, garlic, salt, and capers. Spoon the topping over boiled cauliflower or steamed asparagus. *Polonaise* is a classic French preparation inspired by Polish cuisine.

GRANDMA'S SCOTTISH
SHORTBREAD

GRANDMA'S SCOTTISH SHORTBREAD

My Scottish grandmother was renowned for baked goods,
and these deep shortbread bars are an example of why.
—*Jane Kelly, Wayland, MA*

PREP: 15 MIN. • **BAKE:** 45 MIN. + COOLING • **MAKES:** 4 DOZEN

1 lb. butter, softened
8 oz. superfine sugar (about 1¼ cups)
1 lb. all-purpose flour (3⅔ cups)
8 oz. white rice flour (1⅓ cups)

1. Preheat oven to 300°. Cream butter and sugar until light and fluffy, 5-7 minutes. Combine flours; gradually beat into creamed mixture. Press dough into an ungreased 13x9-in. baking pan. Prick with a fork.

2. Bake until light brown, 45-50 minutes. Cut into 48 bars or triangles while warm. Cool completely on a wire rack.

1 BAR: 139 cal., 8g fat (5g sat. fat), 20mg chol., 61mg sod., 16g carb. (5g sugars, 0 fiber), 1g pro.

PUMPKIN DELIGHT MAGIC BARS

My mother never wrote down her delightful recipes, so I created this recipe as a holiday tribute to her. They're creamy, sweet and a little tart. Eat with a fork so you can scoop up all the delicious topping ingredients that might tumble off.
—*Lisa Glassman, Boynton Beach, FL*

PREP: 20 MIN. • **BAKE:** 45 MIN. + COOLING • **MAKES:** 2 DOZEN

1 pkg. (11 oz.) vanilla wafers
½ cup butter, melted
3 oz. cream cheese, softened
1 can (14 oz.) sweetened condensed milk
½ tsp. pumpkin pie spice
1 can (15 oz.) solid-pack pumpkin
1 cup dried cranberries
1½ cups sweetened shredded coconut
1 cup white baking chips
1 cup chopped pecans

1. Preheat oven to 350°. Place wafers in a food processor; pulse until coarse crumbs form. Drizzle with melted butter; pulse until blended. Press into bottom of a greased 13x9-in. baking pan.

2. In a large bowl, beat cream cheese, milk and pie spice until smooth. Beat in pumpkin; stir in cranberries. Pour over crust. Layer with coconut, baking chips and pecans.

3. Bake until golden brown, 45-55 minutes. Cool in pan on a wire rack 10 minutes.

4. Loosen sides from pan with a knife; cool completely. Cut into bars. Refrigerate leftovers.

1 BAR: 299 cal., 17g fat (8g sat. fat), 25mg chol., 144mg sod., 35g carb. (28g sugars, 2g fiber), 4g pro.

CARAMEL-PECAN DREAM BARS

These ooey-gooey cake bars that pull ever so gently from the
pan and hold a firm cut are a baker's dream come true.

—*Cay Keppers, Nisswa, MN*

PREP: 15 MIN. • **BAKE:** 20 MIN. + COOLING • **MAKES:** 2 DOZEN

1 **pkg. yellow cake mix (regular size)**
½ **cup butter, softened**
1 **large egg, room temperature**

FILLING
1 **can (14 oz.) sweetened condensed milk**
1 **large egg**
1 **tsp. vanilla extract**
1 **cup chopped pecans**
½ **cup brickle toffee bits**

1. Preheat oven to 350°. In a large bowl, beat cake mix, butter and egg until crumbly. Press onto the bottom of a greased 13x9-in. baking pan.

2. In a small bowl, beat milk, egg and vanilla until combined. Stir in pecans and toffee bits. Pour over crust.

3. Bake until golden brown, 20-25 minutes. Cool on a wire rack. Cut into bars.

1 BAR: 239 cal., 12g fat (5g sat. fat), 35mg chol., 222mg sod., 30g carb. (22g sugars, 0 fiber), 3g pro.

MOM'S LEMON SUGAR COOKIES

These tender, soft sugar cookies have just a hint of lemon. If you like more lemon flavor,
go ahead and kick it up a notch. It's also fantastic made with orange instead.

—*Nancy Foust, Stoneboro, PA*

PREP: 15 MIN. + CHILLING • **BAKE:** 10 MIN. PER BATCH • **MAKES:** ABOUT 5 DOZEN

1 **cup butter, softened**
2 **cups sugar**
2 **large eggs, room temperature**
2 **tsp. grated lemon zest**
2 **tsp. lemon extract**
4 **cups all-purpose flour**
1 **tsp. baking soda**
1 **tsp. salt**
1 **cup buttermilk**

1. Cream butter and sugar until light and fluffy, 5-7 minutes. Add eggs, 1 at a time, beating well after each addition. Beat in lemon zest and extract. In another bowl, whisk together flour, baking soda and salt; add to creamed mixture alternately with the buttermilk, beating well after each addition. Cover and refrigerate at least 2 hours.

2. Preheat oven to 375°. Drop by tablespoonfuls 2 in. apart onto ungreased baking sheets. Bake until lightly browned, 7-10 minutes. Remove to wire racks to cool.

NOTE: To substitute for each cup of buttermilk, use 1 Tbsp. white vinegar or lemon juice plus enough milk to measure 1 cup. Stir, then let stand 5 min. Or, use 1 cup plain yogurt or 1¾ tsp. cream of tartar plus 1 cup milk.

1 COOKIE: 88 cal., 3g fat (2g sat. fat), 15mg chol., 95mg sod., 13g carb. (7g sugars, 0 fiber), 1g pro.

SEA SALT MINT WHITE MOCHA COOKIES

This recipe came from my mom's Grandma Alice, who taught her how to bake. Grandma Alice always had a fresh plate of warm cookies on her counter. I learned some of her recipes by heart as a child. This one in particular tastes like Christmas. I've been making these since high school!

—*Kristin Bowers, Rancho Palos Verdes, CA*

PREP: 20 MIN. • **BAKE:** 15 MIN./BATCH • **MAKES:** 26 COOKIES

1 cup butter-flavored shortening
¾ cup sugar
¾ cup packed brown sugar
2 large eggs, room temperature
1 tsp. mint extract
1½ cups all-purpose flour
1 Tbsp. instant espresso powder
1 tsp. sea salt
1 tsp. baking soda
2 cups old-fashioned oats
1 pkg. (10 to 12 oz.) white baking chips

1. Preheat oven to 350°. In a large bowl, cream shortening and sugars until light and fluffy. Beat in eggs and extract. In another bowl, whisk flour, espresso powder, salt and baking soda; gradually beat into creamed mixture. Stir in oats and white chips.

2. Drop dough by scant ¼ cupfuls 2 in. apart onto parchment-lined baking sheets. Bake until the edges begin to brown, 12-15 minutes. Cool on pans 5 minutes. Remove to wire racks to cool. Store in an airtight container.

1 COOKIE: 229 cal., 12g fat (4g sat. fat), 17mg chol., 140mg sod., 28g carb. (19g sugars, 1g fiber), 3g pro.

FROM GRANDMA'S KITCHEN: For a caffeine-free version, simply leave out the espresso powder. Milk or dark chocolate chips can be substituted for white if that's what you have on hand.

BAILEYS & MINT BROWNIE CHEESECAKE BITES

This is a combo of two St. Patrick's Day goodies. You can use any type of chips in the brownies, and you can choose to swirl in the cheesecake instead of using it as a separate topping.
—Teri Rasey, Cadillac, MI

PREP: 25 MIN. • **BAKE:** 45 MIN. + CHILLING • **MAKES:** 64 PIECES

¾ **cup butter, cubed**
1 **cup (6 oz.) dark chocolate chips**
¾ **cup sugar**
2 **large eggs plus**
   1 large egg yolk, room temperature
1 **tsp. vanilla extract**
1 **cup all-purpose flour**
⅓ **cup dark baking cocoa**
½ **tsp. salt**
1 **cup Andes creme de menthe baking chips**

TOPPING
1 **pkg. (8 oz.) cream cheese, softened**
½ **cup sugar**
¼ **cup Irish cream liqueur, such as Baileys**
1 **large egg plus 1 large egg white, room temperature**

1. Preheat oven to 350°. Line an 8-in. square baking pan with parchment, letting ends extend up sides. In a large microwave-safe bowl, microwave butter and chocolate chips on high until butter is melted, about 60 seconds. Stir until chocolate is melted. Whisk in sugar. Cool slightly. Whisk in eggs and yolk, 1 at a time, and vanilla until blended. Stir in flour, baking cocoa and salt; fold in Andes chips. Spread into prepared pan.

2. For topping, in a large bowl, beat cream cheese and sugar until smooth. Beat in liqueur. Add egg and egg white; beat on low speed just until blended. Pour over brownie layer. Bake until center is almost set, 45-50 minutes. Cool 1 hour on a wire rack. Refrigerate at least 3 hours or overnight.

3. Lifting with parchment, remove brownies from pan. Cut into bars. Refrigerate leftovers.

1 PIECE: 96 cal., 6g fat (4g sat. fat), 21mg chol., 54mg sod., 10g carb. (8g sugars, 0 fiber), 1g pro.

FROM GRANDMA'S KITCHEN: These rich little layered treats are perfect for St. Patrick's Day or any Irish menu.

GRANDMA'S SPRITZ COOKIES

I use my grandmother's antique cookie press to make these festive cookies. I'm the only one in the family that can still get it to work!
—*Suzanne Kern, Louisville, KY*

PREP: 15 MIN. • **BAKE:** 10 MIN./BATCH + COOLING • **MAKES:** 6½ DOZEN

1 **cup shortening**	½ **tsp. baking powder**
¾ **cup sugar**	**Dash salt**
1 **large egg, room**	**Optional: Assorted**
temperature	**sprinkles and colored**
1 **tsp. almond extract**	**sugar**
2¼ **cups all-purpose flour**	

1. Preheat oven to 400°. In a large mixing bowl, cream shortening and sugar until light and fluffy, 5-7 minutes. Add egg and almond extract; mix well. Combine the flour, baking powder and salt; add to the creamed mixture until blended.

2. Using a cookie press fitted with the disk of your choice, press dough 2 in. apart onto ungreased baking sheets. If desired, sprinkle with toppings. Bake until set (do not brown), 7-8 minutes.

1 COOKIE: 44 cal., 3g fat (1g sat. fat), 2mg chol., 6mg sod., 5g carb. (2g sugars, 0 fiber), 0 pro.

FROM GRANDMA'S KITCHEN: If your spritz cookies are spreading, there are a few tricks you can try. First, make sure you're using ungreased, unlined cookie sheets, because classic spritz cookies require ungreased metal to grip (and they won't stick when baking!). You can also try slightly refrigerating your dough, but keep an eye on it—the dough needs to be pliable enough to go through the press. A chilled baking sheet can also help in a pinch!

LEBKUCHEN

It's tradition for my family to make these German treats together.
The recipe came from my great-grandmother's cookbook, and judging
from the amount of requests I get, it has certainly stood the test of time.
—*Esther Kempker, Jefferson City, MO*

PREP: 25 MIN. • **BAKE:** 25 MIN. + COOLING • **MAKES:** 3 DOZEN

½ cup butter, softened
½ cup sugar
⅓ cup packed brown sugar
2 large eggs, room temperature
1 cup molasses
¼ cup buttermilk
½ tsp. anise extract
4½ cups all-purpose flour
1½ tsp. baking powder
1 tsp. baking soda
1 tsp. ground cinnamon
½ tsp. salt
½ tsp. each ground allspice, cardamom and cloves
½ cup ground walnuts
½ cup raisins
½ cup pitted dates
½ cup candied lemon peel
⅓ cup sweetened shredded coconut
¼ cup candied orange peel
3 Tbsp. candied pineapple

GLAZE
½ cup sugar
¼ cup water
2 Tbsp. confectioners' sugar

1. Preheat oven to 350°. Line a 15x10x1-in. baking pan with parchment.

2. In a large bowl, cream butter and sugars until light and fluffy, 5-7 minutes. Add eggs, 1 at a time, beating well after each addition. Beat in molasses, buttermilk and extract. In another bowl, whisk flour, baking powder, baking soda, cinnamon, salt, allspice, cardamom and cloves; gradually add to the creamed mixture and beat well. Stir in walnuts.

3. Place raisins, dates, lemon peel, coconut, orange peel and pineapple in a food processor; pulse until chopped. Stir into batter; press into prepared pan. Bake 25-28 minutes or until lightly browned.

4. For glaze, in a small saucepan, bring sugar and water to a boil; boil 1 minute. Remove from heat; whisk in confectioners' sugar. Spread over warm bars. Cool completely in pan on a wire rack.

1 BAR: 187 cal., 4g fat (2g sat. fat), 17mg chol., 137mg sod., 36g carb. (23g sugars, 1g fiber), 2g pro.

CHOCOLATE CHIP
COOKIE BLONDIES

CHOCOLATE CHIP BLONDIE MIX

This recipe has been in my family as long as I can remember. My mom would make these for us when we were young, and I have continued the tradition to my own family. When my husband and I were engaged, I would send these to him during his deployment overseas. In no time, he and his buddies would have the entire container emptied. A jar of this blondie mix makes a great gift!
—*Amanda Green, Salisbury, MO*

PREP: 20 MIN. • BAKE: 15 MIN. + COOLING • MAKES: 1 BATCH (2 DOZEN BLONDIES)

2 cups all-purpose flour
1 tsp. baking soda
1 tsp. salt
¾ cup packed brown sugar
¾ cup sugar
1 cup semisweet chocolate chips

ADDITIONAL INGREDIENTS
2 large eggs, room temperature
¾ cup canola oil
1 tsp. vanilla extract

Whisk flour, baking soda and salt. In a 1-qt. glass jar, layer flour mixture, brown sugar, granulated sugar and chocolate chips in order listed. Cover and store in a cool, dry place up to 3 months.

TO PREPARE BLONDIES: Preheat oven to 375°. Whisk eggs, oil and vanilla until blended. Gradually add blondie mix, mixing well. Spread into a greased 13x9-in. baking pan. Bake until a toothpick inserted in the center comes out clean (do not overbake), 15-20 minutes. Cool completely in pan on a wire rack.

1 BLONDIE: 190 cal., 10g fat (2g sat. fat), 16mg chol., 160mg sod., 26g carb. (17g sugars, 1g fiber), 2g pro.

FROSTED PUMPKIN COOKIES

Fall is the perfect time to turn on the oven and bake up a batch of nicely spiced pumpkin cookies.
—*Carol Preston, Bloomington, IN*

PREP: 15 MIN. • BAKE: 15 MIN./BATCH + COOLING • MAKES: 4 DOZEN

½ cup shortening
1 cup sugar
1 cup canned pumpkin
1 tsp. vanilla extract
2 cups all-purpose flour
1 tsp. baking powder
1 tsp. baking soda
1 tsp. ground cinnamon
Dash salt
1 cup raisins

FROSTING
2 Tbsp. butter
1½ cups confectioners' sugar
2 Tbsp. 2% milk
1 tsp. vanilla extract

1. Preheat oven to 350°. In a large bowl, cream shortening and sugar until light and fluffy, 5-7 minutes. Add pumpkin and vanilla. Combine flour, baking powder, baking soda, cinnamon and salt; add to the creamed mixture and mix well. Fold in the raisins.

2. Using a 1½-in. scoop, drop dough onto greased baking sheets. Bake until lightly browned, 12-14 minutes. Cool on wire racks.

3. For frosting, melt butter in a saucepan. Stir in the sugar, milk and vanilla until smooth. Frost cooled cookies.

1 COOKIE: 84 cal., 3g fat (1g sat. fat), 1mg chol., 44mg sod., 15g carb. (10g sugars, 0 fiber), 1g pro.

"My grandmother used to make cookies very similar to these, and we loved them! So glad when I found this recipe and tried them. Taste very similar to Grandma's! They are a great way to use up leftover pumpkin, too!"
—ONEBUSYLADY, TASTEOFHOME.COM

BLACKBERRY
APPLE PIE,
PAGE 239

GRANDMA'S FAVORITE
CAKES & PIES

—⁂—

A memorable meal calls for one of these
breathtaking centerpieces. They're lovingly
made by Grandma's hand.

LEMON RICOTTA CAKE

This recipe is a family gem that was passed down from my grandmother and mother. Garnished with shaved lemon peel, the moist four-layer cake is the perfect dessert when you want to impress.
—*Nanette Slaughter, Sammamish, WA*

PREP: 1 HOUR + CHILLING • **BAKE:** 30 MIN. + COOLING • **MAKES:** 16 SERVINGS

3 large eggs, room temperature
2 large egg yolks, room temperature
⅔ cup sugar
⅓ cup lemon juice
⅓ cup butter, cubed

CAKE BATTER
1 cup butter, softened
2 cups sugar
3 large eggs, room temperature
1 cup ricotta cheese
1 cup buttermilk
1 Tbsp. grated lemon zest
1½ tsp. vanilla extract
1 tsp. lemon juice
3 cups all-purpose flour
½ tsp. baking powder
½ tsp. baking soda
½ tsp. salt

SUGARED LEMON ZEST
6 medium lemons
¼ cup sugar

FROSTING
⅔ cup butter, softened
5½ cups confectioners' sugar
⅓ cup 2% milk
1½ tsp. grated lemon zest
1½ tsp. vanilla extract
⅛ tsp. salt
Colored sugar, optional

1. For lemon curd, in a small bowl, combine eggs and egg yolks. In a heavy saucepan, cook and stir the sugar, lemon juice and butter over medium heat until smooth. Stir a small amount of hot mixture into eggs; return all to the pan, stirring constantly. Bring to a gentle boil; cook and stir until thickened, about 2 minutes. Cool slightly. Cover and chill until thickened, about 1½ hours or overnight.

2. Preheat oven to 350°. In a large bowl, cream butter and sugar until light and fluffy, 5-7 minutes. Add eggs, 1 at a time, beating well after each addition. Combine the ricotta cheese, buttermilk, lemon zest, vanilla and lemon juice. Combine the flour, baking powder, baking soda and salt; add to the creamed mixture alternately with the buttermilk mixture, beating well after each addition.

3. Pour into 2 greased and floured 9-in. round baking pans. Bake until a toothpick inserted in the center comes out clean, 30-35 minutes. Cool for 10 minutes before removing from pans to wire racks to cool completely.

4. Using a citrus zester, remove zest from lemons in long narrow strips; toss with sugar. Let stand for 30 minutes. (Save fruit for another use.) Meanwhile, to make the frosting, in a large bowl, cream butter until light and fluffy. Add the confectioners' sugar, milk, grated lemon zest, vanilla and salt; beat until smooth.

5. Cut each cake in half horizontally. Place 1 cake layer on a serving plate. Pipe a circle of frosting around edge of cake. Spread a third of the lemon curd inside frosting. Repeat layers twice. Top with remaining cake layer. Frost top and sides. If desired, pipe a decorative border of frosting using a star tip, and decorate sides of cake with colored sugar. Garnish with lemon zest strips. Store in the refrigerator.

1 PIECE: 657 cal., 27g fat (16g sat. fat), 172mg chol., 370mg sod., 98g carb. (77g sugars, 1g fiber), 8g pro.

GRANDMA'S SECRET

The batter mixing method here is for high-ratio cakes—ones where sugar in the recipe outweighs the flour. The few extra mixing steps give you fluffy and light results.

CINNAMON-PEAR RUSTIC TART

I was lucky enough to spend the holidays with my husband's family in Montana. I loved the rustic simplicity of each dish we tasted, especially this rustic pear tart my mother-in-law made.
—*Leah Waldo, Jamaica Plain, MA*

PREP: 45 MIN. + CHILLING • **BAKE:** 45 MIN. • **MAKES:** 8 SERVINGS

2½ cups all-purpose flour
1 tsp. salt
1 cup cold butter, cubed
8 to 10 Tbsp. ice water

FILLING
2 Tbsp. butter
8 medium ripe pears, peeled and thinly sliced
1½ tsp. ground cinnamon
⅓ cup apple cider or juice
¼ cup packed brown sugar
1 tsp. vanilla extract
1 Tbsp. coarse sugar

1. In a large bowl, mix flour and salt; cut in butter until crumbly. Gradually add ice water, tossing with a fork until dough holds together when pressed. Shape into a disk; wrap. Refrigerate 30 minutes or overnight.

2. Preheat oven to 375°. In a large skillet, heat butter over medium-high heat. Add pears and cinnamon; cook and stir until tender, 2-3 minutes. Stir in cider and brown sugar. Bring to a boil; cook and stir until thickened, 8-10 minutes. Stir in the vanilla; cool slightly.

3. On a lightly floured surface, roll dough into a 14-in. circle. Transfer to a parchment-lined baking sheet.

4. Spoon filling over crust to within 2 in. of edge. Fold crust edge over filling, pleating as you go and leaving an opening in the center. Brush folded crust with water; sprinkle with coarse sugar. Bake until crust is golden and filling is bubbly, 45-50 minutes. Transfer tart to a wire rack to cool.

1 PIECE: 512 cal., 27g fat (17g sat. fat), 69mg chol., 506mg sod., 67g carb. (27g sugars, 7g fiber), 5g pro.

BLACKBERRY APPLE PIE

PICTURED ON PAGE 234

My mother made this pie so often she could do it with her eyes closed!
We picked the berries ourselves, and the apples came from the trees in our orchard.
—*Fran Stanfield, Wilmington, OH*

PREP: 20 MIN. • BAKE: 50 MIN. • MAKES: 8 SERVINGS

Pastry for a double-crust pie (9 in.)
5 **cups thinly sliced peeled tart apples (about 5 medium)**
1 **pint fresh blackberries, rinsed and drained**
1 **Tbsp. lemon juice**
¾ **cup sugar**
2 **Tbsp. cornstarch**
2 **Tbsp. butter**
1 **large egg**
1 **Tbsp. water or milk**

1. On a lightly floured surface, roll out half of dough to fit a 9-in. pie plate; trim to 1 in. beyond rim of plate. Top with a thin layer of apples. Combine blackberries and remaining apples; sprinkle with lemon juice. Combine sugar and cornstarch. Add to fruit mixture; toss gently to coat. Spoon into crust; dot with butter.

2. Roll out remaining dough; make a lattice crust. Trim, seal and flute edges. Beat egg with water; brush over lattice top and edges of pie. Bake at 375° for 50 minutes or until filling is bubbly and the apples are tender. Cool on a wire rack. Serve pie warm or at room temperature.

1 PIECE: 415 cal., 18g fat (8g sat. fat), 44mg chol., 238mg sod., 62g carb. (32g sugars, 2g fiber), 3g pro.

DOUGH FOR DOUBLE-CRUST PIE: Combine 2½ cups all-purpose flour and ½ tsp. salt; cut in 1 cup cold butter until crumbly. Gradually add ⅓ to ⅔ cup ice water, tossing with a fork until dough holds together when pressed. Divide dough in half. Shape each into a disk; wrap and refrigerate 1 hour.

FLUTED LEMON CAKE

My great-grandmother used to make this cake, which has been a
family favorite for years. You won't believe it starts with a cake mix!
—*Gail Mast, Clarkson, KY*

PREP: 15 MIN. • BAKE: 45 MIN. + COOLING • MAKES: 12 SERVINGS

1 **pkg. yellow cake mix (regular size)**
1 **pkg. (3.4 oz.) instant lemon pudding mix**
1 **cup apricot nectar**
½ **cup canola oil**
4 **large eggs**
1 **tsp. lemon extract**

LEMON GLAZE
1 **cup confectioners' sugar**
2 **Tbsp. lemon juice**

1. In a large bowl, combine the cake and dry pudding mixes, apricot nectar, oil, eggs and extract; beat on low for 30 seconds. Beat on medium speed for 2 minutes. Pour into a greased and floured 10-in. fluted tube pan.

2. Bake at 350° for 45-55 minutes or until a toothpick inserted in the center comes out clean. Cool for 10 minutes before removing from pan to a wire rack to cool completely.

3. In a small bowl, combine glaze ingredients until smooth; drizzle over warm cake.

1 PIECE: 369 cal., 15g fat (3g sat. fat), 71mg chol., 406mg sod., 55g carb. (38g sugars, 1g fiber), 4g pro.

SALTED DARK CHOCOLATE TART

When I was little, my grandpa kept a bag of caramels in his truck and a few in his pocket. Whether we were camping or going to a movie, he shared them with me. Now I try to put caramel in as many of my desserts as possible, including this sweet and salty tart.
—*Leah Tackitt, Austin, TX*

PREP: 30 MIN. • **COOK:** 15 MIN. + CHILLING • **MAKES:** 16 SERVINGS

1½ cups Oreo cookie crumbs
⅓ cup butter, melted

CARAMEL
¾ cup sugar
3 Tbsp. water
⅓ cup heavy whipping cream
2 Tbsp. butter, cubed
Dash salt

FILLING
4 cups dark chocolate chips
1¼ cups heavy whipping cream
1 tsp. vanilla extract
½ tsp. large-crystal sea salt

1. In a small bowl, combine cookie crumbs and butter; press onto the bottom and up the side of a greased 9-in. fluted tart pan with removable bottom. Cover and refrigerate for 30 minutes.

2. For caramel, in a small saucepan over medium heat, combine sugar and water. Cook, shaking pan occasionally, until sugar is melted and mixture is almost clear (do not boil).

3. Increase heat to medium high; bring to a boil, without stirring. Cover and boil for 2 minutes while tightly holding lid of pan down. Uncover; shake pan. Cook 1-2 minutes longer or until mixture is amber, shaking pan several times.

4. Remove from the heat; stir in cream (mixture will bubble) until smooth. Stir in butter (mixture will bubble) and salt until blended. Pour into crust; refrigerate for 15 minutes.

5. Place chocolate chips in a large bowl. In a small saucepan, bring cream just to a boil. Pour over chocolate; whisk until smooth. Stir in vanilla. Let stand for 20 minutes.

6. Pour chocolate mixture over caramel. Sprinkle with sea salt. Refrigerate for at least 3 hours. Remove from the refrigerator about 45 minutes before serving.

1 PIECE: 552 cal., 37g fat (21g sat. fat), 46mg chol., 200mg sod., 56g carb. (43g sugars, 1g fiber), 5g pro.

PUDDING-FILLED DEVIL'S FOOD CAKE

My grandmother gave me the recipe for her famous homemade chocolate cake.
I remember she often had it when we came over. The creamy chocolate filling
makes it so good, and a fluffy white frosting just puts it over the top.
—*Bonnie Capper-Eckstein, Maple Grove, MN*

PREP: 50 MIN. • **BAKE:** 30 MIN. + COOLING • **MAKES:** 12 SERVINGS

4 **large egg whites**
½ **cup butter, softened**
1¾ **cups sugar**
1 **tsp. vanilla extract**
2 **cups all-purpose flour**
½ **cup baking cocoa**
½ **tsp. baking soda**
¼ **tsp. salt**
1 **cup water**

PUDDING
1 **cup sugar**
¼ **cup all-purpose flour**
½ **tsp. salt**
2 **cups 2% milk**
2 **large egg yolks, beaten**
3 **oz. unsweetened chocolate, chopped**
1 **Tbsp. butter**
1 **tsp. vanilla extract**

FROSTING
1 **cup sugar**
3 **large egg whites**
3 **Tbsp. cold water**
2 **Tbsp. light corn syrup**
½ **tsp. cream of tartar**
⅛ **tsp. salt**
1 **tsp. vanilla extract**

1. Place egg whites in a large bowl; let stand at room temperature for 30 minutes. Meanwhile, in a large bowl, cream butter and sugar until light and fluffy, 5-7 minutes. Beat in vanilla. Combine the flour, cocoa, baking soda and salt; add to the creamed mixture alternately with water, beating well after each addition.

2. Beat egg whites with clean beaters until stiff peaks form; fold into batter. Transfer to a greased 13x9-in. baking pan. Bake at 350° for 30-35 minutes or until a toothpick inserted in the center comes out clean. Cool on a wire rack.

3. For pudding, in a large heavy saucepan, combine the sugar, flour and salt. Stir in milk until smooth. Cook and stir over medium-high heat until thickened and bubbly. Reduce heat to low; cook and stir 2 minutes longer. Remove from the heat.

4. Stir a small amount of hot mixture into egg yolks; return all to the pan, stirring constantly. Bring to a gentle boil; cook and stir 2 minutes longer. Remove from the heat. Stir in chocolate until smooth. Stir in butter and vanilla. Cool to room temperature, stirring occasionally. Spread over cake.

5. In a large heavy saucepan, combine the sugar, egg whites, water, corn syrup, cream of tartar and salt over low heat. With a hand mixer, beat on low speed for 1 minute. Continue beating on low over low heat until frosting reaches 160°, about 8-10 minutes.

6. Pour into a large bowl; add vanilla. Beat on high until stiff peaks form, about 7 minutes. Spread over cake. Store in the refrigerator.

1 PIECE: 495 cal., 14g fat (8g sat. fat), 60mg chol., 342mg sod., 88g carb. (66g sugars, 2g fiber), 8g pro.

"The chocolate cake is good all by itself, but I put it all together and it was delish! I am sure that it also would be good if I substituted whipped topping for the frosting."
—JMELISSAMC, TASTEOFHOME.COM

GRANDMA'S CHOCOLATE MERINGUE PIE

My grandmother served chocolate meringue pie after Sunday dinner each week, usually apologizing that it was too runny or something else was wrong with it. Of course, it was never less than perfect!
—Donna Vest Tilley, Chesterfield, VA

PREP: 30 MIN. • BAKE: 15 MIN. + CHILLING • MAKES: 8 SERVINGS

Dough for single-crust pie
¾ cup sugar
5 Tbsp. baking cocoa
3 Tbsp. cornstarch
¼ tsp. salt
2 cups whole milk
3 large egg yolks, room temperature, beaten
1 tsp. vanilla extract

MERINGUE
3 large egg whites, room temperature
¼ tsp. cream of tartar
6 Tbsp. sugar

GRANDMA'S SECRET
The timing here is a little tricky. Work fast and make sure the chocolate filling is still hot when you spread the meringue on top. A too-cold filling will cause the meringue to weep.

1. On a lightly floured surface, roll dough to a ⅛-in.-thick circle; transfer to a 9-in. pie plate. Trim to ½ in. beyond rim of plate; flute edge. Refrigerate 30 minutes. Preheat oven to 425°.

2. Line unpricked crust with a double thickness of foil. Fill with pie weights, dried beans or uncooked rice. Bake on a lower oven rack until edges are light golden brown, 15-20 minutes. Remove foil and weights; bake until bottom is golden brown, 3-6 minutes longer. Cool on a wire rack. Reduce oven setting to 350°.

3. In a saucepan, mix sugar, cocoa, cornstarch and salt; gradually add milk. Cook and stir over medium-high heat until thickened and bubbly. Reduce heat; cook and stir 2 minutes more. Remove from heat. Stir about 1 cup of the hot filling into the egg yolks. Return to saucepan and bring to a gentle boil. Cook and stir 2 minutes. Remove from the heat and stir in vanilla. Pour hot filling into pie crust.

4. For meringue, immediately beat egg whites with cream of tartar until soft peaks form. Gradually add sugar and continue to beat until stiff and glossy. Spread evenly over hot filling, sealing the meringue to the pie crust. Bake until the meringue is golden brown, 12-15 minutes. Cool 1 hour on a wire rack. Refrigerate at least 4 hours before serving.

1 PIECE: 317 cal., 11g fat (5g sat. fat), 93mg chol., 227mg sod., 49g carb. (31g sugars, 1g fiber), 6g pro.

DOUGH FOR SINGLE-CRUST PIE: Combine 1¼ cups all-purpose flour and ¼ tsp. salt; cut in ½ cup cold butter until crumbly. Gradually add 3-5 Tbsp. ice water, tossing with a fork until dough holds together when pressed. Shape into a disk; wrap and refrigerate 1 hour.

APRICOT MUD HEN CAKE BARS

These mud hen bars have been in my family for generations. My maternal grandmother gave this recipe to my mother, who shared it with me. I've been told the name comes from the speckled meringue topping that resembles the coloring of hens.
—*Kristine Chayes, Smithtown, NY*

PREP: 20 MIN. • **BAKE:** 30 MIN. + COOLING • **MAKES:** 24 SERVINGS

¾ **cup butter, softened**
⅓ **cup sugar**
2 **large egg yolks, room temperature**
1 **tsp. vanilla extract**
1½ **cups all-purpose flour**
⅛ **tsp. salt**

MERINGUE

2 **large egg whites, room temperature**
⅛ **tsp. cream of tartar**
⅓ **cup sugar**
¾ **cup finely chopped pecans**
1 **cup apricot preserves**

1. Preheat oven to 350°. In a large bowl, cream butter and sugar until light and fluffy, 5-7 minutes. Add egg yolks, 1 at a time, beating well after each addition. Beat in vanilla. In another bowl, whisk flour and salt; beat into creamed mixture. Spread into a greased 13x9-in. baking pan. Bake until a toothpick inserted in center comes out clean, 12-15 minutes.

2. Meanwhile for meringue, with clean beaters, beat egg whites with cream of tartar on medium speed until foamy. Gradually add sugar, 1 Tbsp. at a time, beating on high after each addition until sugar is dissolved. Continue beating until stiff glossy peaks form; gently fold in pecans.

3. Spread preserves over hot cake. Spread meringue over preserves, sealing meringue to edges of pan. Bake until meringue is golden brown, 15-20 minutes. Cool completely on a wire rack. Refrigerate leftovers.

1 PIECE: 163 cal., 9g fat (4g sat. fat), 31mg chol., 69mg sod., 21g carb. (12g sugars, 1g fiber), 2g pro.

FROM GRANDMA'S KITCHEN: Raspberry, peach or other preserves may be used in place of apricot.

APPLE PIE

I remember coming home sullen one day because we'd lost a softball game. Grandma, in her wisdom, suggested, "Maybe a slice of hot apple pie will make you feel better." She was right.
—*Maggie Greene, Granite Falls, WA*

PREP: 20 MIN. • **BAKE:** 45 MIN. + COOLING • **MAKES:** 8 SERVINGS

Dough for double-crust pie
⅓ cup sugar
⅓ cup packed brown sugar
¼ cup all-purpose flour
1 tsp. ground cinnamon
¼ tsp. ground ginger
¼ tsp. ground nutmeg

6 to 7 cups thinly sliced peeled tart apples
1 Tbsp. lemon juice
1 Tbsp. butter
1 large egg white
Optional: Turbinado or coarse sugar, ground cinnamon, vanilla bean ice cream and caramel sauce

1. Preheat oven to 375°. On a lightly floured surface, roll half of the dough to a ⅛-in.-thick circle; transfer to a 9-in. pie plate. In a small bowl, combine sugars, flour and spices. In a large bowl, toss apples with lemon juice. Add sugar mixture; toss to coat. Add filling; dot with butter.

2. Roll remaining dough to a ⅛-in.-thick circle. Place over filling. Trim, seal and flute edge. Cut slits in top. Beat egg white until foamy; brush over crust. If desired, sprinkle with turbinado sugar and ground cinnamon. Cover edge loosely with foil.

3. Bake 25 minutes. Remove foil; bake until crust is golden brown and filling is bubbly, 20-25 minutes longer. Cool on a wire rack. If desired, serve with ice cream and caramel sauce.

1 PIECE: 467 cal., 25g fat (15g sat. fat), 64mg chol., 331mg sod., 58g carb. (26g sugars, 2g fiber), 5g pro.

DOUGH FOR DOUBLE-CRUST PIE: Combine 2½ cups all-purpose flour and ½ tsp. salt; cut in 1 cup cold butter until crumbly. Gradually add ⅓ to ⅔ cup ice water, tossing with a fork until dough holds together when pressed. Divide dough in half. Shape each into a disk; wrap and refrigerate 1 hour.

GRANDMA'S RED VELVET CAKE

No one believes it's Christmas at our house until this jolly cake appears.
It's different from other red velvets I've tasted; the icing is as light as snow.
—*Kathryn Davison, Charlotte, NC*

PREP: 30 MIN. • BAKE: 20 MIN. + COOLING • MAKES: 14 SERVINGS

½ cup butter, softened
1½ cups sugar
2 large eggs, room
   temperature
2 bottles (1 oz. each) red
   food coloring
1 Tbsp. white vinegar
1 tsp. vanilla extract
2¼ cups cake flour
2 Tbsp. baking cocoa
1 tsp. baking soda
1 tsp. salt
1 cup buttermilk

FROSTING
½ cup cold water
1 Tbsp. cornstarch
2 cups butter, softened
2 tsp. vanilla extract
3½ cups confectioners' sugar

1. Preheat oven to 350°. Cream butter and sugar until light and fluffy, 5-7 minutes. Add eggs, 1 at a time, beating well after each addition. Beat in food coloring, vinegar and vanilla. In another bowl, whisk together flour, cocoa, baking soda and salt; add to creamed mixture alternately with buttermilk, beating well after each addition.

2. Pour into 2 greased and floured 9-in. round baking pans. Bake until a toothpick inserted in the center comes out clean, 20-25 minutes. Cool layers 10 minutes before removing from pans to wire racks to cool completely.

3. For frosting, combine water and cornstarch in a small saucepan over medium heat. Stir until thickened and opaque, 2-3 minutes. Cool to room temperature. Beat butter and vanilla until light and fluffy. Beat in cornstarch mixture. Gradually add confectioners' sugar; beat until light and fluffy. Spread between layers and over top and side of cake.

1 PIECE: 595 cal., 34g fat (21g sat. fat), 115mg chol., 564mg sod., 71g carb. (52g sugars, 1g fiber), 4g pro.

FROM GRANDMA'S KITCHEN: For a snowy effect, sprinkle confectioners' sugar over the frosted cake top.

NEVER-FAIL PECAN PIE

This incredible pecan pie recipe came from my mother-in-law. Her pies were a
were a hit everywhere she took them, and I never saw anyone not enjoy each mouthful!
She was kind enough to pass this recipe on to me, and it's one that I really enjoy making.
—*Beverly Materne, Reeves, LA*

PREP: 15 MIN. • BAKE: 45 MIN. + COOLING • MAKES: 8 SERVINGS

½ cup sugar
1 Tbsp. all-purpose flour
¼ tsp. salt
2 large eggs, well beaten
1 cup dark corn syrup
1 tsp. vanilla extract
1 cup pecan halves
1 unbaked pastry shell
   (9 in.)

1. In a large bowl, combine the sugar, flour, salt, eggs, corn syrup and vanilla. Stir in pecans. Pour into pastry shell. Cover pastry edges with foil to prevent excess browning.

2. Bake at 350° for 30 minutes. Remove foil and bake another 15 minutes or until golden brown. Cool on a wire rack.

1 PIECE: 401 cal., 18g fat (4g sat. fat), 58mg chol., 253mg sod., 60g carb. (29g sugars, 1g fiber), 4g pro.

OLD-TIME BUTTERMILK PIE

My mother and grandmother made this pie with buttermilk and eggs from our farm and set it on the tables at church meetings and social gatherings. I did the same and now our children make it, too!

—*Kate Mathews, Shreveport, LA*

PREP: 15 MIN. • BAKE: 45 MIN. + COOLING • MAKES: 10 SERVINGS

CRUST
- 1½ cups all-purpose flour
- 1 tsp. salt
- ½ cup shortening
- ¼ cup cold whole milk
- 1 large egg, lightly beaten

FILLING
- ½ cup butter, softened
- 2 cups sugar
- 3 Tbsp. all-purpose flour
- 3 large eggs
- 1 cup buttermilk
- 1 tsp. vanilla extract
- 1 tsp. ground cinnamon
- ¼ cup lemon juice
- Whipped cream and fresh berries, optional

1. Preheat oven to 350°. In a large bowl, mix flour and salt. Cut in shortening until crumbly. Gradually stir in milk and egg. On a lightly floured surface, roll dough to a ⅛-in.-thick circle; transfer to a 9-in. pie plate. Trim pastry to ½ in. beyond rim of plate; flute the edge.

2. For filling, in a large bowl, cream butter and sugar; beat in flour. Add eggs, 1 at a time, beating well after each addition. Stir in the remaining ingredients and mix well. Pour into crust.

3. Bake until center is set, 45-50 minutes. Cool completely on a wire rack. Serve or refrigerate within 2 hours. If desired, top servings with whipped cream and fresh berries.

1 PIECE: 446 cal., 21g fat (9g sat. fat), 111mg chol., 383mg sod., 59g carb. (41g sugars, 1g fiber), 6g pro.

"Excellent! I have used many different recipes over the years, and this one is our favorite. I have also made a version by reducing the butter by half and putting the mixture in custard cups to bake. It's a lower-fat treat and equally delicious!"

—MMDOLL, TASTEOFHOME.COM

MOM'S FAVORITE WHITE CAKE

I received this recipe as part of a wedding gift. I have made it for a couple of summer gatherings with friends and most recently when my husband requested that I make it for his birthday.
—*Tricia Bryan, Bolivar, OH*

PREP: 40 MIN. • **BAKE:** 20 MIN. + COOLING • **MAKES:** 6 SERVINGS

¼ **cup butter, softened**
¾ **cup sugar**
2 **large egg whites, room temperature**
1 **tsp. vanilla extract**
1 **cup plus 2 Tbsp. cake flour**
1½ **tsp. baking powder**
¼ **tsp. salt**
½ **cup 2% milk**

FROSTING/FILLING

½ **cup vanilla or white chips**
1 **envelope whipped topping mix (Dream Whip)**
⅓ **cup 2% milk**
3 **Tbsp. seedless strawberry jam**
½ **cup sliced fresh strawberries**
¼ **cup drained crushed pineapple**

1. In a large bowl, cream butter and sugar until light and fluffy, 5-7 minutes. Add egg whites, 1 at a time, beating well after each addition. Beat in vanilla. Combine the flour, baking powder and salt; add to creamed mixture alternately with the milk. Pour into 2 greased 6-in. round baking pans.

2. Bake at 350° minutes until a toothpick inserted in the center comes out clean, 18-22 minutes. Cool for 10 minutes before removing from pans to wire racks to cool completely.

3. For frosting, in a microwave, melt vanilla chips; stir until smooth. Set aside to cool slightly. In a small bowl, combine topping mix and milk. Beat on high speed for 2 minutes or until thickened. Beat in jam and melted chips until blended. Refrigerate for 15 minutes or until frosting achieves a spreading consistency.

4. For filling, in a small bowl, combine ½ cup frosting with strawberries and pineapple. Place 1 cake layer on a serving plate; spread with filling. Top with remaining cake layer. Frost the top and side of cake with remaining frosting. Store cake in the refrigerator.

1 PIECE: 502 cal., 18g fat (11g sat. fat), 27mg chol., 314mg sod., 79g carb. (56g sugars, 1g fiber), 6g pro.

OLD-FASHIONED PEANUT BUTTER PIE

My mother made a chewy, gooey peanut butter pie
I loved as a child. Now I continue the tradition for
our generation of peanut butter lovers.
—*Brianna DeBlake, Fremont, MI*

PREP: 20 MIN. • **BAKE:** 1 HOUR + COOLING • **MAKES:** 8 SERVINGS

Dough for single-crust pie
1½ **cups light corn syrup**
½ **cup sugar**
½ **cup creamy peanut butter**
¼ **tsp. salt**
4 **large eggs**
½ **tsp. vanilla extract**
Optional toppings: Chopped peanuts, broken Nutter Butter cookies and whipped topping

1. Preheat oven to 350°. On a lightly floured surface, roll dough to a ⅛-in.-thick circle; transfer to a 9-in. pie plate. Trim to ½ in. beyond rim of plate; flute edge.

2. In a large bowl, beat corn syrup, sugar, peanut butter and salt until blended. Beat in eggs and vanilla until smooth. Pour into crust. Bake until the top is puffed and center is almost set, 60-70 minutes; cover top loosely with foil during the last 30 minutes to prevent overbrowning.

3. Remove foil. Cool on a wire rack. (Top may sink and crack slightly upon cooling.) Serve or refrigerate within 2 hours. Top as desired.

1 PIECE: 538 cal., 22g fat (10g sat. fat), 123mg chol., 379mg sod., 82g carb. (65g sugars, 1g fiber), 9g pro.

DOUGH FOR SINGLE-CRUST PIE: Combine 1¼ cups all-purpose flour and ¼ tsp. salt; cut in ½ cup cold butter until crumbly. Gradually add 3-5 Tbsp. ice water, tossing with a fork until dough holds together when pressed. Wrap and refrigerate 1 hour.

BLOOD ORANGE & GOAT CHEESE GALETTE

I made this galette for my mother-in-law's birthday, and it was a sensational hit.
The gorgeous hue of the oranges transforms a rustic pie into an elegant dessert.

—*Tia Laws, Enterprise, OR*

PREP: 1 HOUR + FREEZING • BAKE: 1 HOUR + COOLING • MAKES: 8 SERVINGS (⅔ CUP SAUCE)

1 cup all-purpose flour
2 Tbsp. sugar
½ tsp. salt
⅓ cup cold butter, cubed
¼ cup quick-cooking oats
4 to 6 Tbsp. ice water

FILLING

10 medium blood oranges
¾ cup crumbled goat cheese
3 oz. cream cheese, softened
⅓ cup sour cream
¼ cup honey
2 large egg yolks, divided use
¼ tsp. salt
3 Tbsp. coarse sugar, divided
1 Tbsp. butter
1 Tbsp. water

SAUCE

¼ cup butter, cubed
½ cup packed brown sugar
2 Tbsp. half-and-half cream
2 Tbsp. honey
½ tsp. ground cinnamon

1. In a large bowl, mix flour, sugar and salt; cut in butter until crumbly. Stir in oats. Gradually add ice water, tossing with a fork until dough holds together when pressed. Shape into a disk; cover and refrigerate for 1 hour or overnight.

2. On a lightly floured surface, roll dough to a 13-in. circle. Transfer to a parchment-lined 14-in. pizza pan. Refrigerate, covered, while preparing filling.

3. For filling, cut a thin slice from the top and bottom of oranges; stand oranges upright on a cutting board. With a knife, cut peel and outer membrane from oranges. Cut along the membrane of each segment to remove fruit from 8 oranges. Thinly slice remaining 2 oranges; remove seeds. Place orange segments and slices between layers of paper towels to remove excess moisture; let stand while preparing filling.

4. In a small bowl, beat goat cheese, cream cheese, sour cream, honey, 1 egg yolk and salt until smooth. Spread over crust to within 2 in. of edge. Arrange orange segments over cheese mixture. Sprinkle with 2 Tbsp. coarse sugar; dot with butter.

5. Fold crust edge over filling, pleating as you go and leaving an opening in the center. Whisk remaining egg yolk and 1 Tbsp. water; brush over folded crust. Arrange orange slices over crust to within 1 in. of edge. Sprinkle with remaining 1 Tbsp. coarse sugar. Freeze, covered, overnight.

6. Preheat oven to 375°. Bake until crust is golden and filling is bubbly, 60-70 minutes. Transfer tart to a wire rack to cool.

7. For sauce, in a small saucepan, melt butter over medium heat. Add brown sugar, cream, honey and cinnamon; bring to a boil. Boil 1 minute, stirring constantly to dissolve sugar. Serve with galette.

1 PIECE: 488 cal., 25g fat (15g sat. fat), 79mg chol., 434mg sod., 63g carb. (46g sugars, 4g fiber), 6g pro.

GRANDMA'S SECRET
Feeling fancy? Serve this galette as a cheese course after dinner, then follow it with a plateful of tiny chocolate candies.

PUMPKIN CHIP CAKE WITH WALNUTS

My grandmother gave me this family recipe.
After a few changes, I made the treat even healthier and
tastier. Holidays wouldn't be the same without it!
—*Amy Bridgewater, Aztec, NM*

PREP: 20 MIN. • **BAKE:** 50 MIN. + COOLING • **MAKES:** 16 SERVINGS

- 3 cups all-purpose flour
- 1¼ cups sugar
- 2 tsp. baking powder
- 1 tsp. baking soda
- 2 tsp. ground cinnamon
- ¾ tsp. salt
- ½ tsp. ground cloves
- ¼ tsp. ground allspice
- 4 large eggs, room temperature
- 1 can (15 oz.) pumpkin
- 1 cup unsweetened applesauce
- ¼ cup canola oil
- ¼ tsp. maple flavoring, optional
- ½ cup miniature semisweet chocolate chips
- ½ cup chopped walnuts, toasted
  Confectioners' sugar

1. Preheat oven to 350°. Grease and flour a 10-in. fluted tube pan.

2. In a large bowl, whisk the first 8 ingredients. In another bowl, whisk eggs, pumpkin, applesauce, oil and, if desired, flavoring until blended. Add to flour mixture; stir just until moistened. Fold in chocolate chips and walnuts.

3. Transfer to prepared pan. Bake until a toothpick inserted in the center comes out clean 50-60 minutes or. Cool in pan 10 minutes before removing to a wire rack to cool completely. Dust with confectioners' sugar.

1 PIECE: 261 cal., 9g fat (2g sat. fat), 47mg chol., 260mg sod., 42g carb. (21g sugars, 2g fiber), 5g pro.

FROM GRANDMA'S KITCHEN: To remove cakes easily, use solid shortening to grease plain and fluted tube pans.

OLD-FASHIONED COCONUT CREAM PIE

After their wedding in a small country church, our daughter Angela and her husband, Lonnie, were driven to the reception in a horse-drawn wagon—along the same route that Angela's great-grandparents took in the 1800s! Later, the guests raved over luscious desserts like this old-fashioned pie.
—*Gertrude Gojmerac, Souris, PEI*

PREP: 20 MIN. + CHILLING • **MAKES:** 8 SERVINGS

⅔ cup sugar
¼ cup cornstarch
2 Tbsp. all-purpose flour
¼ tsp. salt
3 cups milk
3 egg yolks, beaten
1 Tbsp. butter
2 tsp. vanilla extract
1 cup sweetened shredded coconut, divided
2 cups whipped cream or whipped topping
1 pastry shell (9 in.), baked

1. In a saucepan, combine sugar, cornstarch, flour and salt; gradually add milk until smooth. Bring to a boil over medium heat. Cook and stir for 2 minutes or until thickened. Remove from the heat. Gradually stir a small amount into egg yolks; return all to the pan, stirring constantly. Bring to a gentle boil; cook and stir for 2 minutes.

2. Remove from the heat; stir in butter and vanilla. Cool to lukewarm; fold in ⅔ cup coconut. Pour into pastry shell. Refrigerate until set, about 3 hours. Meanwhile, toast the remaining coconut. To serve, top pie with whipped cream and sprinkle with toasted coconut. Store in the refrigerator.

1 PIECE: 460 cal., 28g fat (17g sat. fat), 121mg chol., 267mg sod., 46g carb. (28g sugars, 1g fiber), 6g pro.

GRANDMA'S STRAWBERRY PIE

This is one of the first recipes Grandma taught me to make. All summer long, she makes these pies, substituting different seasonal fruits and gelatin flavors. But strawberry has always been the favorite—and it's even better topped with a dollop of whipped cream.
—*Shannon Chabes, Portage, IN*

PREP: 40 MIN. + CHILLING • **MAKES:** 8 SERVINGS

1½ cups all-purpose flour
2 tablespoons sugar
¼ teaspoon salt
½ cup vegetable oil
2 tablespoons 2% milk

FILLING
1 cup sugar
3 Tbsp. plus ½ tsp. cornstarch
1 cup cold water
2 Tbsp. light corn syrup
1 pkg. (3 oz.) strawberry gelatin
4 cups sliced fresh strawberries
½ cup whipped topping

1. In a large bowl, combine the flour, sugar and salt. Gradually add oil and milk, tossing with a fork until dough forms a ball. Press into a 9-in. pie plate.

2. Line unpricked pastry shell with a double thickness of heavy-duty foil. Bake at 450° for 8 minutes. Remove foil; bake until golden brown, 5-7 minutes longer. Cool on a wire rack.

3. In a large saucepan, combine sugar and cornstarch. Stir in water and corn syrup until smooth. Bring to a boil, stirring constantly. Cook and stir for 2-3 minutes or until thickened.

4. Remove from the heat; stir in gelatin until dissolved. Stir in strawberries. Pour into pastry shell. Refrigerate for 4 hours or until set. Garnish with whipped topping.

1 PIECE.: 407 calories, 14g fat (2g sat. fat), 1mg chol., 108mg sod., 68g carb. (44g sugars, 3g fiber), 4g pro.

MOCK APPLE PIE

My mother made this dessert often during the Depression, and our guests
were always astounded that soda crackers could make such convincing apples!
—*Shirley Hunter, St. Paul, MN*

PREP: 20 MIN. + COOLING • BAKE: 25 MIN. • MAKES: 8 SERVINGS

**Dough for double-crust
pie**
18 **saltines, broken in half**
1½ **cups sugar**
1¼ **cups water**
2 **Tbsp. lemon juice**
1 **tsp. cream of tartar**
½ **to 1 tsp. ground cinnamon**
½ **to 1 tsp. ground nutmeg**

1. Preheat oven to 400°. On a lightly floured surface, roll half
of the dough to a ⅛-in.-thick circle; transfer to a 9-in. pie plate.
Trim to ½ in. beyond rim of plate.

2. Layer crackers in shell; set aside. In a small saucepan, combine
the remaining ingredients; bring to a boil. Carefully pour over
crackers (filling will be very thin). Cool for 10 minutes.

3. Roll remaining dough to a ⅛-in.-thick circle; cut into 1-in.-wide
strips. Arrange over filling in a lattice pattern. Trim and seal strips
to edge of bottom crust; flute edge. Bake until crust is golden
brown, 25-30 minutes. Cool on a wire rack.

1 PIECE: 519 cal., 24g fat (15g sat. fat), 60mg chol., 396mg sod.,
73g carb. (39g sugars, 1g fiber), 5g pro.

DOUGH FOR DOUBLE-CRUST PIE: Combine 2½ cups all-purpose
flour and ½ tsp. salt; cut in 1 cup cold butter until crumbly.
Gradually add ⅓ to ⅔ cup ice water, tossing with a fork until dough
holds together when pressed. Divide dough in half. Shape each into
a disk; wrap and refrigerate 1 hour.

FROM GRANDMA'S KITCHEN: Store leftovers of this mock apple pie
in an airtight container in the fridge for up to 3 days.

TRIPLE BERRY LINZER TART

My grandmother gave me her signature lattice-topped tart recipe. The bubbling berry preserves, citrus and nuts fill our home with aromas that bring back warm memories.
—*Michael Compean, Los Angeles, CA*

PREP: 30 MIN. + CHILLING • **BAKE:** 30 MIN. • **MAKES:** 12 SERVINGS

¾ cup unsalted butter, softened
⅓ cup sugar
2 large egg yolks, room temperature
1 Tbsp. grated orange zest
1½ tsp. grated lemon zest
2 cups all-purpose flour
¼ cup ground hazelnuts or blanched almonds
¼ cup ground pecans
¼ cup ground walnuts
1½ tsp. ground cinnamon
½ tsp. baking powder
¼ tsp. salt
¼ tsp. ground cloves
1⅓ cups triple berry preserves
1 Tbsp. lemon juice
Confectioners' sugar, optional

1. In a large bowl, cream the butter and sugar until light and fluffy, 5-7 minutes. Add the egg yolks and citrus zests; mix well. Combine the flour, nuts, cinnamon, baking powder, salt and cloves; gradually add to creamed mixture and mix just until moistened.

2. Divide dough in half and flatten each into a thick rectangle. Wrap and chill until firm, at least 2 hours or overnight.

3. Press 1 portion of dough onto the bottom and up the sides of a lightly greased 14x4-in. fluted tart pan with removable bottom. Cover and refrigerate for about 10 minutes.

4. Combine preserves and lemon juice; spread over crust. Roll remaining dough between 2 pieces of parchment. Make a lattice crust. Trim edges.

5. Bake at 350° for 30-35 minutes or until crust is golden brown and filling is bubbly. Cool on a wire rack. Dust with confectioners' sugar before serving if desired.

1 PIECE: 336 cal., 16g fat (8g sat. fat), 61mg chol., 73mg sod., 46g carb. (27g sugars, 1g fiber), 3g pro.

FROM GRANDMA'S KITCHEN: You may use a greased 9-in. round fluted tart pan with removable bottom instead of a 14-in. x 4-in. pan. Bake as directed.

GRANDMA'S CHRISTMAS CAKE

One bite of this old-fashioned spice cake will bring back memories. Loaded with raisins and nuts, it tastes extra special drizzled with the rich, buttery sauce.
—*Linda Stemen, Monroeville, IN*

PREP: 25 MIN. • **BAKE:** 45 MIN. + COOLING
MAKES: 16 SERVINGS (2⅔ CUPS SAUCE)

2 **cups sugar**	BRANDY BUTTER SAUCE
2 **cups raisins**	1 **cup heavy whipping**
2 **cups water**	**cream**
1 **cup butter, cubed**	1 **cup butter, cubed**
3½ **cups all-purpose flour**	1 **cup sugar**
1 **tsp. baking soda**	4 **large egg yolks, lightly**
1 **tsp. ground cinnamon**	**beaten**
½ **tsp. each ground nutmeg**	¼ **cup brandy**
and cloves	
1 **cup chopped pecans**	

1. In a large saucepan, combine the sugar, raisins, water and butter. Bring to a boil. Reduce heat to medium; cook, uncovered, until sugar is dissolved, about 5 minutes. Remove from the heat and cool.

2. In a large bowl, combine the flour, baking soda, cinnamon, nutmeg and cloves. Add raisin mixture; beat until blended. Fold in the pecans.

3. Pour into a greased and floured 10-in. fluted tube pan. Bake at 350° until cake springs back when lightly touched, 45-55 minutes. Cool for 10 minutes before removing from pan to a wire rack to cool completely.

4. For sauce, in a large saucepan, bring cream to a boil; stir in butter and sugar until smooth. Reduce heat; stir a small amount of hot liquid into egg yolks. Return all to the pan, stirring constantly. Cook until sauce is slightly thickened and coats the back of a spoon (do not boil). Remove from the heat; stir in brandy. Serve warm with cake.

1 PIECE WITH ABOUT 3 TBSP. SAUCE: 624 cal., 35g fat (19g sat. fat), 124mg chol., 271mg sod., 75g carb. (49g sugars, 2g fiber), 5g pro.

SPICED UPSIDE-DOWN APPLE PIE

My grandma taught me to make this pie when I was 4. Over the years I've kept it about the same with just a few changes. Flip it out the second it stops bubbling. The glaze it makes looks like stained glass.
—*Francine Bryson, Pickens, SC*

PREP: 20 MIN. • BAKE: 50 MIN. + COOLING • MAKES: 8 SERVINGS

2 **cups pecan halves**
½ **cup butter, melted**
1 **cup packed brown sugar**
   Pastry for double-crust pie
½ **cup sugar**
3 **Tbsp. all-purpose flour**
1 **Tbsp. apple pie spice**
½ **tsp. ground nutmeg**
6 **cups thinly sliced peeled tart apples**
2 **Tbsp. lemon juice**
1 **tsp. vanilla extract**

1. Arrange pecans, with rounded sides facing down, on the bottom of a 9-in. deep-dish pie plate; drizzle with butter. Sprinkle with brown sugar; press lightly.

2. Roll out dough to fit the pie plate; place over brown sugar. Press the crust firmly against brown sugar and side of pie plate. Trim the edges.

3. In a large bowl, combine the sugar, flour, pie spice and nutmeg. Add the apples, lemon juice and vanilla; toss to coat. Fill crust. Roll out remaining dough to fit top of pie; place over filling. Trim, seal and flute edges. Cut slits in crust.

4. Place a foil-lined baking sheet on a rack below the pie to catch any spills. Bake pie at 450° for 10 minutes. Reduce heat to 350°. Bake pie until the top is golden brown and apples are tender, 40-45 minutes longer. Cool for 10 minutes before inverting onto a serving plate. Serve warm.

1 PIECE: 825 cal., 53g fat (23g sat. fat), 91mg chol., 409mg sod., 87g carb. (50g sugars, 5g fiber), 7g pro.

PASTRY FOR DOUBLE CRUST PIE: Combine 2½ cups all-purpose flour and ½ tsp salt; cut in 1 cup cold butter until crumbly. Gradually add ⅓-⅔ cup ice water, tossing with a fork until the dough holds together when pressed. Divide dough in half. Shape each into a disk; wrap. Refrigerate 1 hour or overnight.

GRANDMA'S SECRET
Don't wait too long before inverting the pie onto a serving plate. If it cools off too much, it might be difficult to remove from the pan.

CHERRY NUT CAKE

My grandmother made up this recipe for her children. None of them liked chocolate or white cake. Using Ozark-grown cherries and walnuts, she invented one they all liked. Granny always used cream from the dairy farm near her home, but the half-and half works well and is easier to find.

—*Diana Jennings, Lebanon, MO*

PREP: 30 MIN. • BAKE: 25 MIN. + COOLING • MAKES: 12 SERVINGS

6 large egg whites
½ cup butter, softened
½ cup shortening
1½ cups sugar
1 cup half-and-half cream
¼ cup maraschino cherry juice
3 cups cake flour
2½ tsp. baking powder
1 tsp. salt
40 maraschino cherries, chopped
½ cup chopped walnuts

TOPPING
1 cup heavy whipping cream
2 Tbsp. confectioners' sugar
1 tsp. vanilla extract
Maraschino cherries with stems, drained and patted dry

1. Place egg whites in a large bowl; let stand at room temperature 30 minutes. Preheat oven to 350°. Line bottoms of 2 greased 9-in. round baking pans with parchment; grease parchment.

2. In a large bowl, cream butter, shortening and sugar until light and fluffy, 5-7 minutes. In a small bowl, mix cream and cherry juice. In another bowl, whisk flour, baking powder and salt; add to creamed mixture alternately with cream mixture, beating well after each addition. Fold in cherries and walnuts. With clean beaters, beat egg whites on medium speed until stiff glossy peaks form. Fold into batter.

3. Transfer batter to prepared pans. Bake until a toothpick inserted in center comes out clean, 25-30 minutes. Cool in pans 10 minutes before removing to wire racks; remove paper. Cool completely.

4.For topping, in a large bowl, beat cream until it begins to thicken. Add confectioners' sugar and vanilla; beat until stiff peaks form. Place 1 cake layer on a serving plate; spread top with half the whipped cream. Top with remaining cake layer; spread with remaining whipped cream. Decorate with cherries.

1 PIECE: 540 cal., 28g fat (13g sat. fat), 53mg chol., 402mg sod., 66g carb. (39g sugars, 1g fiber), 7g pro.

HEAVENLY SURPRISE MINI CUPCAKES

My grandmother was an accomplished baker, and this was one of the many special treats she liked to make. It's fun to bite into these dense chocolate cupcakes and discover a surprise inside.
—*Jorun Meierding, Mankato, MN*

PREP: 35 MIN. • **BAKE:** 15 MIN./BATCH + COOLING • **MAKES:** 6 DOZEN

FILLING
- **1 pkg. (8 oz.) cream cheese, softened**
- **⅓ cup sugar**
- **1 large egg**
- **⅛ tsp. salt**
- **1 cup sweetened shredded coconut**
- **1 cup finely chopped walnuts**
- **1 cup miniature semisweet chocolate chips**

BATTER
- **2 cups sugar**
- **1½ cups water**
- **¾ cup canola oil**
- **2 large eggs, room temperature**
- **2 tsp. vanilla extract**
- **1 tsp. white vinegar**
- **3 cups all-purpose flour**
- **½ cup baking cocoa**
- **1 tsp. baking soda**
- **1 tsp. salt**

FROSTING
- **1⅓ cups semisweet chocolate chips**
- **½ cup heavy whipping cream**

1. For filling, in a small bowl, beat cream cheese and sugar until light and fluffy, 5-7 minutes. Add egg and salt; mix well. Stir in the coconut, walnuts and chocolate chips.

2. For batter, in a large bowl, beat the sugar, water, oil, eggs, vanilla and vinegar until well blended. Combine the flour, cocoa, baking soda and salt; gradually beat into oil mixture until blended.

3. Fill paper-lined miniature muffin cups one-third full with batter. Drop filling by teaspoonfuls into center of each. Top with additional batter, filling muffin cups three-fourths full.

4. Bake at 350° until a toothpick inserted in the cake portion of a cupcake comes out clean, 12-15 minutes. Cool for 10 minutes before removing from pans to wire racks to cool completely.

5. For frosting, in a small saucepan, melt chocolate with cream over low heat; stir until blended. Remove from the heat. Cool to room temperature. Frost cupcakes. Refrigerate leftovers.

1 CUPCAKE: 130 cal., 7g fat (3g sat. fat), 15mg chol., 71mg sod., 15g carb. (10g sugars, 1g fiber), 2g pro.

FROM GRANDMA'S KITCHEN: Cupcakes may also be baked in 30 paper-lined muffin cups for 20-25 minutes.

BANANA SKILLET
UPSIDE-DOWN CAKE

BANANA SKILLET UPSIDE-DOWN CAKE

My grandmother gave me my first cast-iron skillet, and I've been cooking and baking with it ever since. Sometimes I add drained maraschino cherries to this banana skillet dessert and serve it with ice cream.
—*Terri Lynn Merritts, Nashville, TN*

PREP: 25 MIN. BAKE 35 MIN. • **MAKES:** 10 SERVINGS

1 pkg. (14 oz.) banana quick bread and muffin mix
½ cup chopped walnuts
¼ cup butter, cubed
¾ cup packed brown sugar
2 Tbsp. lemon juice
4 medium bananas, cut into ¼-in. slices
2 cups sweetened shredded coconut

1. Preheat oven to 375°. Prepare banana bread batter according to package directions; stir in walnuts.

2. In a 10-in. ovenproof skillet, melt butter over medium heat; stir in brown sugar until dissolved. Add lemon juice; cook and stir until slightly thickened, 2-3 minutes longer. Remove from heat. Arrange bananas in a single layer over brown sugar mixture; sprinkle with coconut.

3. Spoon prepared batter over coconut. Bake until dark golden and a toothpick inserted in center comes out clean, 35-40 minutes. Cool 5 minutes before inverting onto a serving plate. Serve warm.

1 PIECE: 554 cal., 22g fat (10g sat. fat), 49mg chol., 459mg sod., 82g carb. (30g sugars, 2g fiber), 6g pro.

MOM'S CHEESE PIE

My mother brought this traditional recipe with her from Ukraine. A sprinkling of cinnamon enhances the pie's subtly sweet flavor.
—*Anne Kulick, Phillipsburg, NJ*

PREP: 20 MIN. • **BAKE:** 45 MIN. + COOLING • **MAKES:** 4 SERVINGS

2 large eggs
1 sheet refrigerated pie pastry
1 tsp. ground cinnamon, divided
1¾ cups ricotta cheese
4 oz. cream cheese, softened
3 Tbsp. confectioners' sugar
1½ tsp. cornstarch
½ tsp. vanilla extract
½ tsp. salt

1. Separate 1 egg. In a small bowl, lightly beat egg white. In another small bowl, combine egg and egg yolk. On a lightly floured surface, unroll pastry; cut in half. Roll out half of pastry into an 8-in. circle. Transfer to a 7-in. pie plate; trim pastry even with edge. Brush with egg white; sprinkle with ½ tsp. cinnamon.

2. In a large bowl, combine cheeses, confectioners' sugar, cornstarch, vanilla, salt and the egg mixture. Pour into pastry.

3. Roll out remaining pastry to fit top of pie. Place over filling. Trim, seal and flute edges. Cut slits in pastry. Brush egg white over pastry; sprinkle with remaining ½ tsp. cinnamon.

4. Bake at 350° until a knife inserted in the center comes out clean, 45-50 minutes. Cool completely on a wire rack.

1 piece: 561 cal., 37g fat (20g sat. fat), 191mg chol., 745mg sod., 39g carb. (13g sugars, 0 fiber), 20g pro.

7UP POUND CAKE

My grandmother gave me my first cake recipe—a pound cake using 7UP—and her grandmother had given it to her. On top of being delicious, this cake represents family tradition, connection and love.
—*Marsha Davis, Desert Hot Springs, CA*

PREP: 25 MIN. • **BAKE:** 65 MIN. + COOLING • **MAKES:** 16 SERVINGS

1½ **cups butter, softened**
3 **cups sugar**
5 **large eggs, room temperature**
2 **Tbsp. lemon juice**
1 **tsp. vanilla extract**
3 **cups all-purpose flour**
¾ **cup 7UP soda**

GLAZE
1½ **cups confectioners' sugar**
1 **Tbsp. lemon or lime juice**
1 **to 2 Tbsp. 7UP soda**
½ **tsp. grated lemon or lime zest, optional**

1. Preheat oven to 350°. Grease and flour a 10-in. fluted or plain tube pan.

2. In a large bowl, cream butter and sugar until light and fluffy, 5-7 minutes. Add eggs, 1 at a time, beating well after each addition. Beat in lemon juice and vanilla. Add flour alternately with 7UP, beating well after each addition.

3. Transfer batter to prepared pan. Bake until a toothpick inserted in center comes out clean, 65-75 minutes. Cool in pan 20 minutes before removing to a wire rack to cool completely.

4. For glaze, in a small bowl, mix confectioners' sugar, lemon juice and enough 7UP to reach desired consistency. If desired, stir in zest. Drizzle over cake.

1 PIECE: 457 cal., 19g fat (11g sat. fat), 104mg chol., 177mg sod., 69g carb. (50g sugars, 1g fiber), 5g pro.

"I have used this recipe several times. I even made some as Christmas gifts. This is really a beautiful cake."
—SAMARA, TASTEOFHOME.COM

PRALINE PUMPKIN PECAN PIE

My husband and I are not big fans of traditional pumpkin pie; however my mother and others are. Because of this, we must have pumpkin pie as one of the desserts at Thanksgiving. I decided to meet everyone halfway with this recipe, and it was a hit. Now I bring it to Thanksgiving every year. My mother doesn't even feel the need to bake her own pumpkin pie.
—*Emily Reese, Glade Hill, VA*

PREP: 25 MIN. • BAKE: 50 MIN. + COOLING + CHILLING • MAKES: 8 SERVINGS

1 cup crushed gingersnaps (about 20 cookies)
¾ cup finely chopped pecans
⅓ cup packed light brown sugar
⅛ tsp. salt
3 Tbsp. unsalted butter, melted

FILLING
2 large eggs, lightly beaten
1 can (15 oz.) pumpkin
1 can (14 oz.) sweetened condensed milk
1½ tsp. ground cinnamon
½ tsp. ground ginger
½ tsp. ground nutmeg
½ tsp. salt

TOPPING
1 cup packed light brown sugar
¼ cup heavy whipping cream
2 Tbsp. light corn syrup
2 Tbsp. unsalted butter
1 Tbsp. white vinegar
1 cup coarsely chopped pecans
1 Tbsp. vanilla extract

1. Preheat oven to 325°. In a large bowl, mix crushed cookies, pecans, brown sugar and salt; stir in butter. Press onto bottom and up side of a greased 9-in. deep-dish pie plate. Bake until lightly browned, 5-7 minutes. Cool on a wire rack.

2. For filling, in a large bowl, beat eggs, pumpkin, milk, spices and salt. Pour into crust. Bake on a middle oven rack until center is set, 50-60 minutes. Cool on a wire rack 1 hour.

3. For topping, in a large heavy saucepan, combine brown sugar, cream, corn syrup, butter and vinegar. Bring to a boil over medium heat. Cook and stir until a candy thermometer reads 240° (firm-ball stage), stirring occasionally. Remove from heat; stir in pecans and vanilla. Pour over pie immediately. Refrigerate at least 4 hours or overnight.

1 PIECE: 684 cal., 35g fat (11g sat. fat), 91mg chol., 372mg sod., 89g carb. (74g sugars, 5g fiber), 10g pro.

CHALLAH
BREAD PUDDING,
PAGE 273

GRANDMA'S FAVORITE

DESSERTS

We're sweet on heavenly trifles, pastries, custards
and cobblers at Grandma's house. The best part of the
meal is always the delightful finish.

MANGO GLACE WITH PINEAPPLE POMEGRANATE SALSA

I'd like to say this dish was a brilliant idea that came from expert planning. But the truth is that with the quickly ripening fruit on my counter and the 100-degree heat, this dessert pretty much invented itself! Very ripe fruit eliminates the need for added sugar.

—Jodi Taffel, Altadena, CA

PREP: 45 MIN. + FREEZING • MAKES: 1 DOZEN

4 medium ripe mangoes, peeled and chopped
1 fresh ripe pineapple, peeled and cut into ½-in. pieces
2 Tbsp. lime juice

SALSA
1 cup finely chopped fresh pineapple
2 Tbsp. pomegranate seeds
1 Tbsp. minced fresh mint

1. Combine mangoes, pineapple and lime juice in a blender. Cover and process until smooth. Strain through a fine-mesh strainer into a large bowl. Pour into 1¾-in. silicone ice cube trays. Freeze until firm, 8 hours or overnight.

2. Combine salsa ingredients; cover and refrigerate overnight.

3. Take cubes out of freezer 10 minutes before serving. Run a small spatula around the edges of each fruit cube to loosen; remove from trays. Serve with salsa.

1 CUBE WITH 4 TSP. SALSA: 114 cal., 1g fat (0 sat. fat), 0 chol., 2mg sod., 29g carb. (24g sugars, 3g fiber), 1g pro.

RICE PUDDING

For an old-fashioned sweet treat just like Grandma made, try this creamy pudding. It has a rich cinnamon flavor. The whipped cream folded in at the end gives it a wonderful light texture.

—Jennifer Bennett, Salem, IN

PREP: 15 MIN. • COOK: 3 HOURS + CHILLING • MAKES: 4 SERVINGS

1¼ cups 2% milk
½ cup sugar
½ cup uncooked converted rice
½ cup raisins
2 large eggs, lightly beaten
1 tsp. ground cinnamon
1 tsp. butter, melted
1 tsp. vanilla extract
¾ tsp. lemon extract
1 cup heavy whipping cream, whipped
Optional: Additional whipped cream and ground cinnamon

1. In a 1½-qt. slow cooker, combine the first 9 ingredients. Cover and cook on low for 2 hours; stir. Cover and cook 1-2 hours longer or until rice is tender. Transfer to a small bowl; cool. Refrigerate until chilled.

2. Just before serving, fold in whipped cream. If desired, garnish with additional whipped cream and cinnamon.

¾ CUP: 437 cal., 17g fat (10g sat. fat), 157mg chol., 87mg sod., 63g carb. (39g sugars, 1g fiber), 8g pro.

MANGO GLACE
WITH PINEAPPLE
POMEGRANATE SALSA

BITTERSWEET CHOCOLATE CHEESECAKE

While it's usually the case that one generation passes recipes down to the next, sometimes there's one that's so good, it goes the other way. That's the case here: I'm a great-grandmother and I received this recipe from my niece! My whole family enjoys this dessert—it's so very chocolaty.

—*Amelia Gregory, Omemee, ON*

PREP: 20 MIN. • **BAKE:** 1 HOUR + CHILLING • **MAKES:** 16 SERVINGS

- 1 cup chocolate wafer crumbs
- ½ cup finely chopped hazelnuts, toasted
- ⅓ cup butter, melted
- 3 pkg. (8 oz. each) cream cheese, softened
- 1 cup sugar
- 12 oz. bittersweet chocolate, melted and cooled
- 1 cup sour cream
- 1½ tsp. vanilla extract
- ½ tsp. almond extract
  Dash salt
- 3 large eggs, room temperature, lightly beaten

GLAZE
- 4 oz. bittersweet chocolate, chopped
- ¼ cup heavy whipping cream
- 1 tsp. vanilla extract
  Optional: Whipped cream and additional toasted hazelnuts

1. Preheat oven to 350°. Mix wafer crumbs, hazelnuts and melted butter; press onto bottom of an ungreased 9-in. springform pan.

2. Beat cream cheese and sugar until smooth. Beat in cooled chocolate, then sour cream, extracts and salt. Add eggs; beat on low speed just until blended. Pour over crust. Place pan on a baking sheet.

3. Bake until center is almost set, 60-65 minutes. Cool on a wire rack 10 minutes. Loosen rim from pan with a knife; cool 1 hour longer. Refrigerate 3 hours.

4. For glaze, in a microwave, melt chocolate with cream; stir until smooth. Stir in vanilla. Spread over chilled cheesecake. Refrigerate, covered, overnight. Remove rim from the pan. If desired, serve with whipped cream and additional hazelnuts.

1 PIECE: 484 cal., 39g fat (21g sat. fat), 112mg chol., 235mg sod., 34g carb. (24g sugars, 3g fiber), 8g pro.

FROM GRANDMA'S KITCHEN: You can use semisweet baking chocolate instead of bittersweet chocolate.

CHALLAH BREAD PUDDING

PICTURED ON PAGE 268

When my mother-in-law told me that she liked bread pudding, I went on a mission to create a version that was so good she'd ask me for the recipe. It worked! This can be served for breakfast, brunch or dessert.

—*Marsha Ketaner, Henderson, NV*

PREP: 25 MIN. • BAKE: 40 MIN. • MAKES: 16 SERVINGS

1 cup sugar
1 cup packed brown sugar
7 large eggs
½ cup butter, melted
2 cans (12 oz. each) evaporated milk
2 cups half-and-half cream
1½ Tbsp. vanilla extract
1 tsp. ground nutmeg
1 tsp. ground cinnamon
¼ tsp. ground cloves
¼ tsp. ground ginger
10 cups torn challah or egg bread (about a 20-oz. loaf)
1 cup raisins
2 medium tart apples, peeled and chopped
1 cup chopped walnuts
¼ cup cold butter, cubed
   Vanilla ice cream, optional

1. Preheat the oven to 350°. In a large bowl, whisk the first 11 ingredients until blended. Gently stir in bread; let stand until bread is softened, about 15 minutes. Stir in the raisins, apples and walnuts. Dot with cold butter.

2. Transfer to a greased 13x9-in. baking dish. Bake until puffed and golden and a knife inserted near the center comes out clean, 40-45 minutes. Serve warm, with ice cream if desired.

¾ CUP: 498 cal., 24g fat (11g sat. fat), 152mg chol., 300mg sod., 59g carb. (40g sugars, 2g fiber), 12g pro.

FROM GRANDMA'S KITCHEN: Instead of challah or egg bread, you can use a day-old loaf of cinnamon raisin bread, or a combination of cinnamon-raisin bread and croissants.

APPLE KOLACHES

APPLE KOLACHES

A fellow home cook shared the recipe for this sweet, fruit-filled pastry. Even my son, who isn't a dessert fan, was disappointed when he came home to find his dad had polished off the last kolache in the batch.
—*Ann Johnson, Evansville, IN*

PREP: 30 MIN. + CHILLING • BAKE: 10 MIN./BATCH • MAKES: 2½ DOZEN

1 cup butter, softened
1 pkg. (8 oz.) cream cheese, softened
2 cups all-purpose flour
1½ cups finely chopped peeled apples
¼ tsp. ground cinnamon

ICING
1 cup confectioners' sugar
4½ tsp. 2% milk
½ tsp. vanilla extract

1. In a large bowl, beat butter and cream cheese until light and fluffy. Gradually add flour and mix well. Divide dough into 2 portions; cover and refrigerate for 2 hours or until easy to handle.

2. Preheat oven to 400°. In a small bowl, combine apples and cinnamon. On a lightly floured surface, roll 1 portion of dough into a 15x9-in. rectangle; cut into fifteen 3-in. squares. Place a teaspoon of apple mixture in center of each square. Overlap 2 opposite corners of dough over filling; pinch tightly to seal.

3. Repeat with remaining dough and apple mixture. Place 2 in. apart on ungreased baking sheets. Bake 10-12 minutes or until bottoms are lightly browned. Cool 1 minute before removing from pans to wire racks. Combine icing ingredients; drizzle over kolaches.

1 PASTRY: 129 cal., 9g fat (6g sat. fat), 24mg chol., 66mg sod., 11g carb. (4g sugars, 0 fiber), 2g pro.

MEXICAN ICE CREAM

I made this ice cream for my grandma and her friends, and they were delighted. This simple, fun dessert is also a perfect way to get kids involved in the kitchen.
—*Ben Phipps, Lima, OH*

PREP: 20 MIN. + FREEZING • MAKES: 4 SERVINGS

2 cups vanilla ice cream
½ cup frosted cornflakes, crushed
¼ cup sugar
1 tsp. ground cinnamon
¼ cup honey

1. Place four ½-cup scoops of ice cream on a waxed paper-lined baking sheet. Freeze for 1 hour or until firm.

2. In a shallow bowl, combine the cornflake crumbs, sugar and cinnamon. Roll ice cream in crumb mixture to coat. Freeze until serving. Drizzle each serving with 1 Tbsp. honey.

1 SERVING: 266 cal., 7g fat (4g sat. fat), 29mg chol., 79mg sod., 51g carb. (43g sugars, 1g fiber), 3g pro.

LAYERED LEMON DESSERT SQUARES

I found this recipe in an old cookbook and changed it to be extra citrusy.
If you're a fan of Key lime pie, try lime flavors instead of lemon.
—*Dawn Lowenstein, Huntingdon Valley, PA*

PREP: 30 MIN. + CHILLING • MAKES: 15 SERVINGS

3½ cups graham cracker
crumbs
1¾ cups sugar, divided
1 Tbsp. ground cinnamon
1¼ cups butter, melted
2 pkg. (8 oz. each) cream
cheese, softened
2 cups heavy whipping
cream
1 tsp. lemon extract
2 jars (10 oz. each) lemon
curd or 1 can (15¾ oz.)
lemon pie filling

1. In a large bowl, mix cracker crumbs, ¾ cup sugar and cinnamon; stir in butter. Reserve half of mixture for topping. Press remaining crumb mixture onto bottom of a greased 13x9-in. baking dish.

2. In a large bowl, beat cream cheese and remaining sugar until smooth. Gradually beat in the cream and extract until soft peaks form. Spread half of the cream cheese mixture over the crust. Gently spread the lemon curd over cream cheese layer. Spread with remaining cream cheese mixture. Sprinkle with reserved cracker crumb mixture. Refrigerate, covered, overnight.

FREEZE OPTION: After assembling, cover and freeze dessert. To use, thaw in refrigerator overnight.

1 PIECE: 676 cal., 42g fat (25g sat. fat), 136mg chol., 361mg sod., 71g carb. (56g sugars, 1g fiber), 5g pro.

DATE-WALNUT PINWHEELS

Every time someone drops in for coffee, I bake up a batch of these fruit and nut cookies—I always keep the ingredients in my pantry. The recipe's a cinch to double, too, so it's good for parties and potlucks.
—*Lori McLain, Denton, TX*

TAKES: 25 MIN. • MAKES: 1 DOZEN

3 Tbsp. sugar
½ tsp. ground cinnamon
1 sheet refrigerated pie
crust
1 Tbsp. apricot preserves
⅔ cup finely chopped pitted
dates
½ cup finely chopped
walnuts

1. Preheat oven to 350°. Mix sugar and cinnamon. On a lightly floured surface, unroll crust; roll crust into a 12-in. square. Spread preserves over top; sprinkle with dates, walnuts and cinnamon sugar.

2. Roll up jelly-roll style; pinch seam to seal. Cut crosswise into 12 slices about 1 in. thick. Place 1 in. apart on an ungreased baking sheet. Bake until golden brown, 12-14 minutes. Remove from pan to a wire rack to cool.

1 COOKIE: 155 cal., 8g fat (2g sat. fat), 3mg chol., 68mg sod., 21g carb. (11g sugars, 1g fiber), 2g pro.

GRILLED HONEY-BALSAMIC GLAZED FRUIT

One summer my mother-in-law made us grilled peaches basted with a sweet and tangy sauce. These are so good I'm always tempted to eat the whole batch.

—*Kristin Van Dyken, Kennewick, WA*

TAKES: 25 MIN. • **MAKES:** 6 SERVINGS (½ CUP GLAZE)

½ cup balsamic vinegar
½ cup honey
Dash salt

6 medium peaches or nectarines, halved and pitted
Vanilla ice cream, optional

1. In a small saucepan, combine vinegar, honey and salt; cook and stir over low heat until blended, 2-3 minutes. Reserve ⅓ cup mixture for brushing peaches.

2. Bring remaining mixture to a boil over medium heat; cook and stir just until mixture begins to thicken slightly (do not overcook), 4-6 minutes. Remove from heat.

3. Brush peaches with some of the reserved balsamic mixture. Grill, covered, on a greased rack over medium heat until caramelized, brushing occasionally with remaining reserved balsamic mixture, 6-8 minutes on each side. Serve with glaze and, if desired, ice cream.

1 SERVING: 164 cal., 0 fat (0 sat. fat), 0 chol., 26mg sod., 43g carb. (40g sugars, 2g fiber), 1g pro.

"What an amazing combination! Just delicious. Perfect dessert for a nice summer outdoor dinner with company. They will gobble it up and wish for more! I followed the recipe exactly and wouldn't change a thing. Do use the ice cream."

—HAVINGFUNWITHMYFAMILY, TASTEOFHOME.COM

HONEY GINGERBREAD TRIFLE

My husband's grandma made the most amazing honey gingerbread. It's wonderful all
on its own, but when you add it to a trifle, your guests are sure to ask for the recipe.
—*Tami Kuehl, Loup City, NE*

PREP: 25 MIN. + CHILLING • **BAKE:** 25 MIN. + COOLING • **MAKES:** 12 SERVINGS

1 cup sour cream
1 cup honey
1 large egg, room
   temperature
¼ cup canola oil
2½ cups all-purpose flour
½ tsp. salt
1 tsp. baking soda
1 tsp. baking powder
2 tsp. ground ginger
½ tsp. ground cinnamon

PUDDING LAYER
2 cups 2% milk
1 pkg. (3.3 oz.) instant white
   chocolate pudding mix

PUMPKIN MOUSSE LAYER
1 cup 2% milk
1 pkg. (3.4 oz.) instant
   pumpkin spice pudding
   mix
1 carton (8 oz.) frozen
   whipped topping, thawed

1. Preheat oven to 350°. Beat sour cream, honey, egg and oil until
well blended. In another bowl, whisk together next 6 ingredients;
gradually beat into sour cream mixture. Transfer to a greased
9-in. square baking pan. Bake until a toothpick inserted in center
comes out clean, 25-30 minutes. Cool in pan 5 minutes. Remove
to a wire rack to cool completely.

2. Meanwhile, for the pudding layer, whisk the milk and white
chocolate pudding mix for 2 minutes. Let stand until soft-set,
about 5 minutes. Refrigerate. For the mousse layer, whisk milk
and pumpkin spice pudding mix in another bowl for 2 minutes.
Fold in whipped topping. Refrigerate.

3. To assemble, cut the cake into 1-in. cubes. In a 3-qt. trifle bowl
or other glass serving dish, layer a third of the cake cubes, white
chocolate pudding and pumpkin mousse. Repeat layers twice.
Refrigerate, covered, 4 hours or overnight.

1 CUP: 413 cal., 14g fat (7g sat. fat), 25mg chol., 514mg sod.,
64g carb. (44g sugars, 1g fiber), 6g pro.

GRANDMA'S SECRET

This gingerbread has a slightly coarser crumb than most and stands up well to the moist pudding layers. The longer it sits, the more tender the cake will become.

PUMPKIN RUGELACH WITH CREAM CHEESE ICING

My twist on this classic pastry adds pumpkin to the filling and a rich cream cheese icing on top. Because you can make the dough ahead and refrigerate it, the recipe is ideal for the busy holiday season.
—*Justine Duffy, Wooster, OH*

PREP: 40 MIN. + CHILLING • **BAKE:** 20 MIN./BATCH + COOLING
MAKES: 3 DOZEN

2 cups butter, softened
12 oz. cream cheese, softened
⅛ tsp. salt
3¾ cups all-purpose flour
1 can (15 oz.) pumpkin
3 Tbsp. plus 1 cup sugar, divided
3 Tbsp. honey
1 tsp. vanilla extract
4½ tsp. ground cinnamon
1 large egg, room temperature
1 Tbsp. 2% milk

ICING
12 oz. cream cheese, softened
1 cup confectioners' sugar
⅔ cup 2% milk
1 tsp. vanilla extract

1. In a large bowl, cream butter, cream cheese and salt until blended. Gradually beat in flour. Divide dough into 3 portions. Shape each into a disk; wrap and refrigerate 1 hour.

2. Preheat oven to 350°. In a small bowl, combine pumpkin, 3 Tbsp. sugar, honey and vanilla. Mix cinnamon and remaining 1 cup sugar. On a lightly floured surface, roll each portion of dough into a 14-in. circle. Spread each with a third of the pumpkin mixture and sprinkle with ¼ cup sugar mixture.

3. Cut dough into 12 wedges. Roll up from wide ends; place 2 in. apart on parchment-lined baking sheets, point side down. Whisk together egg and milk; brush over pastries. Sprinkle with the remaining sugar mixture.

4. Bake until bottoms are browned, 18-22 minutes. Remove from pans to wire racks to cool completely. In a small bowl, beat icing ingredients; drizzle over pastries. Let stand until set.

1 RUGELACH: 258 cal., 17g fat (10g sat. fat), 52mg chol., 154mg sod., 24g carb. (13g sugars, 1g fiber), 3g pro.

VANILLA BEAN CHEESECAKE WITH CHOCOLATE GANACHE

This recipe is the most recent cheesecake I gave to my mother for her birthday, and we all just loved it—too much! There's a hint of orange in the chocolate crust that makes every bite worth savoring.

—Jenn Tidwell, Fair Oaks, CA

PREP: 50 MIN. • BAKE: 1 HOUR + CHILLING • MAKES: 16 SERVINGS

2 cups chocolate graham cracker crumbs (about 16 graham crackers)
4 tsp. grated orange zest
⅓ cup butter, melted

FILLING
3 pkg. (8 oz. each) cream cheese, softened
1 cup sugar
1 cup sour cream
1 vanilla bean or 1 Tbsp. vanilla extract
3 large eggs, lightly beaten

TOPPING
1 cup semisweet chocolate chips
⅔ cup heavy whipping cream
2 cups fresh raspberries

1. Preheat oven to 325°. Place a greased 9-in. springform pan on a double thickness of heavy-duty foil (about 18 in. square). Wrap foil securely around pan.

2. In a small bowl, mix cracker crumbs and orange zest; stir in butter. Press onto bottom and 2 in. up side of prepared pan. Refrigerate 5 minutes.

3. In a large bowl, beat cream cheese and sugar until smooth. Beat in sour cream. Split vanilla bean lengthwise; using the tip of a sharp knife, scrape seeds from the center into cream cheese mixture. Add eggs; beat on low speed just until blended. Pour into crust. Place springform pan in a larger baking pan; add 1 in. of hot water to larger pan.

4. Bake 60-70 minutes or until center is just set and top appears dull. Remove springform pan from water bath. Cool cheesecake on a wire rack 10 minutes. Loosen rim from pan with a knife; remove foil. Cool 1 hour longer. Refrigerate overnight, covering when completely cooled.

5. For topping, place chocolate chips in a small bowl. In a small saucepan, bring cream just to a boil. Pour over chocolate chips; stir with a whisk until smooth. Cool to room temperature or until mixture thickens to spreading consistency, about 10 minutes.

6. Remove rim from springform pan. Spread chocolate mixture over the cheesecake. Refrigerate 1 hour longer or until set. Top cheesecake with raspberries before serving.

1 PIECE: 431 cal., 31g fat (17g sat. fat), 109mg chol., 281mg sod., 36g carb. (26g sugars, 2g fiber), 6g pro.

BROWNIE TORTE

My mother-in-law first shared this recipe, and now it's often requested for birthdays and other special occasions. I like to serve it at Christmastime on an antique platter surrounded by ornaments.
—*Candace McClure, Brookville, IN*

PREP: 30 MIN. • **BAKE:** 15 MIN. + COOLING • **MAKES:** 12 SERVINGS

1 cup miniature semisweet chocolate chips
⅔ cup butter, cubed
4 large eggs, room temperature
1½ cups sugar
1½ cups all-purpose flour
1 tsp. baking powder
½ tsp. salt
½ cup coarsely chopped walnuts

FROSTING
2 cups heavy whipping cream
¼ cup confectioners' sugar
1 tsp. vanilla extract
1 cup miniature semisweet chocolate chips
 Additional miniature semisweet chocolate chips, optional

1. Preheat the oven to 350°. Line a 15x10x1-in. baking pan with parchment.

2. In a microwave, melt chocolate chips and butter; stir until smooth. Cool slightly. In a large bowl, beat eggs and sugar. Stir in chocolate mixture. In another bowl, mix flour, baking powder and salt; gradually add to chocolate mixture, mixing well. Fold in walnuts.

3. Transfer to prepared pan. Bake until a toothpick inserted in the center comes out clean, 15-20 minutes (do not overbake). Cool for 10 minutes. Invert onto a flat surface dusted with confectioners' sugar. Gently peel off paper. Cool completely.

4. In a bowl, beat cream, confectioners' sugar and vanilla until stiff peaks form. Fold in chocolate chips. Trim cake edges; cut crosswise into fourths. Place 1 layer on a serving plate; top with ¾ cup frosting. Repeat twice. Top with remaining layer. Frost top, sides and ends of cake. If desired, sprinkle with additional chocolate chips. Store in the refrigerator.

1 PIECE: 586 cal., 38g fat (22g sat. fat), 134mg chol., 258mg sod., 60g carb. (45g sugars, 2g fiber), 7g pro.

"Delicious! I will definitely make this again. The cake was brownie-like with a soft consistency. The simple whipped cream frosting was the perfect topper, not too sweet. Everyone loved this, and it was easy to make. It also looked beautiful!"
—KCHEEKERS, TASTEOFHOME.COM

DIRTY BANANA TRIFLE

What could be better than bananas, cookies and Kahlua? You can adjust this to suit your taste, depending on whether you like a stronger or weaker Kahlua flavor.

—*Laurie Handlin, Ocean View, DE*

PREP: 40 MIN. + CHILLING • **MAKES:** 24 SERVINGS

2 pkg. (8 oz. each) cream cheese, softened, divided
2 cans (14 oz. each) sweetened condensed milk, divided
1½ cups Kahlua (coffee liqueur), chilled
2½ cups cold 2% milk, divided
2 pkg. (3.9 oz. each) instant chocolate pudding mix
3 cartons (8 oz. each) frozen whipped topping, thawed, divided
9 whole chocolate graham crackers, coarsely crushed
2 pkg. (3.4 oz. each) instant banana cream pudding mix
1½ cups coarsely crushed vanilla wafers (about 45 wafers)
5 medium bananas, sliced
Additional wafers, crushed chocolate graham crackers and sliced bananas

1. In a large bowl, beat 1 package cream cheese and 1 can condensed milk until blended. Beat in Kahlua, ½ cup milk and chocolate pudding mixes until thickened, about 2 minutes. Fold in 1 carton whipped topping, then chocolate graham crackers. Set aside.

2. In another large bowl, beat the remaining cream cheese and condensed milk until blended. Beat in the remaining 2 cups milk and the banana pudding mixes until thickened, about 2 minutes. Fold in 1 carton whipped topping, vanilla wafers and bananas.

3. Spread chocolate pudding mixture in the bottom of a 6- or 7-qt. trifle bowl or glass bowl. Layer with 1½ cups whipped topping and banana pudding mixture; top with remaining 1½ cups whipped topping. Cover and refrigerate overnight.

4. Garnish with additional wafers, crushed chocolate graham crackers and sliced bananas before serving.

1 CUP: 381 cal., 16g fat (11g sat. fat), 33mg chol., 326mg sod., 46g carb. (33g sugars, 1g fiber), 5g pro.

DESSERTS

284

LIME PUDDING CAKES

This old-time dessert was always a real treat. My mother, Lois, baked it for us. Now I share it with my loved ones, too.
—*Ethel Kozma, Westport, NY*

PREP: 20 MIN. • BAKE: 40 MIN. • MAKES: 6 SERVINGS

2 **Tbsp. butter, softened**	½ **cup lime or lemon juice**
1½ **cups sugar**	1¼ **cups 2% milk**
⅓ **cup all-purpose flour**	3 **large eggs, room**
¼ **tsp. salt**	**temperature, separated**
1 **tsp. grated lime or lemon zest**	

1. Preheat oven to 325°. In a small bowl, beat butter and sugar until crumbly. Add flour, salt, lime zest and juice; mix well. Beat in milk and egg yolks until smooth. In another bowl, beat egg whites until stiff peaks form; gently fold into batter.

2. Place 6 ungreased 6-oz. custard cups in a baking pan large enough to hold them without touching. Pour egg mixture into cups. Place pan on oven rack; add very hot water to pan to within ½ in. of top of cups.

3. Bake, uncovered, until a knife inserted in the centers comes out clean and tops are golden, 40-45 minutes. Immediately remove cups from water bath to a wire rack. Serve warm or at room temperature.

1 PUDDING CAKE: 324 cal., 8g fat (4g sat. fat), 121mg chol., 181mg sod., 60g carb. (53g sugars, 0 fiber), 6g pro.

LEMON CUSTARD CAKE

My grandma gave me this recipe—it's nice to whip up when unexpected company stops in. It's a cool, creamy dessert that tastes sophisticated—proof that a simple meal doesn't have to go without dessert.
—*Sue Gronholz, Beaver Dam, WI*

TAKES: 15 MIN. • MAKES: 12 SERVINGS

1 **prepared angel food cake (8 to 10 oz.)**	Tear angel food cake into bite-sized pieces. Place in a 13x9-in. pan. In a bowl, combine the pudding mix, milk and sour cream. Beat until thickened, about 2 minutes. Spread over cake. Spoon pie filling on top. Chill until serving time.
1 **pkg. (3.4 oz.) instant lemon pudding mix**	
1½ **cups cold 2% milk**	
1 **cup sour cream**	
1 **can (21 oz.) cherry or strawberry pie filling**	

1 SERVING: 184 cal., 5g fat (3g sat. fat), 7mg chol., 270mg sod., 31g carb. (18g sugars, 1g fiber), 3g pro.

LAYERED STRAWBERRY POUND CAKE DESSERT

My mother's cousin shared this recipe more than 50 years ago. Our family has enjoyed it ever since, especially on hot New Mexico days! It can be made the day before.
—*Vickie Britton, Hobbs, NM*

PREP: 20 MIN. + CHILLING • MAKES: 24 SERVINGS

1 loaf (10¾ oz.) frozen pound cake, thawed
1 pkg. (8 oz.) cream cheese, softened
1 can (14 oz.) sweetened condensed milk
⅓ cup lemon juice
1 carton (12 oz.) frozen whipped topping, thawed
1 container (16 oz.) frozen sweetened sliced strawberries, thawed

1. Cut pound cake into ½-in. slices; place in bottom of a 13x9-in. baking dish. In a large bowl, beat cream cheese until smooth. Beat in milk and lemon juice until blended. Fold in 2⅔ cups whipped topping and 1½ cups strawberries with juice.

2. Spread mixture over pound cake. Top with remaining 2⅔ cups whipped topping. Refrigerate, covered, at least 4 hours or overnight. Top with remaining ½ cup strawberries in juice before serving.

1 PIECE: 195 cal., 10g fat (7g sat. fat), 34mg chol., 88mg sod., 24g carb. (20g sugars, 0 fiber), 3g pro.

MOM'S CINNAMON-APPLE CRISP

I was fortunate enough to have a dear friend share this recipe with me more than 50 years ago. The sweet-smelling combination of apples, cinnamon, sugar and nutmeg has been a welcome scent in my house ever since.
—*Cleo Lightfoot, Southlake, TX*

PREP: 20 MIN. • BAKE: 40 MIN. • MAKES: 9 SERVINGS

6 cups thinly sliced peeled tart apples
½ cup sugar
1 Tbsp. all-purpose flour
¼ tsp. ground cinnamon
2 Tbsp. butter

TOPPING
1 cup all-purpose flour
1 cup sugar
1 tsp. baking powder
¼ tsp. ground nutmeg
½ cup cold butter, cubed
1 large egg, lightly beaten
Vanilla ice cream, optional

1. Combine the apples, sugar, flour and cinnamon in a large bowl. Transfer to an 11x7-in. baking dish; dot with butter.

2. For topping, combine the flour, sugar, baking powder and nutmeg in another large bowl. Cut in the butter until mixture resembles coarse crumbs. Stir in egg just until moistened; sprinkle over filling.

3. Bake, uncovered, at 375° for 40-45 minutes or until topping is golden brown and apples are tender. Serve warm, with ice cream if desired.

1 SERVING: 341 cal., 14g fat (8g sat. fat), 55mg chol., 163mg sod., 54g carb. (41g sugars, 1g fiber), 3g pro.

LAYERED STRAWBERRY
POUND CAKE DESSERT

CHOCOLATE MALT CHEESECAKE

For a change of pace, substitute pretzel crumbs for the graham cracker crumbs. They make a surprisingly good crust!
—*Anita Moffett, Rewey, WI*

PREP: 25 MIN. • BAKE: 1 HOUR + CHILLING • MAKES: 14 SERVINGS

- 1 cup graham cracker crumbs (about 16 squares)
- ¼ cup sugar
- ⅓ cup butter, melted

FILLING
- 3 pkg. (8 oz. each) cream cheese, softened
- 1 can (14 oz.) sweetened condensed milk
- ¾ cup chocolate malted milk powder
- 4 large eggs, room temperature, lightly beaten
- 1 cup semisweet chocolate chips, melted and cooled
- 1 tsp. vanilla extract Confectioners' sugar, optional

1. Preheat oven to 325°. Combine the cracker crumbs, sugar and butter. Press onto the bottom of a greased 9-in. springform pan; set aside.

2. In a large bowl, beat cream cheese and milk until smooth. Add malt powder; beat well. Add eggs; beat on low speed just until combined. Stir in the melted chocolate and vanilla just until blended. Pour over crust. Place pan on a baking sheet.

3. Bake until center is almost set, 60-65 minutes. Cool on a wire rack for 10 minutes. Carefully run a knife around edge of pan to loosen; cool 1 hour longer. Refrigerate overnight, covering when completely cooled.

4. Remove rim of pan. Sprinkle with confectioners' sugar if desired. Refrigerate leftovers.

1 PIECE: 369 cal., 19g fat (11g sat. fat), 101mg chol., 291mg sod., 47g carb. (35g sugars, 1g fiber), 7g pro.

ORANGE-ALMOND CHOCLAVA

A twist on classic baklava, this recipe adds semisweet chocolate to the nut filling and drizzles more chocolate on top. Christmas gift-giving has never been yummier!

—Nella Parker, Hersey, MI

PREP: 1 HOUR • **BAKE:** 50 MIN. + CHILLING • **MAKES:** ABOUT 6 DOZEN

1 lb. slivered almonds
1 cup semisweet chocolate chips
¾ cup sugar
2 Tbsp. grated orange zest
1½ cups butter, melted
1 pkg. (16 oz., 14x9-in. sheets) frozen phyllo dough, thawed

SYRUP
1¼ cups orange juice
¾ cup sugar
½ cup honey
2 Tbsp. lemon juice

DRIZZLE
2 oz. semisweet chocolate, chopped
3 Tbsp. water

1. Preheat oven to 325°. Place almonds and chocolate chips in a food processor; pulse until finely chopped. In a large bowl, combine the almond mixture, sugar and orange zest. Brush a 15x10x1-in. baking pan with some of the butter.

2. Unroll phyllo dough. Layer 10 sheets of phyllo in prepared pan, brushing each with butter. Keep remaining phyllo covered with a damp towel to prevent it from drying out. Sprinkle with a third of the almond mixture. Repeat layers twice. Top with the remaining phyllo sheets, brushing each with butter. Cut into 1-in. diamonds. Bake until golden brown, 50-60 minutes. Meanwhile, in a saucepan, combine syrup ingredients; bring to a boil. Reduce heat; simmer, uncovered, 20 minutes.

3. In a small heavy saucepan, heat chocolate and water over very low heat until melted and smooth, stirring constantly. Pour syrup over warm baklava; drizzle with chocolate mixture. Cool completely in pan on a wire rack. Refrigerate, covered, several hours or overnight. Serve at room temperature.

1 PIECE: 123 cal., 8g fat (3g sat. fat), 10mg chol., 55mg sod., 13g carb. (8g sugars, 1g fiber), 2g pro.

"Amazing! I would recommend this dish to anyone who likes baklava."

— ABBYSCHULTZ, TASTEOFHOME.COM

APPLE
CORNBREAD
CRISP

APPLE CORNBREAD CRISP

With its hearty ingredients and quick prep time, this warm apple crisp makes a smart dessert for any fall night. It reminds me of the recipe my grandmother would serve after our big family seafood dinners. It's absolutely wonderful topped with ice cream.
—*Julie Peterson, Crofton, MD*

PREP: 10 MIN. • BAKE: 30 MIN. • MAKES: 6 SERVINGS

4 cups sliced peeled tart apples (4-5 medium)
¾ cup packed brown sugar, divided
1 pkg. (8½ oz.) cornbread/muffin mix
½ cup quick-cooking oats
1 tsp. ground cinnamon (or to taste)
5 Tbsp. cold butter, cubed

1. Preheat oven to 350°. Stir together apples and ¼ cup brown sugar. In another bowl, combine cornbread mix, oats, cinnamon and remaining brown sugar. Cut in butter until crumbly.

2. Add ½ cup cornbread mixture to apples. Transfer to a greased 8-in. square baking dish. Sprinkle remaining cornbread mixture over top. Bake until filling is bubbly and topping golden brown, 30-35 minutes. Serve warm.

1 SERVING: 421 cal., 15g fat (7g sat. fat), 26mg chol., 413mg sod., 70g carb. (43g sugars, 5g fiber), 4g pro.

QUICK & EASY BAKLAVA SQUARES

I love baklava but rarely indulge because it takes so much time to make. Then a friend of mine gave me this simple recipe. I've made it for family, friends and co-workers—they can't get enough. I'm always asked to bring these squares to special gatherings and parties, and I even give them as gifts during the holidays.
—*Paula Marchesi, Lenhartsville, PA*

PREP: 20 MIN. • BAKE: 25 MIN. + COOLING • MAKES: 2 DOZEN

1 lb. (4 cups) chopped walnuts
1½ tsp. ground cinnamon
1 pkg. (16 oz., 14x9-in. sheets) frozen phyllo dough, thawed
1 cup butter, melted
1 cup honey

1. Preheat oven to 350°. Coat a 13x9-in. baking dish with cooking spray. Combine walnuts and cinnamon.

2. Unroll phyllo dough. Layer 2 sheets of phyllo in prepared pan; brush with butter. Repeat with 6 more sheets of phyllo, brushing every other 1 with butter. (Keep remaining phyllo covered with a damp towel to prevent it from drying out.)

3. Sprinkle ½ cup nut mixture in pan; drizzle with 2 Tbsp. honey. Add 2 more phyllo sheets, brushing with butter; sprinkle another ½ cup nut mixture and 2 Tbsp. honey over phyllo. Repeat layers 6 times. Top with remaining phyllo sheets, brushing every other 1 with butter.

4. Using a sharp knife, score surface to make 24 squares. Bake until golden brown and crisp, 25-30 minutes. Cool on a wire rack 1 hour before serving.

1 PIECE: 294 cal., 21g fat (6g sat. fat), 20mg chol., 145mg sod., 26g carb. (13g sugars, 2g fiber), 5g pro.

STRAWBERRY-LEMON CREPE CAKE

Each year for my husband's birthday I make him a different lemon cake
(a tradition started by his mother). A couple of years ago I made a lemon crepe cake and
it was really good. This spring I added fresh strawberries and the cake was fabulous!
I like to make the crepe batter and lemon curd the night before and assemble the next morning.
—Lora Roth, Seneca, SC

PREP: 1 HR. + CHILLING • COOK: 35 MIN. • MAKES: 10 SERVINGS PLUS 5 LEFTOVER CREPES

1 tsp. unflavored gelatin
2 Tbsp. cold water
4 large eggs
1 cup sugar
¾ cup lemon juice
6 large egg yolks
2 Tbsp. grated lemon zest
6 Tbsp. butter, cubed

CREPES
1¼ cups 2% milk
3 large eggs, room
  temperature
⅓ cup melted butter
1 tsp. vanilla extract
¾ cup all-purpose flour
½ cup sugar
¼ tsp. salt

FILLING/TOPPING
1½ cups heavy whipping
  cream
¼ cup confectioners' sugar
1 pkg. (16 oz.) fresh
  strawberries, hulled and
  thinly sliced

1. Sprinkle gelatin over cold water; let stand for 5 minutes.

2. In a small heavy saucepan over medium heat, whisk the eggs, sugar, lemon juice, egg yolks and lemon zest until blended. Add butter; cook, whisking constantly, until mixture is thickened and coats the back of a spoon. Remove from the heat; stir in softened gelatin until completely dissolved. Transfer to a large bowl; cool. Press waxed paper onto surface of lemon curd; refrigerate overnight or until chilled.

3. Meanwhile, for the crepes, in a small bowl, whisk the milk, eggs, melted butter and vanilla. Combine the flour, sugar and salt; add to milk mixture and mix well. Cover and refrigerate for 2 hours or overnight.

4. Heat a lightly greased 8-in. nonstick skillet over medium heat; pour 2 Tbsp. batter into center of skillet. Lift and tilt the pan to coat bottom evenly. Cook until top appears dry; turn and cook 15-20 seconds longer. Remove to a wire rack. Repeat with remaining batter, greasing skillet as needed. When cool, stack crepes with waxed paper or paper towels in between.

5. In a large bowl, beat the cream until it begins to thicken. Add confectioners' sugar; beat until stiff peaks form. Set aside 1 cup for the topping; cover and refrigerate. In a large bowl, gradually whisk whipped cream into lemon curd.

6. To assemble, place 1 crepe on a cake plate. Spread with 3 Tbsp. filling and layer with 2 Tbsp. strawberries. Repeat the layers until 15 crepes are used (save remaining crepes for another use). Cover cake and remaining lemon curd mousse; refrigerate until serving.

7. Just before serving, top cake with whipped cream. Garnish with remaining strawberries. Serve crepe cake with additional lemon curd mousse.

1 PIECE WITH A SCANT ¼ CUP LEMON CURD MOUSSE: 461 cal., 30g fat (17g sat. fat), 328mg chol., 186mg sod., 42g carb. (33g sugars, 1g fiber), 8g pro.

PUMPKIN
BREAD PUDDING CUPCAKES

Every fall when I was young, my mom made bread pudding cupcakes. Today I keep up her tradition with my daughter and three grandkids by baking these treats.

—*Terrel Porter-Smith, Los Osos, CA*

PREP: 35 MIN. + CHILLING • **BAKE:** 25 MIN. + COOLING • **MAKES:** 2 DOZEN

4 **large eggs**	1½ **tsp. vanilla extract,**
4½ **cups canned pumpkin**	**divided**
1½ **cups 2% milk**	10 **cups cubed French bread**
1 **cup sugar**	**(1-in. pieces)**
1 **cup half-and-half cream**	½ **cup butter, cubed**
1 **tsp. ground cinnamon**	1 **cup packed brown sugar**
½ **tsp. salt**	1 **Tbsp. light corn syrup**
½ **tsp. ground nutmeg**	1 **cup chopped pecans**

1. In a large bowl, whisk eggs, pumpkin, milk, sugar, cream, cinnamon, salt, nutmeg and ½ tsp. vanilla until blended. Gently stir in bread. Refrigerate, covered, 1 hour.

2. Preheat oven to 350°. Fill foil-lined muffin cups with bread pudding mixture. Bake 20-25 minutes or until firm to the touch.

3. Meanwhile, in a small heavy saucepan, melt butter. Stir in the brown sugar and corn syrup. Bring to a boil, stirring constantly. Cook, without stirring, 2-3 minutes longer or until slightly thickened. Remove from heat; stir in pecans and remaining vanilla.

4. Spoon 1 Tbsp. sauce over each cupcake. Bake 5-6 minutes longer or until topping is set. Cool 10 minutes before removing from pans to wire racks. Serve warm. Refrigerate leftovers.

1 CUPCAKE: 224 cal., 10g fat (4g sat. fat), 47mg chol., 181mg sod., 31g carb. (22g sugars, 2g fiber), 4g pro.

CLASSIC BLUEBERRY BUCKLE

This blueberry buckle recipe came from my grandmother. As children, my sister
and I remember going to Pennsylvania for blueberry picking. Mother taught
us to pick only perfect berries, and those gems went into this wonderful recipe.
—*Carol Dolan, Mount Laurel, NJ*

PREP: 20 MIN. • BAKE: 40 MIN. • MAKES: 9 SERVINGS

¼ **cup butter, softened**
¾ **cup sugar**
1 **large egg, room**
  temperature
2 **cups all-purpose flour**
2 **tsp. baking powder**
¼ **tsp. salt**
½ **cup 2% milk**
2 **cups fresh blueberries**

TOPPING
⅔ **cup sugar**
½ **cup all-purpose flour**
½ **tsp. ground cinnamon**
⅓ **cup cold butter, cubed**
  Whipped cream, optional

1. Preheat oven to 375°. In a small bowl, cream butter and sugar until light and fluffy, 5-7 minutes. Add egg; beat well. In another bowl, combine the flour, baking powder and salt; add to creamed mixture alternately with milk, beating well after each addition. Fold in blueberries. Spread into greased 9-in. square baking pan.

2. For topping, in a small bowl, combine the sugar, flour and cinnamon; cut in butter until crumbly. Sprinkle over blueberry mixture.

3. Bake until a toothpick inserted in the center comes out clean, 40-45 minutes. Cool on a wire rack. If desired, serve with whipped cream and additional blueberries.

NOTE: If using frozen blueberries, use without thawing to avoid discoloring the batter.

1 PIECE: 390 cal., 13g fat (8g sat. fat), 54mg chol., 282mg sod., 64g carb. (36g sugars, 2g fiber), 5g pro.

GRANDMA'S SECRET
Buckle gets its name from the heavy streusel topping that weighs the batter down while the dessert bakes, causing the top of the cake to buckle in spots.

SUGAR PLUM PHYLLO KRINGLE

Thanks to store-bought phyllo dough, this pastry
is easier to make than it looks. Serve it not only for
breakfast, but also for dessert with a scoop of ice cream.
—*Johnna Johnson, Scottsdale, AZ*

PREP: 30 MIN. • **BAKE:** 20 MIN. + COOLING • **MAKES:** 6 SERVINGS

¾ **cup chopped dried
    apricots**
½ **cup dried cherries**
⅓ **cup water**
¼ **cup sugar**
¼ **cup raisins**
¾ **cup chopped walnuts**
1 **Tbsp. lemon juice**

1 **pkg. (8 oz.) cream cheese,
    softened**
12 **sheets (14x9 in. each)
    phyllo dough
    Butter-flavored cooking
    spray
    Confectioners' sugar**

1. Preheat oven to 375°. In a large saucepan, bring the apricots,
cherries, water, sugar and raisins to a boil. Reduce heat; simmer,
uncovered, until liquid is thickened, 6-8 minutes. Stir in walnuts
and lemon juice. Remove from heat; cool completely.

2. In a small bowl, beat cream cheese until smooth. Place 1 sheet
of phyllo dough on a work surface; spritz with the cooking spray.
Layer with remaining phyllo, spritzing each layer. Spread cream
cheese over phyllo to within 2 in. of edges; top with dried fruit
mixture. Fold in the edges; roll up, starting with a long side.

3. Place in a parchment-lined 15x10x1-in. baking pan, seam side
down. Spritz top with cooking spray. Bake until golden brown,
20-25 minutes. Cool on a wire rack. Sprinkle kringle with
confectioners' sugar.

1 PIECE: 446 cal., 25g fat (9g sat. fat), 38mg chol., 224mg sod.,
52g carb. (31g sugars, 3g fiber), 7g pro.

EGGNOG CREAM PUFFS

If you want to receive rave reviews and recipe requests, combine two Christmas classics: eggnog and cream puffs. When it comes to Santa, this recipe goes on the nice list!
—*Kristen Heigl, Staten Island, NY*

PREP: 40 MIN. • **BAKE:** 30 MIN. + COOLING • **MAKES:** ABOUT 2 DOZEN

1 **cup water**
½ **cup butter, cubed**
⅛ **tsp. salt**
1 **cup all-purpose flour**
¾ **tsp. ground nutmeg**
4 **large eggs, room temperature**

WHIPPED CREAM
1½ **cups heavy whipping cream**
1½ **cups confectioners' sugar**
¼ **cup eggnog**
1 **tsp. vanilla extract**
⅛ **tsp. ground nutmeg**
Additional confectioners' sugar

1. Preheat oven to 400°. In a large saucepan, bring water, butter and salt to a rolling boil. Add flour all at once; add nutmeg and stir until blended. Cook over medium heat, stirring vigorously until mixture pulls away from side of pan. Remove from heat; let stand 5 minutes.

2. Add eggs, 1 at a time, beating well after each addition until smooth. Continue beating until mixture is smooth and shiny. Drop dough by rounded tablespoonfuls 1 in. apart onto greased baking sheets. Bake 30-35 minutes or until puffed, very firm and golden brown. Pierce side of each puff with tip of a knife. Cool on wire racks. Cut top third off each puff.

3. In a large bowl, beat cream until it begins to thicken. Add confectioners' sugar, eggnog, vanilla and nutmeg; beat until soft peaks form. Just before serving, fill cream puffs with whipped cream; replace tops. Dust with additional confectioners' sugar. Serve immediately.

1 CREAM PUFF: 127 cal., 9g fat (5g sat. fat), 51mg chol., 52mg sod., 10g carb. (7g sugars, 0 fiber), 2g pro.

DOUBLE-CHOCOLATE TOFFEE ICEBOX CAKE

My mother-in-law taught me that anything tastes good if you use enough chocolate or cream. This no-bake dessert proves she was right.
—*Bee Engelhart, Bloomfield Township, MI*

PREP: 30 MIN. + CHILLING • **MAKES:** 8 SERVINGS

3 **cups 2% milk**
1 **pkg. (5.9 oz.) instant chocolate pudding mix**
1½ **cups heavy whipping cream**
2 **pkg. (9 oz. each) chocolate wafers**
2 **Heath candy bars (1.4 oz. each), crushed**

1. In a large bowl, whisk milk and pudding mix 2 minutes. Let stand 2 minutes or until soft-set. In another large bowl, beat cream until stiff peaks form.

2. Arrange 20 cookies on the bottom of an 8-in. square baking dish. Spread a fourth of the chocolate pudding and a fourth of the whipped cream over cookies. Repeat layers 3 times. Sprinkle with crushed candy bars. Refrigerate overnight.

1 PIECE: 538 cal., 28g fat (14g sat. fat), 64mg chol., 493mg sod., 68g carb. (40g sugars, 3g fiber), 8g pro.

PUMPKIN CHARLOTTE

My mother-in-law gave me this recipe a while back and I just love it!
I make it for my husband and his friends during hunting season and it's a big hit.
—*Lorelle Edgcomb, Granville, IL*

PREP: 30 MIN. + CHILLING • **MAKES:** 12 SERVINGS

2 pkg. (3 oz. each) ladyfingers, split
6 oz. cream cheese, softened
2 Tbsp. sugar
2¼ cups heavy whipping cream, divided
3 Tbsp. confectioners' sugar, divided
1 cup cold 2% milk
2 pkg. (3.4 oz. each) instant vanilla pudding mix
½ tsp. ground cinnamon
¼ tsp. ground ginger
¼ tsp. pumpkin pie spice
1 can (15 oz.) solid-pack pumpkin
Additional ground cinnamon

1. Arrange split ladyfingers on the bottom and upright around the side of an ungreased 9-in. springform pan, trimming to fit if necessary. Set aside.

2. In a large bowl, beat cream cheese and sugar until smooth. In a small bowl, beat 1¾ cups whipping cream and 2 Tbsp. confectioners' sugar until stiff peaks form. Set ½ cup aside. Fold remaining whipped cream into cream cheese mixture. Spread into prepared pan.

3. In a bowl, combine the milk, pudding mixes and spices; beat on low speed for 1 minute. Add pumpkin; beat 1 minute longer. Fold in reserved whipped cream. Pour over cream cheese layer. Cover and refrigerate for 8 hours or overnight.

4. Just before serving, beat remaining cream and confectioners' sugar until stiff peaks form. Spoon over pumpkin layer. Sprinkle with cinnamon. Remove side of pan. Refrigerate the leftovers.

1 PIECE: 275 cal., 21g fat (13g sat. fat), 98mg chol., 173mg sod., 21g carb. (16g sugars, 2g fiber), 3g pro.

GRANDMA'S SECRET
If you plan to keep leftovers for several days, skip the whipped cream topping or keep it separate from your finished dessert. Sprinkle the top with cinnamon for a simple garnish.

RECIPE INDEX